Karin Hansson

The Autonomous and the Passive Progressive in 20th-Century Irish

**UPPSALA
UNIVERSITET**

Dissertation for the degree of Doctor of Philosophy in Celtic Languages presented at Uppsala University in 2004

ABSTRACT

Hansson, K. 2004. The Autonomous and the Passive Progressive in 20th-Century Irish. Acta Universitatis Upsaliensis. *Studia Celtica Upsaliensia* 5. 176 pp. Uppsala. ISBN 91-554-5899-8.

The present study deals with the use of two Irish verb constructions, the auto-nomous (e.g. cuireadh litreacha chun bealaigh, 'letters were dispatched') and the passive progressive (e.g. bhí m'athair á leigheas acu, 'my father was being cured by them'), in a corpus of 20th-century texts. From this corpus, 2,956 instances of the autonomous and 467 instances of the passive progressive were extracted and included in the analysis. Dialectal variation concerning the use of these two constructions is also surveyed.

The study explores and compares the use of the autonomous and the passive progressive. The main aim of the study is to investigate the two constructions with regard to their textual functions. The features studied relate to verb and clause type, as well as the measuring of topicality of patients, implicit agents, and—in the passive progressive only—overt agents.

The autonomous tends to be used when the patient is topical, or central, in the text. The passive progressive, on the other hand, is mainly used with an overt agent that is considerably more topical than the patient. In agent-less passive progressives, patients and implicit agents are equally low in topicality. The autonomous occurs about equally often in main and subclauses, while the passive progressive is used primarily in subclauses, mainly non-finite ones. This difference is connected to the finding that 24% of the clauses containing the autonomous denote events as part of a sequentially ordered chain of events, compared to 4% of those containing the passive progressive.

The most salient dialectal variation concerns the frequency of the passive progressive: 73% of the instances of the passive progressive in the database occur in the Munster texts, compared to 22% in Connacht 5% in Ulster. The autonomous, in contrast, is fairly evenly distributed across the dialects.

Key words: autonomous, agent, corpus linguistics, impersonal, discourse function, Irish, passive, passive progressive, patient, topicality

Karin Hansson, Celtic Section, University of Uppsala, Box 527, S-751 20 Uppsala, Sweden

ISSN 1104-5515
ISBN 91-554-5899-8

Typesetting: Uppsala University, Editorial Office
Printed in Sweden by Elanders Gotab, Stockholm 2004
Distributor: Uppsala University Library, Box 510, SE-751 20 Uppsala, Sweden
www.uu.se, acta@ub.uu.se

ACTA UNIVERSITATIS UPSALIENSIS
Studia Celtica Upsaliensia
5

For
Edith, Olov, Anna,
Pétur, Hanna,
Margit, Tinna, Alvar

Contents

Tables

Preface

Many people have kindly assisted and supported me during my work on this book. My heartfelt thanks are due to the following:

my supervisor Professor Ailbhe Ó Corráin, who got me back on the Irish track when my interest was drifting into other directions, and always encouraged me with his expertise;

my assistant supervisor Docent Ingegerd Bäcklund, who fearlessly plunged into the world of Irish, and in her firm but always friendly way guided me through the everyday routine of thesis-writing;

Professor Merja Kytö, who generously helped me with my many queries, and who welcomed me into the English linguistics seminar;

Dr. Mícheál Ó Flaithearta, who has been an inspiring and helpful colleague;

all colleagues, past and present, at the Department of English and the Celtic Section, who made my time at the department a happy one;

the members of the English linguistics seminar for their interest and many insightful comments;

my friends and colleagues Ylva Berglund, Astrid Sandberg and Hanna Sveen, who enlightened and supported me in many ways;

all my past students, who helped me widen my perspective on Irish grammar.

Special thanks are due to Ola Johanson, Ulrica Källén, Susanne Schaffer, Anders Sveen, Lisa Thiel, Tomas Thiel and Emma Wikstad, who apart from monitoring my social life found the time to read parts of my manuscript.

Introduction

1 Background and aim

The passive as a category has attracted considerable attention among linguists. It is generally agreed that practically all languages have the means of presenting information so that some element other than the agent is in focus, thus contrasting with constructions where the most important participant is the one responsible for the action. Active constructions, where the agent is in focus, are regarded as unmarked since this is the usual way of presenting information. Passive constructions, on the other hand, where a non-agent is in focus, are regarded as marked. A number of studies have been made of passive constructions in Irish but there have been very few corpus-based studies.[1]

The present study is a corpus-based survey of the use of the passive in Modern Irish. The aim of the study is to investigate the use, frequency and distribution of the two main passive constructions in Modern Irish literature. The constructions in question are the so-called *autonomous* verb form (henceforth, the autonomous), as in (1), and the *passive progressive*, shown in (2).[2]

The term passive is here used to denote all constructions that realise passivisation as it is defined by, for example, Givón (1979a: 186): "Passivization is the

---

[1] However, see Noonan (1994) (Modern Irish), and Müller (1994, 1999) (Old Irish), which are presented in section 3 below.

[2] Several terms are used to refer to these constructions. The autonomous is also referred to as autonomous impersonal (Stenson 1989), autonomous/passive (Ó Corráin 2001), impersonal (forms), (*Graiméar Gaeilge na mBráithre Críostaí* 1999, Greene 1979, Hartmann 1977, Ó Siadhail 1989), impersonal passive (Guilfoyle 1991, Nolan 2001, Noonan 1994), impersonal verb (Stenson 1981). The passive progressive is also referred to as passive progressive aspect (Ó Siadhail 1989), progressive passive (Guilfoyle 1991, Noonan 1994, Stenson 1981). 'Autonomous' is the usual rendering of the Irish term *an briathar saor/an saorbhriathar*, 'the free verb', (see, for example, *New Irish Grammar by The Chrisitian Brothers* 1986, *Graiméar Gaeilge na mBráithre Críostaí* 1999, Ó Cadhlaigh 1940; compare Ó Dónaill 1992 and de Bhaldraithe 1987), besides being a frequently used term (see Guilfoyle 1991, Ó Corráin 2001, Stenson 1981, Stenson 1989). As for the passive progressive, this term passive progressive was chosen because the construction is generally described as passive as well as progressive (see further below). Further, I chose the term passive progressive rather than progressive passive since I take it to be the passive variant of the active progressive (compare Ó Siadhail's (1989) term passive progressive aspect) rather than a progressive variant of the passive since there is no non-progressive passive.

(1) **Cuireadh** *litreacha* *chun* *bealaigh.*
    send-PST-AUT letters to way-GEN

'Letters **were dispatched**.' (Co. *Feamainn Bhealtaine*: 289)[3]

(2) *Bhí* *m'athair* *á* **leigheas** *dá ainneoin* *acu* *mar sin,* *níor*
    be-PST my+father to+his cure-VBN in spite of it by-3PL thus COP-NEG-PRT

    chás *dhuit* *a* *rá.*
    case to-2SG to say-VBN

'My father was **being cured** by them in spite of it, of course.' (Mu. *Na hAird Ó Thuaidh*: 129)

process by which a nonagent is promoted into the role of main topic of the sentence."[4] This definition covers the autonomous as well as the passive progressive, which represent two different passivisation strategies. The first of these is to let a non-agent occupy the subject position, i.e. promote the patient, as in the Irish passive progressive. The other strategy involves the demotion of the agent from the focus of attention which is generally associated with the agent (in subject position). This can be done in at least three ways. The agent can be excluded altogether, or included in a demoted position. The third possibility is that the agent is left unspecified. The first two ways to demote the agent apply to the passive progressive, while in the autonomous the agent is demoted since it is not overtly expressed and thus unspecified. For a unified description and discussion of the autonomous and the passive progressive in the present study, the term agent is used to denote the agent phrase in an agented passive progressive as well as the implied agents of agent-less passive progressives and autonomous clauses. It should be pointed out from the start that there is no non-progressive passive in Irish that corresponds formally to the passive progressive.

The autonomous is a verb form characterised structurally by its ending (for example, *cuireadh* in (1) above), which indicates an agent whose identity is unspecified.[5] An important feature of the autonomous is that an agent phrase cannot normally be used with it, that is, the agent is not be overtly expressed.[6] Therefore,

---

[3] For explanations of the grammatical annotations, translations and references of the examples, see section 5 below.

[4] See also Givón (1982), Keenan (1985), Shibatani (1985).

[5] The assumption that the autonomous form 'contains' a subject (although unspecified) is based on the fact that the object form is used to denote the patient, for example, *é*, 'him, it', instead of *sé*, 'he, it'; see, for example, Bondaruk and Charzynska-Wójcik (2003), Stenson (1981), and Stenson (1989). This distinction between subject and object form is only found in third person pronouns. In Old Irish, the patient of the passive construction (which later developed into the Modern Irish autonomous construction, as explained in section 2 below) was normally in the nominative case.

[6] See, for example, Ó Cadhlaigh (1940: 56f.), Ó Siadhail (1989: 294), Stenson (1989: 382). Ó Cadhlaigh (1940: 69ff.) points out that the agent was often overtly expressed with the autonomous in earlier stages of the Irish language. He gives several examples of agented autonomous forms from works by, for example, the writers Geoffrey Keating (c. 1570–c. 1650) and Peadar Ó Laoghaire (1839–1929). (The present corpus contains one text by Peadar Ó Laoghaire, see section 4 below). I have not found a single instance of an agented autonomous clause in the present material.

(3) *Cá* **suífear?**
     where sit-FUT-AUT

'Where **will one sit**?' (Co. *Feamainn Bhealtaine*: 110)

(4a) *Chuireadar* *litreacha* *chun* *bealaigh.*
      send-PST-3PL letters to way-GEN

'They dispatched letters.'

(4b) *Chuir* *siad* *litreacha* *chun* *bealaigh.*
      send-PST they letters to way-GEN

'They dispatched letters.'

the autonomous is usually referred to as an impersonal, or impersonal passive, construction (see, for example, *Graiméar Gaeilge na mBráithre Críostaí* 1999: 166, and Noonan 1994: 284). Practically all verbs, both transitive and intransitive, have an autonomous form for each tense. A transitive verb in the autonomous was shown in (1). An example of the autonomous of an intransitive verb is found in (3). The autonomous contrasts mainly with personal active forms, exemplified in (4a) and (4b), which are active clauses corresponding to the autonomous clause in (1). In (4a) a personal ending, –(e)adar, is used to denote third person plural, whereas in (4b) a pronoun, *siad,* 'they', is used.[7]

Although, in principle, all verbs can form the autonomous, there are some restrictions as to the types of verb that are actually used in the autonomous. Stenson (1989: 386) points out that "verbs whose meaning is such that no agent, even implicit, is possible" are not used in the autonomous. One group of such verbs comprises those that describe natural phenomena, as in (5). Instead of the autonomous an active verb form is used without a subject/agent, as in (6). On the other hand, there are cases where the autonomous is used although "no null agent or experiencer can plausibly be identified with subject position", as in (7) (Stenson 1989: 387). In (7) the transitive verb *caill*, which normally means 'lose', has the force of the intransitive verb 'die'. Stenson (1989: 388) concludes that examples like (7) represent "for the most part idiosyncratic usages of verbs which have a broader range of meaning as well, especially in their nonimpersonal [active] forms".

The other construction investigated in the present study, the passive progressive, is a periphrastic construction consisting of an auxiliary, the so-called substantive verb *bí,* 'be', followed by a verbal noun phrase. Like the active progressive, the passive progressive is characterised by the verbal noun phrase introduced by a preposition indicating that the action denoted by the verbal noun is

---

[7] In Irish, person and number can be expressed either synthetically, as in *chuireadar,* 'they put', or analytically, as in *chuir siad,* 'they put', where the verb form *chuir* is neutral as to person and number. In most tenses, and in most persons, both possibilities exist and are accepted in the standard grammar.

(5) *Neartaíodh   ar   an   ngaoth.
     strengthen-PST-AUT   on   the wind

     'The wind **strengthened**.' (Stenson 1989: 387)

(6) _Neartaigh_   ar   an   ngaoth.
     strengthen-PST   on   the wind

     'The wind strengthened.' (Stenson 1989: 386, her translation)

(7) **Cailleadh**   a   hathair.
     lose-PST-AUT   her father

     'Her father **died**.' (Stenson 1989: 387, her translation)

on-going. The subject is inserted between the auxiliary and the verbal noun phrase. This verbal noun phrase contains the preposition _do_, 'to', a possessive pronoun and a verbal noun. The agent may be omitted or overtly expressed in a phrase introduced by the preposition _ag_, 'at, by'. An example of the passive progressive has already been given in (2). A more detailed description of (2) showing its constituents is given below.

(2)	_Bhí_	_m'athair_	_á_		**leigheas**	_dá ainneoin_	_acu,_
	be-PST	my father	to+his		cure-VBN	in spite of it	by-3PL
	auxiliary verb	subject/patient	preposition _do_, 'to'+ possessive pronoun _a_				agent

	mar sin,	_níor_	_chás_	_dhuit_	_a_	_rá._
	thus	COP-NEG-PRT	case	to-2SG	to	say-VBN

'My father was **being cured** by them in spite of it, of course.' (Mu. _Na hAird Ó Thuaidh_: 129)

The subject of the substantive verb, _m'athair_, 'my father', is also the object of the verbal noun, _leigheas_, 'curing', that is, the patient is the grammatical subject—in contrast to the autonomous, where the patient is the grammatical object. Formally, the passive progressive contrasts primarily with the active progressive; an active progressive corresponding to the passive progressive example (2) is given in (8). In conclusion, the passive progressive and the autonomous share one important feature despite their formal differences: the promotion of the patient. In the autonomous the agent is left unspecified, and in the passive progressive, the patient appears in subject position.

   Taking into account what the autonomous and the passive progressive have in common, as well as their formal differences, I base my study of these two constructions on one main question: what differences in use are there between the autonomous and the passive progressive? The study will deal with factors that may have an influence on the use of the two constructions. Such factors include verb type, clause type and type of patient and agent. Formal characteristics of the two constructions as well as the function of the autonomous and the passive

(8) *Bhí*   *siad*   *ag*   *leigheas*   *m'athar.*
     be-PST they   at   cure-VBN   my father-GEN

'They <u>were curing</u> my father.'[8]

progressive from an information packaging perspective will be considered. A secondary aim of the study is to investigate possible differences in the use of the autonomous and the passive progressive among the three main dialects of Modern Irish (Connacht, Munster, and Ulster).

2 Overview of the autonomous, the passive progressive, and related constructions in Irish

Naturally, the autonomous and passive progressive constructions are variously described in Modern Irish grammars. Below (under The autonomous and the passive progressive in grammars of Modern Irish), I will refer to accounts of the autonomous and the passive progressive in three comprehensive grammars, Ó Cadhlaigh (1940), *Graimeár Gaeilge na mBráithre Críostaí* (1999, henceforth *Graiméar*), and Ó Searcaigh (1954), as well as Ó Siadhail (1989).[9] There are several studies concerned with passive constructions in Modern as well as Old Irish that are relevant to the present investigation. These will be presented in section 3.

The autonomous and the passive progressive in grammars of Modern Irish

The autonomous and the passive progressive are dealt with to a varying extent in Ó Cadhlaigh (1940), *Graiméar* (1999), and Ó Searcaigh (1954). The most comprehensive of the grammars, Ó Cadhlaigh (1940) and *Graiméar* (1999), devote whole sections to the autonomous, while Ó Searcaigh (1954) merely mentions examples of the autonomous as part of his account of verb inflections. In *Graiméar* (1999: 140), the autonomous is defined as an impersonal form, since it is "free from person and number". Ó Cadhlaigh (1940: 54) states that the autonomous is used when the agent is unknown or when one does not want to mention it (see also *Graiméar* 1999: 166). One examples of the autonomous from Irish literature given by Ó Cadhlaigh (1940) is found in (9). As mentioned above, no overt agent is normally expressed with the autonomous, but an inanimate instrument may be included in a prepositional phrase introduced by *le*, 'with'

---

[8] *M'athar* is the genitive singular of *m'athair*. The direct object of a verbal noun is usually in the genitive case.
[9] The autonomous is not dealt with in Ó Searcaigh (1954), although examples of the autonomous occur as parts of the account of verb inflections.

(9) **Chuirtí**   na   ba   agus na   caoirigh ar   an   sliabh   i   dtús   an
     put-IPF-AUT   the cows and   the sheep   on   the mountain in beginning the-GEN

   tsamhraidh agus **d'fhágtaí**   ann   iad   go   deireadh an   **fhóghmhair.**
   summer-GEN   and   leave-IPF-AUT   there them to   end   the-GEN   autumn-GEN

   'The cows and the sheep **were put** on the mountain in the beginning of the summer and they
   were left there until the end of the autumn.' (Ó Cadhlaigh 1940: 56)

(10a) **Do leagadh**   an   fear agus   mise   ag   gabháil   thar brághaid.
      knock down-PST-AUT   the man   and   I-EMPH   at   going-VBN past

   'The man **was knocked down** as I was going past.' (Ó Cadhlaigh 1940: 58, his translation)

(10b) **deisíodh**   an   rothar
      repair-PST-AUT   the bike

   'the bike **was repaired**' (*Graiméar* 1999: 166)

(11a) **deirtear**
      say-PRS-AUT

   'it **is said**' (*Graiméar* 1999: 167)

(11b) tá   <u>daoine</u> á   rá
      be-PRS   people   to+its   say-VBN

   '<u>people</u> are saying' (*Graiméar* 1999: 167)

(Ó Cadhlaigh 1940: 69, Greene 1979: 134). It is pointed out that the autonomous
used with transitive verbs often corresponds to passive constructions in other
languages (*Graiméar* 1999: 166, Ó Cadhlaigh 1940: 58). This is exemplified for
English in (10a) an (10b). However, Ó Cadhlaigh (1940: 72) claims that as a
consequence of the fact that the autonomous is used to avoid mentioning the
agent, the Irish equivalent of an agented passive clause in English is an Irish
active clause. Further, it is mentioned that both transitive and intransitive verbs
can form the autonomous (*Graiméar* 1999: 166). Finally, it is pointed out that
there are active constructions that are used with the same meaning as the autonomous (*Graiméar* 1999: 167, Ó Cadghlaigh 1940: 61). *Daoine*, 'people', in (11b),
and *siad*, 'they', in (12b), are examples of subjects used in active clauses, corresponding to the autonomous in (11a) and (12a).[10] For comparison, my constructed
example in (12a) is an autonomous version of (12b).

---

[10] In an earlier edition of *Graiméar* (1999), *Graiméar Gaeilge na mBráithre Críostaí* (1960: 205 n.),
it is noted that since the autonomous is an impersonal verb form, it is normally not followed by a
relative clause where the antecedent appears in the autonomous clause, as in *táthar ann a deir*, 'there
are people who say', which is described as an exceptional use of the autonomous. Instead, an active
structure is recommended: *tá daoine ann a deir*, 'there are people who say', where *daoine*, 'people'
is the subject and antecedent (*Graiméar Gaeilge na mBráithre Críostaí* 1960: 205 n.).

(12a)	*Táiliúir*	*na*	*gCos*	*a*	**thugtaí**	*orm.*
	tailor	the-GEN	feet-GEN	REL	give-IPF-AUT	on-1SG

'I **used to be called** The Foot Tailor.'

(12b)	*Táiliúir*	*na*	*gCos*	*a*	*thugaid*	<u>*siad*</u>	*orm.*
	tailor	the-GEN	feet-GEN	REL	give-IPF	they	on-1SG

'<u>They</u> used to call me The Foot Tailor.' (Ó Cadhlaigh 1940: 61)

The passive progressive is dealt with in less detail in the grammars. It is noteworthy that the passive progressive is treated as a variant of the active progressive, rather than a separate construction assigned a label of its own. The only explicit reference to the passive progressive as a passive construction is found Ó Searcaigh (1954). In the discussion of the active progressive, Ó Searcaigh (1954: 48) notes that the passive progressive is used to express a continuous action in the passive voice, as in (13). Ó Searciagh (1954: 48) also points out that the agent is often not mentioned.[11] In Ó Cadhlaigh (1940: 67f.) we are told that the passive progressive, as in (14), is used when one wishes to express continuous action without stating the agent (unknown or known) (compare Ó Searcaigh 1954: 48). Ó Siadhail (1989: 297) notes that in the passive progressive, as in (15a), "the grammatical subject /.../ is the object in the corresponding active construction", given in (15b) (see also *Graiméar* 1999: 202). Further, Ó Siadhail (1989) points out that there is some dialectal variation concerning the use of the passive progressive. First, he notes that the passive progressive is considerably more common in Munster Irish than in the other dialects. Second, Ó Siadhail (1989: 298) claims that in Munster, the agented passive progressive has replaced the active progressive "when the object of a verbal noun does not immediately precede it".[12] Second, the agent is often placed before the verbal noun phrase in the Munster dialect, as in (16), instead of after the verbal noun phrase as is normally the case (Ó Siadhail 1989: 298).[13]

Finally, there is one interesting feature of the passive progressive that relates to the autonomous. As mentioned above, the passive and active progressive are constructed in a similar way: the auxiliary verb *bí*, 'be', is followed by a verbal noun phrase which indicates an on-going action. It is pointed out in *Graiméar* (1999: 207) that the active and passive progressive may coincide formally in the

---

[11] It may be noted that this is mentioned in Ó Searcaigh (1954) which is an account of Ulster Irish. As is shown in Chapter 5, the lowest frequency is of agented passive progressives is found in the Ulster texts in the corpus.

[12] Compare Greene (1979: 134), who points out that the dialect of West Munster, "shows a great preponderance of the 'passive' construction [i. e. the passive progressive] in active meaning in progressive tenses with transitive verbs"; see also Sjoestedt-Jonval (1938: 155) who makes a similar observation.

[13] Dialectal variation in the use of the autonomous and the passive progressive in the present corpus is dealt with in Chapter 5.

(13)　*Tá*　　*teach*　**dhá**　　**dhéanamh**　*ag*　*Tomás.*
　　be-PRS　house　to+its　make-VBN　by　Tomás

'A house is **being built** by Tomás.' (Ó Searcaigh 1954: 48)

(14)　*Bhí*　　*amhráin*　*agus*　*filidheacht*　**dá**　　　**gcumadh.**
　　be-PST　songs　and　poetry　to+their　compose-VBN

'Songs and poems were **being composed**.' (Ó Cadhlaigh 1940: 68)

(15a)　*Tá*　　*<u>an</u>　<u>doras</u>*　**dhá**　　**phéinteáil**　*agam*
　　be-PRS　the　door　to+its　paint-VBN　by-1SG

'<u>The door</u> is **being painted** by me (lit. <u>The door</u> is **to its painting** by me) (Ó Siadhail 1989: 297, his translation)

(15b)　*Tá*　　*mé*　*ag*　*péinteáil*　*<u>an</u>*　*<u>dorais</u>*
　　be-PRS　I　at　paint-VBN　the-GEN　door-GEN

'I am painting <u>the door</u>' (Ó Siadhail 1989: 297, his translation)

(16)　*Ní*　*raibh*　*aon*　*ní*　*<u>aige</u>*　*á*　　**dhéanamh**
　　NEG　be-PST　any　thing　by-3SGM　to+its　do-VBN

'<u>He</u> was **doing** nothing' (Ó Siadhail 1989: 298, his translation)

(17)　*tá*　　*Tomás*　*á*　　**mholadh**
　　be-PRS　Tomás　to+his　praise-VBN

'Tomás is **being praised**' or 'Tomás is **praising** him' (*Graiméar* 1999: 207, their translation)

third person. This is illustrated in (17). As indicated, both a passive and an active interpretation of (17) are possible. In the passive interpretation *á*, 'at his', refers to *Tomás*, the patient, while in the active interpretation *á* refers to some other person (masculine third person singular) who is then the patient. It is mentioned in *Graiméar* (1999: 207) that when the passive interpretation is intended, ambiguity can be avoided by using the autonomous with the active progressive instead of the passive progressive, as shown in (18).[14] The combination of the autonomous and the active progressive can then be said to correspond to the agent-less passive progressive since it denotes an on-going action where the agent is implicit.

In sum, the autonomous is described in grammars of Modern Irish as an impersonal construction that is used when the agent is not mentioned. The passive progressive is described as a progressive construction in which the patient appears as the grammatical subject.

---

[14] See also Stenson (1981: 153f.), and examples in Ó Cadhlaigh (1940: 67f.) and Ó Searcaigh (1954: 48).

(18) *táthar*   *ag*   *moladh*   *Thomáis*
      be-PRS-AUT   at   praise-VBN   Tomás-GEN

'Tomás is being praised' (*Graiméar* 1999: 207)

Two passive-like constructions

There are two other constructions in Modern Irish that formally resemble the passive progressive, namely, the perfect, as in (19), and the passive prospective, as in (20).[15]

(19) *tá*   *an* *doras* *dúnta*   *ag*   *Pól*
     be-PRS   the door shut-VBA by-1SG Pól

'Pól has shut the door' (*Graiméar* 1999: 139)

(20) *Tá*   *an* *leabhar* *le* *léamh*   *agam*
     be-PRS   the book to read-VBN by-1SG

'The book is to be read by me/I have to read the book' (Ó Siadhail 1989: 299, his translation)

Like the passive progressive, both the perfect and the passive prospective are formed with the substantive verb as auxiliary, together with a verbal adjective phrase in the perfect, and a verbal noun phrase in the passive prospective. The patient is in subject position in both constructions, and, optionally, the agent can be included as a prepositional phrase containing the preposition *ag*, 'by'.[16] Despite the similarities with the passive progressive, the perfect and the passive prospective are generally not considered primarily passive in function. McCloskey (1996: 255) points out that the perfect "is simply the formal means used to express a particular aspectual category—a recent perfective or completive aspect" (cf. *Graiméar* 1999: 139). As regards the passive prospective, Stenson refers to it as a 'non-passive' construction (Stenson 1981: 150). In conclusion, the perfect and the passive prospective are not considered primarily as passive constructions. Therefore, they are not included in the present investigation.

Development of the autonomous and the passive progressive

The Modern Irish autonomous form has developed from the Old Irish passive. In Old Irish (600–900), there was an inflection forming a passive where the patient

---

[15] Other terms are also used for these constructions. The perfect has been referred to as participial/ergative (Noonan 1994), passive perfective (Ó Siadhail 1989), perfective passive (McCloskey 1996, Guilfoyle 1991), perfective/passive (Stenson 1981), stative/perfective (Stenson 1981). The passive prospective is also called the necessitative/prospective (Noonan 1994). The term perfect was chosen here because that is the term used in *New Irish Grammar by The Christian Brothers* (1986), and in *Graiméar* (1999) (see also Greene 1979), and since this construction is not generally regarded as a primarily passive construction (as explained below). The term passive prospective is used in Ó Siadhail's (1989).

[16] For a comment on the development of the perfect in Irish, see Dillon (1941).

is the grammatical subject. However, this inflection was incomplete: there were personal endings in the third person only, as in the present singular *carth(a)ir*, 'he is loved' and plural *cart(a)ir*, 'they are loved' (Thurneysen 1980: 349). The third person singular passive verb form was used for all persons except the third person plural. To mark the first and second persons, infixed pronouns were used, for example, *no-m-charthar*, 'I am loved'.[17] The same set of infixed pronouns marking first- and second-person patients were used in passive as well as active clauses, as shown in the active clause, *no-m-chara*, 'he loves **me**'. Since there were separate verb forms for third persons only and since there is some fluctuation between the use of the nominative and the accusative to mark the subject, we may conclude that the passive in Old Irish was a mixed passive/impersonal inflection.

One of the major Middle Irish (900–1200) developments was the growing use of independent object (and to a lesser extent subject) pronouns. Still rare in 12th-century manuscripts, these pronouns gradually replaced the Old Irish infixed pronouns. The use of independent pronouns indicating the patient instead of infixed pronouns seems to have been established early in the passive/impersonal (McCone 1987: 192). This development is illustrated by the replacement of *no-b-mairfider* by *mairfidir sib* for, '**you** (plural) will be killed'/'someone will kill **you**' (Vendryes 1956: 188). This, together with the spreading use of third person singular verb forms with third person plural pronouns or plural nouns, marked the transition from passive to impersonal. Once this transition had started, the trend was towards one general impersonal form (which developed from the third person singular), accompanied by an object pronoun (or noun) to express a patient, that is, the Modern Irish autonomous. Although the Old Irish construction is in general referred to as a passive, it was always primarily an impersonal verb form, rather than a personal passive (see Vendryes 1956: 191).

The passive progressive developed in the Middle Irish period (900–1200) from the active progressive.[18] An early example of the passive progressive is *atu-sa secht mbliadna ico-m mess o na dib rigu sechtmogat-sa*, 'I have been **judged** now for seven years by those seventy two judges' (Ó Corráin 1997: 165). The active progressive construction had been in use since the Old Irish period (600–900). This active progressive construction consisted of an auxiliary verb together with the preposition *oc* (Modern Irish *ag*), 'at', and a verbal noun, as in *boi in drui occ airi na rind*, 'the druid was **watching** the stars' (Ó Corráin 1997: 163).

---

[17] In Old Irish a distinction is made between so-called absolute (independent) and conjunct (dependent) verb forms. Absolute verb forms are used when the verb is not preceded by a verbal particle, as in *carth(a)ir*. Conjunct forms, such as *c(h)arthar*, are used when the verb is preceded by a verbal particle, for example *no* in *no-m-charthar* (see Thurneysen 1980: 350). Thus, this is the reason why the verb appears in a different shape in these two clauses.

[18] See, however, Greene (1979: 134), who claims that the passive progressive in Early Modern Irish (looking like the Modern Irish form) disappeared, being replaced by the Modern Irish passive progressive construction, which is mainly active in meaning (compare also Greene 1979/1980).

3 Previous research

Relatively few extensive studies have been made of the autonomous and the passive progressive in Irish. The majority of these are concerned with the autonomous only. Below (under Studies of the autonomous and the passive progressive in Irish), a number of studies of the autonomous and the passive progressive that are relevant to the present investigation are presented. As is well known, much research has been done on the passive in certain other languages, especially English. Studies of particular relevance to the present investigation are presented below, under Topicality and the passive.

Topicality and the passive

Empirical research has shown that the passive exists in most natural languages (Keenan 1985: 47). It has also been shown that passive constructions are considerably less common than active ones. Therefore, the focus of interest has usually been the function of the passive, i.e. the marked form, as opposed to the active, unmarked form. It has been observed that in an active declarative sentence, the subject/agent is normally the most topical, or central, element in the sentence, and thus more topical than the patient/object. In the passive, on the other hand, a non-agent is more topical than the agent (Givón 1979a: 57). Foley and Van Valin (1985: 282) illustrate this with two sentences, one active and one passive, which refer to the same situation.

(1)   a. The boy hit the ball

       b. The ball was hit by the boy
(Foley and Van Valin's numbering).

Foley and Van Valin (1985: 282) point out that "[w]e ordinarily understand each of the sentences in (1) as being about their subjects: about *the boy* (1a) and about the *the ball* (1b)". Since the same situation is presented differently in the active and the passive in English, Foley and Van Valin (1985: 291) conclude that in English, the passive is a syntactic information packaging device. In passive constructions, a non-agent is in subject position and the agent phrase is optional (as in the passive progressive in Irish). In impersonal passives (such as the Irish autonomous) the agent is implicit and therefore automatically less topical than the patient. Considering these formal characteristics, one obvious way of approaching the question of the function of the passive is to measure the topicality of patients and agents of passive clauses. The topicality of patients and agents in passive clauses can then be compared to those of subjects and objects in active clauses. Features associated with assessing the topicality of participants are presented and discussed below. As will be shown, these features are definite vs. indefinite, given vs. new, continuity, and parallel surface structure.

From an information packaging perspective, the choice between a definite and an indefinite expression is related to whether or not the speaker/author assumes that the hearer/reader can uniquely identify the referent of the NP in question. Obviously, there is a correlation between given information and the definite expression of a nominal element since an element that is active in the reader or hearer's mind because it has been mentioned earlier in a text or conversation is often uniquely identifiable and thus subject to a definite form of expression. Chafe (1976: 42f.) remarks that the use of an indefinite NP to refer to a participant that represents given information is rather unlikely. It has been pointed out that some things do not need to be activated in discourse to be identifiable by the addressee, for example, when *your father* is introduced in the utterance *I saw your father yesterday* (Chafe 1976: 30). In this case *your father* is classified as new information although it does not represent information that is in any way new to the addressee. Chafe notes that "[t]he point is that the speaker has assumed that the addressee was not thinking about his father at the moment" (Chafe 1976: 30). Extralinguistic factors can also play an important role in establishing givenness: "If the speaker sees the addressee looking at a certain picture on his wall, for example, he might say out of the blue *I bought it last week*, where the idea of the picture is treated as given" (Chafe 1976: 31). 'The picture' is therefore pronominalised as *it* by the speaker.

One way of assessing the topicality of an element is to measure its continuity, that is, whether, and for how long, the element in question stays in the discourse after it has been introduced. The basic assumption is that the more topical, or central, an element is in the discourse, the longer it lingers. Consequently, preceding as well as following discourse may be considered when measuring the continuity of a participant. To assess the degree of continuity, Givón (1983b: 13ff.) has introduced two measures: referential distance and persistence.[19] Referential distance (also called 'look-back') is a count of the number of clauses since the last reference. It is given a value from 1 to 20, the lower the value the higher the degree of continuity. The value 1 means that the closest reference is in the immediately preceding clause. The value 20 indicates that the closest reference is in the 20th (or higher) clause preceding the clause in question. Persistence (also called 'decay') is a measure of the number of successive clauses where the participant under investigation is mentioned in the following discourse. High topicality is indicated by low values for referential distance and high values for persistence.

Thompson (1987b) investigates factors influencing the choice of the passive over the active from a discourse perspective in a corpus of spoken and written English. Her conclusion is that there are two discourse strategies influencing the choice of a passive construction over an active construction, one concerning the choice of an agent-less passive construction, and the other concerning the choice

---

[19] Referential distance and persistence have been used to measure topicality in a number of languages in Givón (1983a).

of an agent-less passive construction, as formulated below (Thompson 1987b: 497).

> A. If the agent is not to be mentioned, use the passive.
> B. If the agent is to be mentioned, then use the passive only when the non-agent is more closely related than the agent either
>> B1. to the 'theme' of the 'paragraph', or
>> B2. to a participant in the immediately preceding clause.

As regards the agent-less passive in English, Thompson (1987b: 499) notes that "there is relatively little controversy over the claim that the agent which is not expressed is either inferable from the context or has a referent whose exact identity is not important." Examples of these two types in Thompson's material are found in (21) and (22), respectively.

(21) I left under circumstances of considerable honor. I was given a farewell luncheon by half the staff of the law firm, meaning the lawyers themselves. *I was asked to make a speech and I was much applauded.* (Thompson 1987b: 499, her italics)

In (21), the agent (in italics) is inferable from the preceding sentence ('half the staff of the law firm') (Thompson 1987b: 499).

(22) In the olden days, the maintenance of the cemetery was left to the individual family. One family would pay and the others didn't. You would have weeds in one area and someplace else cared for. Today, in a modern cemetery, you have trust funds. Whenever a family purchases, a part of that money is put into a trust. This trust is inviolate. In this state it's held by a third party, a bank. You know that the cemetery *is gonna be cared for.* (Thompson 1987b: 499, her italics)

In (22), the type of agent (but not its identity) of the passive *is gonna be cared for* is inferable from the context. The meaning of the passive clause may thus be interpreted as "the trust fund pays for groundkeepers to care for the cemetery" (Thompson 1987b: 499). The agented passive, on the other hand, is used, as mentioned above (B), when "the referent of the non-agent subject unequivocally either is, or is intimately related to, the 'theme' of the paragraph, or what the paragraph is 'about', while the agent is more incidental to this 'theme'" (Thompson 1987b: 502). Examples of the strategies B1 and B2 in Thompson's material are given in (23) and (24), respectively.

(23) I was a young Columbia man while I worked in a cafeteria from 6:30 A.M. to 3:00 P.M. *I was much respected by the management,* even though I drove the people I worked with insane, because I had standards they couldn't cope with. (Thompson 1987b: 503, her italics)

(24) Lorenzo arrived in Paris as a down-at-heel political refugee without friends or money: luckily for him France at that time was ruled by an Italian, Cardinal Mazarin, in the minority of the twelve-year-old Louis XIV. (Thompson 1987b: 506, her italics)

Thompson (1987b: 506) points out that the strategies B1 and B2 are related: "The greater the number of connections we can establish between identical or related participants, the more cohesive and continuous the discourse is, and presumably, the easier it is to process."

After a closer study of her material, Thompson (1987b: 507) concludes that "[o]ne of the most striking ways in which the subject of the passive clause relates to a participant in the immediately preceding clause is in a reduced relative clause." This reduced relative subclause is a non-finite participial subclause, as exemplified in (25).

(25) ... At the very least the government is expected to order the police to seize the thirty businesses and hotels. and more than twenty-five farms, *owned by the Mitterand company*, a company *set up by the Patriotic Front* ostensibly to help rehabilitate former guerrillas from Mr. Nkomo's ZIPRA force... (Thompson 1987b: 507, her italics)

Thompson finds that subclauses like those in (25) play an important part in the choice of an agented passive construction over an active one. Each of the reduced relative subclauses in (25), *owned by the Mitterand company* and *set up by the Patriotic Front*, "is coded in the passive in order to render it a subject relative, i e., a relative clause in which the noun identical to the head noun is the subject" (Thompson 1987b: 507). In her corpus, "when a patient is relativized it is twice as likely [...] to occur as the subject of a passive than as the object of an active clause" (Thompson 1987b: 508). Furthermore, 83% of the passive clauses with relativized subjects in Thompson's material are reduced relative subclauses. Thompson therefore argues that reduced relative clauses provide "topic continuity between clauses in which the non-agent in the second clause is identical to a participant in the first" (Thompson 1987b: 508). Continuity is thus a crucial factor for choosing the passive over the active.[20]

These results presented in Thompson (1987b) point to a feature that is related to continuity, namely, parallel surface structure. Parallel surface structure, as defined by Weiner and Labov (1983), occurs when the referent of a passive patient is co-referential with the subject of an active clause in an uninterrupted chain of up to five neighbouring clauses. The main distinction of participants with respect to function is that between subjects and non-subjects, since the subject position is generally regarded as the most topical position. The main findings of Weiner and Labov's study is that the choice of a passive construction over an active one may be motivated by a wish on the part of the speaker to keep a participant in focus. Weiner and Labov's investigation deals with several factors that may influence the use of an agent-less passive in spoken English, such as given vs. new, parallel surface structure, and preceding passives. The results of Weiner and Labov's

---

[20] Compare Givón (1983b: 23f.), who points out that although main clauses normally are more continuous than subclauses, one type of (non-finite) subclause often functions as a topic continuity device, namely participial subclauses, as in *Having finished, he left*. Further, Pinkster (1985: 125ff.) finds that the passive in classical Latin is used to create continuity (keep perspective) as well as discontinuity (change perspective).

study indicate that, in their material, parallel surface structure is the factor that most strongly triggers the use of a passive construction, that is, "passives are favoured when the logical object moves into a position parallel with its co-referents" (Weiner and Labov 1983: 47). Another concept that is related to continuity and parallel surface structure is cohesion or cohesiveness. In Risselada's (1991) study of classical Latin, active and passive clauses are compared with regard to discourse cohesiveness (also called cohesion), which is defined in the following way. "A constituent C is considered *cohesive* if a constituent that is coreferential with C or in some way semantically or pragmatically related to C figures somewhere in the same sentence or in the surrounding (preceding or following) context." (Risselada 1991: 406, his italics). He distinguishes between sentence-internal and sentence-external cohesiveness, and between cohesion with subjects and with non-subjects. The results of Risselada's study indicate that subjects, that is, agents of active clauses and patients of passive clauses, are more cohesive than non-subjects, that is, patients of active clauses and agents of passive clauses. His study also shows that cohesive subjects are more often co-referential with subjects than with non-subjects. Risselada's (1991: 406f.) conclusion is that active agents and passive patients are more topical than non-subjects. In other words, the passive in Latin is used when the patient is more cohesive than the agent, that is, to a higher extent co-referential with, or closely semantically or pragmatically related to, some other constituent in the surrounding context.

  When it comes to the implicit agents of agent-less passive clauses, it is generally argued that the reason the agent is not explicitly mentioned in agent-less passive clauses is that its identity is either unimportant or easily inferable from the context (see, for example, Givón 1979a and Thompson 1987b). The recoverability of implicit agents indicates how the reader/hearer identifies, or recovers, the agent (Givón 1979a: 63). Givón outlines two ways of doing this: either the exact identity of the agent is inferred from the surrounding discourse, or the type of agent is inferred from the reader/hearer's "background knowledge of a general pragmatic sort" (Givón 1979a: 63).

  Since topicality has been shown to be a decisive factor in connection with passive constructions, the choice of features to examine in the present study is based on the factors described above. These features will be further discussed in Chapter 1.

Studies of the autonomous and the passive progressive in Irish

The research studies of the autonomous and the passive progressive that are relevant to the present study in Irish are presented below in chronological order, as displayed in Table 1. The earliest study, Hartmann (1954), is a mainly semantic, diachronic study of the passive in Irish, as well as in Welsh, Latin, Iranian languages and Indic. The passive is defined as "forms and expressions which denote that which comes into effect and that which is effected by force through an agent as well as that which is affected by a force" (Hartmann 1954: 13, my translation).[21] Hartmann includes in this definition the autonomous and the passive progressive, as well as other constructions that share the feature that the actor (or experiencer) is not the grammatical subject. Hartmann concludes that the Irish passive is used when the agent is under some outside force and "feels compelled to give in", or when the agent is unknown or unimportant (Hartmann 1954: 29, cf. 104–5). When it comes to the passive progressive, Hartmann (1954: 92) defines it as the progressive construction used when the process and the agent—instead of the patient—are highlighted. His main findings are that the different passive constructions in Irish, among them, the autonomous and the passive progressive, are closely related to certain areas of terminology. In Modern Irish, the most important area where the autonomous is used is what Hartmann terms 'das Messen der Kräfte' ('trial of strength'), as in (26), which is a command, one of the subcategories of 'das Messen der Kräfte' (Hartmann 1954: 89). According to Hartmann (1954), 'das Messen der Kräfte' is also associated with the use of the passive progressive, as in (27).[22] Apart from 'das Messen der Kräfte', there are six areas closely related to the passive progressive according to Hartmann (1954), namely, physical processes, right and wrong, mental qualities, sickness and health, matchmaking, handcraft and meals. Examples of the passive progressive used in clauses denoting a mental quality and matchmaking are found in (28) and (29) respectively.

Stenson (1981), the next study mentioned in Table 1, seeks a unified definition of the passive constructions (the autonomous, the passive progressive and a few other periphrastic constructions sharing features with the autonomous and the passive progressive) in Modern Irish. Following Langacker and Munro (1975) she concludes that the common features of Irish passive constructions are the embedding of a clause with an unspecified subject to the verb 'be' as a subject complement, and the topicalisation of the underlying object (Stenson 1981: 156). In a later study, Stenson (1989) investigates the autonomous and other constructions where the logical agent is not expressed. By comparing the autonomous with other constructions, Stenson's main aim is to determine the

---

[21] It should be noted that Hartmann (1954) has been severely criticised by the Celticist Heinrich Wagner (1956: 141–45). Wagner's main point of criticism is that Hartmann includes in his definition of the passive many kinds of constructions that are too dissimilar to be discussed together. According to Wagner, all these formally, historically and functionally different constructions cannot fit into a single system. Moreover, Hartmann's claim that "the belief in an 'Allkraft', *Nert*, ('strength'), lies behind the development of passive constructions in Irish and other languages that pushed aside the older tendency to use subject-active expressions" (Wagner 1956: 143, my translation) is hardly convincing in Wagner's view. Wagner also points out that Hartmann uses, and sometimes misinterprets, his (admittedly extensive) material to suit his purpose. Wagner (1956: 144) concludes that the strength of Hartmann's study lies in his extensive material and the great number of examples given to illustrate the use of the autonomous and the passive progressive and other passive-like constructions.

[22] For a discussion of this and other examples, see Hartmann (1954: 92–96). Most of his examples are from Peadar Ó Laoghaire's novel *Scéal Shéadna* (first published 1904).

Table 1. Research studies on the autonomous and the passive progressive

author	year of publ.	aut.	pass. prog.	material	language period	remark
Hartmann	1954	x	x	spoken and written	old and modern	incl. other passive/passive-like constructions[a]
Stenson	1981	x	x	constructed examples	modern	incl. other passive/passive-like constructions[a]
Stenson	1989	x		spoken and written	modern	
Noonan	1994	x	x	spoken and written	modern	incl. other passive/passive-like constructions[a]
Müller	1994	x		written	old	i.e. Old Irish passive
Müller	1999	x		written	old	i.e. Old Irish passive, incl. other passive/passive-like constructions[a]
Ó Corráin	2001	x		written	old and modern	incl. other passive/passive-like constructions[a]

[a] Mainly the perfect and the passive prospective presented above (under Two passive-like constructions).

(26) *Éistear*   *liom*
    listen-PRS-AUT   to-1SG

'**Let** me **be listened** to', 'Listen!' (Hartmann 1954: 89)

(27) *...go* *raibh* *breis* *mhór agus* *a* *gceart acu* ***d'á*** ***fhagháil***
    CONJ be-PST addition big and their due by-3PL to+its get-VBN

'...that far more than their due was **being got** by them' (Hartmann 1954: 93, his translation)

(28) *ní* *riabh* *aon* *phioc* ***d'á*** ***chuimhneamh*** *aige* *go...*
    NEG be-PST any bit to+its think-VBN by-3SGM that...

'it was not a bit **being thought** by him that...' (Hartmann 1954: 95, his translation)

(29) *tá* *cleamhnas* *aige* ***dhá*** ***dhéanamh***
    be-PRS wedding-match by-3SGM to+its make-VBN

'a wedding-match is **being made** by him' (Hartmann 1954: 96, his translation)

(30) ***Briseadh*** *an* *fhuinneog.*
    break-PST-AUT the window

'The window **was broken**.' (Stenson 1989: 385, her translation)

(31) <u>*Bhris*</u> *an* *fhuinneog.*
    break-PST the window

'The window <u>broke</u>.' (Stenson 1989: 385, her translation)

nature of the null subject. of autonomous clauses.[23] For example, Stenson (1989: 386) points out the contrast found in transitive verbs between the autonomous, as

---

[23] Stenson's study is conducted from a Government-Binding perspective. Her conclusion is that the subject of the Modern Irish autonomous verb form is arbitrary PRO (Stenson 1989: 404).

in (30), and what Stenson calls an 'ergative' use of active verb forms, as in (31).[24] In (30) the patient is the grammatical object of the autonomous verb. In (31), in contrast, "an underlying object, the patient NP, has been moved to fill an empty subject position" (Stenson 1989: 386). Syntactically, then, *an fhuinneog*, 'the window', is the subject in (31) although it is not the logical agent of the clause. In neither sentence is an agent overtly expressed, but the autonomous in (30) implies the presence of an outside agent, whereas the analytic form in (31) does not—it denotes a "spontaneous event" (Stenson 1989: 385f.).[25]

Another survey of Modern Irish autonomous and passive progressive is found in a corpus-based study by Noonan (1994). Noonan applies an information packaging perspective, which is of particular interest for the present study. The main aim of Noonan's study is to compare the autonomous and the passive progressive with each other and with active constructions with regard to the topicality of patients and overt agents. Under the heading of passive, Noonan includes the passive progressive and the passive prospective (see section 2 above). The active constructions included in the study are the simple active and various periphrastic constructions that share with the passive progressive the feature that the main verb is expressed as a verbal noun. The periphrastic constructions are grouped together as nominal constructions, while the autonomous and the simple active are labelled verbal constructions. In a corpus of written as well as spoken material, Noonan measures the topicality of the patients and agents of autonomous and passive progressive clauses and, for comparison, also of active clauses.[26] Noonan uses Givón's two topicality measures, referential distance and persistence, as described above, under Topicality and the passive. The mean referential distance and persistence values are calculated for patients and agents in both passive/impersonal and active sentences, one value each for the spoken and written material. Table 2 shows the types and numbers of constituents whose referential distance and persistence are measured by Noonan (1994). The average referential distance and persistence values are then analysed to reveal patterns of high and low topicality within each construction.

The results of Noonan's survey show that patients of autonomous clauses display topicality values like those of agents of active transitive and intransitive

---

[24] Compare the definition of ergative found in Crystal (1991: 124). See also Shibatani (1985: 827).

[25] Compare McCloskey (1996: 242f.., 251) who discusses two groups of verbs that can be used without an overt subject, the so-called 'salient unaccusatives', such as **laghdaigh** *ar a neart*, 'decreased on his strength/his strength **decreased**', and 'putative unaccusatives', as in **neartaigh** *a ghlór*, '**strengthened** his voice/his voice **strengthened**'. For an analysis and discussion of these and other examples, see McCloskey. Compare the so-called impersonal use of active verb forms, as in *bhris ar an fhoighne aige*, 'he lost his patience', quoted in *Graiméar* (1999: 167), see also Ó Cadhlaigh (1940: 73). See also the discussion of the examples (5) and (6) above.

[26] Noonan's corpus consists of 400 spoken and 400 written sentences (see Noonan 1994: 291). The written material is taken from three books: *Lig Sin i gCathú* by Breandán Ó hEithir (first published in 1976), *Deoraíocht* by Pádraic Ó Conaire (first published in 1910), and three short stories by Pádraic Pearse: *Íosagán, Eoghainín na nÉan* and *Na Bóithre* (first published in 1907). No details about the spoken sources are given.

Table 2. Constructions and constituents studied by Noonan (1994) as regards referential distance and persistence

nominal constructions			verbal constructions		
construction	constituent	n	construction	constituent	n
passive[a], agented	patient	34	autonomous	patient	84
	agent	34			
passive[a], agent-less	patient	8			
Total		42	Total		84
active[b], transitive	patient	44	active, transitive	patient	169
	agent	44		agent	169
active[b], intransitive	agent	15	active, intransitive	agent	85
Total		59	Total		254

[a] passive progressive and passive prospective
[b] active progressive and active prospective

clauses, as opposed to those of patients of active transitive clauses. This he interprets as a sign of patient topicalisation in the autonomous. Noonan finds that the implicit autonomous agents are mostly either contextually redundant, as in (32), or irrelevant, as in (22) (Noonan 1994: 292).[27] Noonan also analyses the autonomous with regard to stativisation, a feature that Langacker and Munro (1975) have associated with passive constructions (see further below). Noonan finds that stativisation is not a feature of the autonomous. To establish this, he shows that the autonomous can be used in the imperative, as in (34). Moreover, the autonomous can be combined with the progressive aspect, as in (35). Finally, Noonan notes that the imperative as well as the progressive aspect are inconsistent with stativisation (Noonan 1994: 292).

Turning to the passive progressive, Noonan draws four conclusions. First, patients of passive progressive clauses are less topical than both patients in active progressive sentences and agents in the passive progressive. He concludes that, patients are not topicalised in the passive progressive, as opposed to in the autonomous. Second, he finds that passive progressive agents are much more topical than passive progressive patients. A typical example of the (agented) passive progressive in Noonan's material is (36) (Noonan 1994: 294). Third, Noonan contrasts passive progressive agents with subjects of the active constructions presented in Table 2 and observes that passive progressive agents are more topical than many of these subjects. Finally, he finds that 81% (34/42) of the passive progressive clauses in his corpus are agented.[28] Noonan therefore concludes that the passive progressive in Irish is not characterised by agent deletion/defocusing (Noonan 1994: 297).

---

[27] Compare the "idiosyncratic usages" identified by Stenson (1989) mentioned in section 1.
[28] The proportion of agented passive progressive clauses in the spoken material is 91% and in the written material 67%.

(32) **Cailleadh**   *m'athair*   *agus*   *mo*   *mháthair...*
    lose-PST-AUT   my father   and   my   mother

'My father and my mother **were lost**...' (Noonan 1994: 292, his translation)

(33) ...**cuireadh**   *í*
    bury-PST-AUT   her

'...she **was buried**' (Noonan 1994: 292, his translation)

(34) **Bristear**   *é!*
    break-PRS-AUT   it

'**Let** it **be broken**', '**Let someone break** it!' (Noonan 1994: 292, his translation)

(35) *Táthar*   **á**   **bhriseadh**
    be-PRS-AUT   to+its   break-VBN

'It's **being broken**' (Noonan 1994: 292, his translation)

(36) *tá*   *a*   *cuid*   *gruaige*   **á**   **cíoradh**   *aici*
    be-PRS-AUT   her   share   hair-GEN   to+its   comb-VBN   by-3SGF

'Her hair is **being combed** by her' (Noonan 1994: 294, his translation)

Noonan finds the explanation why the Irish constructions have these topicality patterns in the information structure of Irish sentences. Noonan argues that in Irish, the immediate postpredicate position in a clause is reserved for arguments of high topicality. There are two positions for participants of low (lower) topicality: the position following the postpredicate position and the prepredicate position. Consequently, according to Noonan, there is a pattern where the element with the highest topicality is the agent in the passive progressive and the patient in the autonomous (Noonan 1994: 295, 302f.). This pattern is displayed in Table 3. As can be seen in Table 3, patients and agents have different levels of topicality depending on the syntactic structure. In the autonomous, the patient is highly topical since it follows immediately after the predicate. Conversely, in the corresponding active construction (active non-progressive), it is the agent that appears in the post-predicate high topicality slot, while the patient is in a low topicality position. As opposed to the autonomous, patients of the passive progressive occupy the prepredicate low topicality position, while agents appear in the postpredicate high topicality slot. Interestingly, the passive progressive also contrasts with the active progressive with regard to topicality. In the active progressive, agents occur in the prepredicate low topicality position and patients in the postpredicate high-topicality position.[29] Noonan compares his results with the

---

[29] In Noonan's (1994: 293) study, the passive progressive (and the passive prospective) in the written material (30/44 instances) diverge from the information structure pattern shown in Table 3 in that the agents are more topical than the patients. Noonan (1994: 304) states: "I have no wholly convincing explanation for this single anomaly in what is otherwise a very regular pattern".

Table 3. Topicality of constituents in passive progressive, autonomous and active clauses, adapted from Noonan (1994: 303)
(The examples inserted are my own.)

construction	(auxiliary)	low topicality	predicate	high topicality	low topicality
autonomous	-	-	autonomous form	patient	-
	-	-	*léitear*	*leabhar*	-
			'one reads'	'a book'	
			'one reads a book', 'a book is read'		
passive progressive		**patient**	verbal noun phrase	**agent**	-
	tá	*leabhar*	*á léamh*	*aige*	
	'is'	'a book'	'at its reading'	'by him'	
	'a book is being read by him', 'he is reading a book'[a]				
active non-progressive	-	-	active verb form	**agent**	**patient**
	-	-	*léann*	*sé*	*leabhar*
			'reads'	'he'	'a book'
			'he reads a book'		
active progressive		**agent**	verbal noun phrase	**patient**	-
	tá	*sé*	*ag léamh*	*leabhair*	-
	'is'	'he'	'at reading'	'of a book'	
	'he is reading a book'				

[a]An active translation of this clause is suitable, since Noonan's conclusion is that the passive progressive does not function as a passive construction.

functional characteristics of the passive as defined by Langacker and Munro (1975).[30] In their analysis, the passive in general is characterised by three features (Noonan 1994: 279):

– patient topicalisation
– agent deletion/defocusing
– stativisation

Based on this comparison, Noonan concludes that the passive progressive is formally a passive, but not functionally, and, conversely, that the autonomous is functionally a passive but not formally.[31] His main claim is that "the arrangement of high and low topicality in Irish is organised in terms of position relative to the semantic predicate" (Noonan 1994: 306). Noonan thus finds that Irish deviates from what according to him is the basic assumption held by most linguists, namely, that "high and low topicality are arranged within a sentence on a

---

[30] Compare Stenson (1981), who also refers to Langacker and Munro (1975) when analysing passive constructions in Irish.
[31] Compare Greene (1979: 134) who claims that the agented passive progressive is passive in structure but "active in meaning", while the agent-less passive progressive is an impersonal construction.

continuum of high first/low last, with little regard for the syntactic or semantic status of the items contained within the sentence" (Noonan 1994: 305). Instead, in Irish, the topicality of a constituent depends on its position relative to the predicate of the sentence (see Table 3 above).

Noonan's application of an information packaging perspective on the autonomous and the passive progressive makes his survey particularly relevant to the present study. There are, however, problems concerning the evaluation of Noonan's results, mainly since he describes neither the collection of the spoken material nor his selection of the written material in sufficient detail.

Two other studies devoted to information packaging in relation to the passive are by Müller (1994 and 1999). Müller (1994) investigates the functions of the Old Irish passive construction (which was later to develop into the Modern Irish autonomous; cf. section 2, Development of the autonomous and the passive progressive, above) in three versions of the medieval tale *Táin Bó Cúailgne*, 'The Cattle Raid of Cooley'. Her study is based on theories of information flow, and more precisely the concept of pivot presented in Foley and Van Valin (1985). The term pivot denotes "a particular NP type which is privileged in controlling a great deal of the language's syntax" (Foley and Van Valin 1985: 305). Consequently, the pivot is usually the subject, since it is the subject that controls verb agreement. Müller concludes that in early Irish the choice of pivot depends on discourse requirements, that is, early Irish has pragmatic pivot. This means that when the patient and not the agent/subject of an active sentence is the pivot, the passive is used, where the patient/subject—the pivot—controls verb agreement (Müller 1994: 197). After analysing her data, Müller finds that the early Irish passive has three functions: to background the agent, to foreground the patient, and to foreground the verb itself (Müller 1994: 196). The third of these functions is not discussed in Müller's article and therefore not exemplified below. The first of the functions listed by Müller, to background the agent, is shown in (37).[32] In (37) the agent is well known in the context, it is the hero (*Cú Chulainn*), who is also the main character of the story. Omitting the agent is thus possible without obscuring the meaning of the sentence (Müller 1994: 197). The second function of the Old Irish passive construction in Müller's survey, to foreground the NP patient, occurs, for example, when this patient is a new topic, as in (38), where *culén*, 'a whelp', appears for the first time in the text (Müller 1994: 197f.).

In a later study of early Irish prose, Müller (1999) further investigates the nature of agents, and to some extent also patients. One construction under investigation is the Old Irish passive. Müller analyses the internal structure of the Old Irish passive with regard to, among other things:

---

[32] The translations of the examples from Müller (1994) are Müller's. Where necessary, I have added a more literal translation. In addition to the grammatical annotations listed in section 5 below, the following abbreviations occur in (29)–(32): INF = infixed pronoun, PASS = passive voice (described in section 2 above), PERF = perfect tense, PRT = preterite tense.

(37)

Ansait	and sin	trá	*corrubad*		and	Cáur mac Da Láth	7
stay-PRT-3PL	there	then	until+slay-PRT-PASS-3SG		there	Cáur...		and

Láth mac Da Bró	7	*Foirc mac Trí nAignech*	7	*Srubgaile mac Eóbith.*	Ar	galaib
Láth...	and	Foirc...		and	Srubgaile...	at	combat

óenfhir	*ro gáeta*	uli
one man-GEN	slay-PRT-PASS-3PL	all

'They stayed there until Cáur... and Láth... and Srubgaile <u>were slain</u>. They <u>were</u> all <u>killed</u> in single combat.' (Müller 1994: 197, her translation)

(38)

Ebéltair	culén	din	chúani	chétna	*lem-sa*	duit,	7
raise-FUT-PASS	whelp	from+the	litter	same	by-1SG-EMPH	for-2SG	and

bíam	cú-sa	do	imdegail	do	chethra...
COP-FUT-1SG	hound	to	guard-VBN	your-SG	cattle

'<u>I will raise</u> a whelp from the same litter for you, and I will be a hound to guard your cattle...' (Müller 1994: 197, her translation, lit. 'a whelp <u>will be raised</u> <u>by me</u> from the same litter for you, ...')

– the definiteness of agents and patients
– the contrast between given and new information
– continuity, where she looks at the occurrence and semantic role of an element in the preceding (retrospective continuity) and/or following (prospective continuity) main clause that is co-referential with the passive agent or patient (retrospective continuity).

Müller's survey of the definiteness of patients and agents shows that the agents are always definite. In contrast, a majority of the patients are indefinite. Further, Müller (1999: 151) found that 91% of the agents of passive clauses refer to given participants. Patients, however, are more often new (56%) than given (33%); in a few instances patients are inferable (11%), that is, not overtly expressed.[33]

As regards continuity, Müller finds that continuity is more common among agents (47% of them display retrospective continuity, and 61% prospective continuity) than among patients (23% retrospective continuity, 19% prospective continuity) (Müller 1999: 155). For both patients and agents retrospective continuity is slightly more frequent than prospective continuity. As for the semantic role of the continuing element, Müller (1999) finds that there is a fairly even distribution across the various semantic roles. However, it seems that the agents of passive clauses are most often co-referential with subjects of active clauses. The sentence in (39) and (40) contain examples of prospective and retrospective continuity, respectively. In (39) the subject and addressee of the imperative in the first sentence, *Collaa dún, a popa Loíg*, 'Go for me, friend Láeg',

---

[33] Since Müller (1999) is primarily concerned with agents, only agented passives have been included in her study.

(39)

Collaa	dún,	a popa	Loíg...	co	n-airlither	Lugaid...	dús
go	for me	friend	Láeg	so that	consult-PRS-SUBJ-2SG	Lugaid	to know

cía	dotháet... .	*Iarfaighter*	co lléir	7	a	imchomarc	*lat'*.
who	come-PRS-3SG	question-IPV-PASS-3SG	closely	and	his	greeting	by-2SG

"Go for me, friend Láeg... and consult Lugaid and find out who is coming... Question him closely and greet him."' (Müller 1999: 156, her translation, lit. '... let him be questioned closely... by you')

(40)

In	*fer*	*déideanach*	*níndránic*		*acht*	*ind*	*mbéimme*
the	man	last	NEG+INF-him+reach-PRT/PERF-3SG		but	end	blow-GEN

conid		*corastair*	*i*	*mmúaidhi.*	*Anachtai-side*		*la*
so that+INF-3SGM		put-PRT-3SG	in	a swoon	rescue-PRT-PASS-3SG+EMPH		by

Coin Culaind	*íarom.*
Cú Chulainn	afterwards

'The last man, he only received a glance of a blow, so that he fell into a swoon. He was rescued by Cú Chulainn later.' (Müller 1999: 156, her translation)

is resumed in the following sentence as the agent *lat*, 'by you', of the passive *iarfaighter*, 'let him be questioned' (Müller 1999: 156). In (40) the patient of the passive *anachtai-side*, 'he was rescued', in the second sentence refers back to the subject of the first sentence, *in fer déideanach*, 'the last man' (Müller 1999: 156).

Ó Corráin (2001), the final study mentioned in Table 1, is a diachronic investigation of voice in Irish. One of the constructions studied is the autonomous, along with so-called impersonal active and nominal formations. These constructions share the feature that the grammatical subject does not refer to the participant responsible for the action. Ó Corráin's (2001: 119) main finding is that in Irish the most important contrast as regards voice is that between active and middle, rather than that between active and passive.[34] As a consequence, there is a formal distinction between volition and non-volition, which is reflected, for example, in the use of the autonomous. Ó Corráin (2001: 118) finds that "Irish tends to reserve the structure *Active Verb + Subject* for situations where the subject is the willing agent of an action", which, according to Ó Corráin, motivates the use of the autonomous in certain cases. For example, the use of the autonomous in the sentence **baineadh** *gáire as*, 'it made him laugh', lit. 'a laugh **was taken** out of him', indicates non-volition on the part of the participant referred to by the prepositional pronoun *as*, 'out of him', while in the active clause *lig sé gáire*, 'he laughed', lit. 'he **let out** a laugh', the use of an active verb form indicates that the subject *sé*, 'he', is " the willing agent of an action" (Ó Córráin 2001: 118). Further examples that illustrate "the disinclination [in Irish] to subjectivize logical patients" are, for instance, **baineadh** *tuisle as*, 'he tripped', lit. 'a trip **was taken** out of him' (Ó Corráin 2001: 98, 108 f.). Based on the analysis of these and other examples Ó Corráin (2001: 115) concludes that

---

[34] Ó Corráin (2001: 108, 110) mentions 'fail', 'succeed', 'become angry' as typical middle concepts.

"[t]he Irish passive or autonomous is to be regarded, along with other formations, as a subspecies of the middle voice".

Finally, one may note that dialectal variation in the use of the autonomous and the passive progressive is not touched upon in any of the sources referred to in sections 3 and 4 above, except for remarks concerning the relatively frequent use of the passive progressive in Munster (see above, section 3, under Topicality and the passive).

4 Material and data

The Corpus

As mentioned above, the main aim of the present study is to compare the use of the autonomous and the passive progressive. The choice was to work with an electronic corpus since the use of electronic material enhances the application of a new methodology on a large number of texts. This was also justified by the fact that the few existing corpus-based studies that are relevant to the present study were based on a relatively small amount of material. When I started the compilation of the corpus used for the present study, there was one electronic corpus available to me, the Gaelic Text Database ('Gaeldict'), first compiled by Ciarán Ó Duibhín in 1995.[35] The version of the Gaeldict corpus used (1998) contains 27 Ulster texts (by 7 authors), 2 Connacht texts (by 2 authors) and one text from Munster. In addition, the corpus contains 4 texts in Scots Gaelic (4 authors) and 3 English texts by 2 authors (the Irish translations of which are included in the Ulster part of the corpus). All texts are included in their entirety. The total number of words is 1,997,043 (of which the Ulster texts comprise 1,470,301 words, the Connacht texts 99,701 words, Munster 57,965 words, Scots Gaelic 100,535 words, and English 268,541).

The present corpus consists of eleven complete texts (with two exceptions, as explained below) by ten authors, evenly distributed across the three main dialects Connacht, Munster and Ulster. The corpus is presented in Table 4. The total number of words is around 600,000. Connacht and Ulster are represented by four texts each, by four and three authors respectively. The remaining three texts in the corpus are by three Munster writers. The corpus was compiled from sources of two kinds. Seven of the texts are part of the Gaelic Text Database. To make up

---

[35] The corpus is downloadable from the Internet. The Internet release used is from November 1998, downloaded from address: <ftp://ftp.heanet.ie/pub/itdb>, now available from <http://www.ceantar.-org/Comp/GAELDI98.HTML>. The Gaeldict Corpus was first released in 1995. Several revised and enlarged versions have been released, the latest release is from November 2003.
The 15 Million word National Corpus of Irish (Corpas Náisiúnta na Gaeilge) which would have been a highly useful tool for a corpus-based study of Modern Irish texts had not yet been released at the time of the compilation of the present corpus.

Table 4. Presentation of the texts included in the corpus
(Unless otherwise stated, the whole text is included in the corpus. Gael. = Gaelic
Text Database, scan. = scanned.)

title	source	genre	author	dialect	year of publ.	no. of words
An Mothall sin ort	Gael.	non-fiction	Seán Ó Ruadháin b. 1883	Co.	1967	40,742
Feamainn Bhealtaine	Gael.	auto-biogr.	Máirtín Ó Direáin b. 1910	Co.	1961	58,959
Dúil	scan.	fiction	Liam Ó Flaithearta b. 1897	Co.	1978 (1953)	55,198
An tSraith ar lár (p. 9–184)	scan.	fiction	Máirtín Ó Cadhain b. 1906	Co.	1967	49,733
				Total Connacht		204,632
Na hAird Ó Thuaidh	Gael.	auto-biogr.	Pádraig Ua Maoileoin b. 1913	Mu.	1960	57,965
Fiche bliain ag Fás	scan.	auto-biogr.	Muiris Ó Súilleabháin b. 1911	Mu.	1976 (1933)	117,359
Mo Scéal Féin (p. 7–101)	scan.	auto-biogr.	Peadar Ó Laoghaire b. 1839	Mu.	(1917)[a]	28,068
				Total Munster		203,392
Dochartach Duibhlionna	Gael.	fiction	Seosamh Mac Grianna b. 1901	Ul.	1926	15,084
Saoghal Corrach	Gael.	auto-biogr.	Séamus Ó Grianna b. 1889	Ul.	1945	95,707
Crathadh an Phocáin	Gael.	fiction	Seaghán Mac Meanman b. 1886	Ul.	1955	66,637
Rácáil agus Scuabadh	Gael.	fiction	Seaghán Mac Meanman b. 1886	Ul.	1955	25,606
				Total Ulster		203,034
				Total		611,058

[a] The year of publication of the edition included in the present corpus is not mentioned in the printed book.

for the uneven distribution of texts across dialects in the Gaeldict corpus, I have added four books to the material selected from that corpus, two each in the Munster and Connacht dialects. This additional material was scanned in order to have the whole corpus in electronic format. To create a corpus with the same amount of material from each dialect (c. 200,000 words per dialect), two of the scanned texts have not been included in their entirety, *An tSraith ar lár* and *Mo Scéal féin*. As shown in Table 4, my corpus includes the two Connacht texts, the Munster text and four of the Ulster texts from the Gaeldict corpus. The selected Ulster texts are by the three authors that are most frequently represented in the Gaeldict corpus. The compiler has provided information about the exact number of words in each text of the Gaeldict corpus.[36] For the remaining texts, *Dúil*, *An tSraith ar Lár*, *Fiche Bliain ag Fás* and *Mo Scéal Féin* (totalling 685 pages), I

---

[36] Ciarán Ó Duibhín, personal communication.

judged it sufficient for the purpose of my study to estimate the number of words based on the number of words per page found on the ten first pages.[37]

As can be noted in Table 4, the texts are published within a time-span of 50 years: the earliest text was first published in 1917 and the latest in 1967. However, the most important factor considered when selecting the texts from the Gaeldict corpus and the additional texts has been the language aspect: I have sought to include authors well-known for writing genuine, idiomatic Irish. Other factors that have determined the choice of texts have been availability, and, in the case of the scanned material, printing quality.

As regards genre, the texts selected for inclusion in the present corpus are mainly of two types. Five of the texts are autobiographical novels or collections of short stories (comprising approximately 359,000 words). Five of the texts are fictional novels or collections of short stories (comprising approximately 212,000 words). Finally, there is one text (*An Mothall sin ort*) that has been classified as non-fiction (40,742 words). This text is a collection of pieces (originally published in a newspaper) on various topics. The tone is informal and the subject matter often resembles that of the autobiographical texts. In conclusion, while the corpus is somewhat heterogeneous with respect to genre, all texts share the feature that they are basically narrative.

Data retrieval and statistical method

The relevant data was collected in two steps. Automated searches using the programme WordSmith (version 3) yielded 94% of the instances in the database. The remaining 6% of the instances included in the database were selected manually from the printed originals of the scanned texts. This was necessary since there were several errors in the scanned texts, mainly due to poor printing quality of the original texts and restrictions in the OCR program available to me for the interpretation of the scanned material (OmniPage Pro 9.0). As for the texts from the Gaeldict corpus, I am confident that the quality of the electronic texts is adequate for the purpose of the present study. I have referred to the original printed texts when classifying each instance of the autonomous and the passive progressive in the database, with the exception of two texts from the Gaeldict Corpus, *An Mothall sin ort* and *Dochartach Duibhlionna*, whose printed originals were not available to me.

As a statistical tool in the analysis of quantitative findings, I used the chi-square test to determine whether my results are statistically significant or not. Throughout, the level of significance used is 0.05, the significance level generally encountered in linguistic surveys. The chi-square test is a useful tool when interpreting the results; attested statistical significance of variation supports conclusions drawn concerning differences between the use of the autonomous and

---

[37] I have used the same method of counting words as the compiler of the Gaeldict corpus, that is, contractions, such as *ina = i + a*, and compound words are counted as two words (see the Gaeldict documentation file gaeldi98.text).

the passive progressive. However, it should be kept in mind that the chi-square test has certain limitations. Most importantly, sample size may affect the result: the greater the sample size, the stronger the probability of obtaining a statistically significant result. Further, it is recommended that none of the expected frequencies in the table that is to be tested is below five for obtaining a reliable result. When the obtained chi-square value is greater than the relevant critical value, and none of the expected frequencies are below five, the result is statistically significant.[38] In the text, only statistically significant chi-square values are given, together with the critical value with which the chi-square value is compared (see, for example, Oakes (1998: 266) for a table of critical values).

5 The examples

Throughout the thesis, examples of the autonomous and the passive progressive are presented and discussed. The translations of the examples are not intended to be literal, but rather correspond to current English versions of the Irish original sentence. As a consequence, the Irish autonomous and the passive progressive verb forms may not be translated as passives in the English version. To facilitate the interpretation of the examples, the autonomous and the passive progressive verb forms are shown in bold-face in the Irish sentence. The corresponding verb forms in the English sentence are also shown in bold-face. In some examples, a part of the sentence is underlined in the Irish as well as the English versions to highlight a feature or features relevant to the discussion. The sentences selected for the examples have been checked against the original printed text (with two exceptions, as mentioned in section 4 above). The spelling in the original printed text has been retained, except in obvious cases of misprints. The source text of the examples from the corpus is stated together with the code Co. (Connacht), Mu. (Munster) or Ul. (Ulster) indicating the dialect, and a reference to the page where the example begins. When no specific reference is stated, the example is my own. The abbreviations used for grammatical annotations are AUT = autonomous verb form, COMP = comparative, COND = conditional mood, CONJ = conjunction, COP = the copula, DIM = diminutive, EMPH = emphatic, F = feminine, FUT = future tense, GEN = genitive case, INT = interrogative, IPF = imperfect tense, IPV = imperative mood, M = masculine, NEG = negative, PL = plural, PRS = present tense, PST = past tense, REL = relative, SG = singular, SUBJ = subjunctive mood, SUP = superlative, VBA = verbal adjective, VBN = verbal noun, VOC = vocative case.[39] These annotations have been included to help the reader interpret the examples; they are not intended to be exhaustive.

---

[38] For more detailed information on the testing of correlation using the chi-square test, see, for example, Brown (1988), Oakes (1998), Reynolds (1984), and Woods (1986).
[39] Unless otherwise stated, verbs are in the indicative mood.

6 Plan of the thesis

The remaining six chapters of the present thesis are organised in the following way. Chapter 1 is a presentation of the principles of classification of the instances of the autonomous and passive progressive in the database. In Chapter 2 the results of the classification of verb and clause types are presented and discussed. The results of the classification of patients and agents are presented and discussed in Chapter 3. Chapter 4 contains an analysis of dialectal variation in the use of the autonomous and the passive progressive. In Chapter 5, the study of a subset of the autonomous and the passive progressive clauses in the main database in more detail is presented. The thesis concludes with a summary and a discussion of the most important results of the study.

CHAPTER 1
Method

In the Introduction, section 2, I formulated my main research question, namely, 'What differences in use are there between the autonomous and the passive progressive?' To find an answer to this question, the 600,000 word corpus consisting of eleven texts was compiled, as described in the Introduction, section 4. All instances of the autonomous and the passive progressive were extracted from the corpus and gathered in a database. The instances were then classified according to two sets of variables.[1] The first set of variables concerns mainly the verb types that form the autonomous and the passive progressive and the clause types where the autonomous and the passive progressive occur. In addition, since the passive progressive can be used in non-finite subclauses, passive progressive clauses were classified with regard to finite vs. non-finite subclause structure. One aim of investigating the features concerning verbs and clauses is to form a basis for the analysis of the autonomous and the passive progressive with respect to information packaging, as will be shown in Chapter 5 (see also Chapter 2). The second set of variables deals with the classification of the patients and agents of the autonomous and passive progressive, overt as well as implicit. As the focus is on the comparison of the two constructions with respect to the information packaging, the second set of variables studied were selected since they are factors that have been shown to be connected to the measuring of the topicality of the participants. The selected features are definite vs. indefinite form, given vs. new information, continuity, and syntactic function of continuity creating elements. In addition, the recoverability of implicit agents is studied. Recoverability concerns the way implicit agents are identified; this feature is thus linked to the concept of information packaging. As highlighted in the Introduction, section 3, the topicality of participants is relevant in the discussion of the function of the passive, since in previous research, high topicality of non-agents is considered a basic part of the definition of the passive. One aim of investigating the topicality of the patients and agents in the database is thus to try to determine whether the autonomous and the passive progressive differ regarding passive function.

---

[1] A subset of the instances of autonomous and the passive progressive in the database have been classified according to a third set of variables, as presented in Chapter 5.

1.1 Verbs and clauses

The variables that concern verbs and clauses and the co-occurrence of their values with the autonomous and the passive progressive are presented in Table 1.1.

Table 1.1. Variables concerning verbs and clauses

variable	value	autonomous	passive progressive
verb type	monotransitive, direct	yes	yes
	monotransitive, indirect	yes	no
	ditransitive	yes	yes
	intransitive	yes	no
	auxiliary	yes	no
clause type	main clause	yes	yes
	subclause, adverbial	yes	yes
	subclause, nominal	yes	yes
	subclause, relative	yes	yes
subclause structure	finite	no	yes
	non-finite	no	yes

The classification of verbs and clauses is based on the description of the autonomous and the passive progressive in grammars of Modern Irish (see the Introduction, section 2) as well as the analysis of the instances of the autonomous and the passive progressive in the present database. The three variables and their values, displayed in Table 1.1, will now be presented in more detail.

1.1.1 Verb type

The variable verb type is based primarily on the kind of object, if any, taken by the verb in question. Four structural types are distinguished: monotransitive with a direct object (monotransitive direct) or with an indirect object, that is, a prepositional object (monotransitive indirect), ditransitive, that is, verbs that take one direct object and one prepositional object, and intransitive.[2] As mentioned above (the Introduction, section 1), a direct object is required in a passive progressive clause, since the direct object is the grammatical subject of the clause. Therefore, only monotransitive verbs that take direct objects and ditransitive verbs can be used in the passive progressive. An example of a passive progressive verb form of the monotransitive direct type is given in (1). In (2) the autonomous clause includes a verb of the monotransitive indirect type. Ditransitive verbs take one direct object and one prepositional object, as in (3), which is an example of the passive progressive.

---

[2] Compare *Graiméar* (1999: 14, 16, 320), where direct object is the only object type recognised, while prepositional objects are defined as complements.

(1)

Coinnle	céarach	a	bhíodh	in	úsáid	ar	an	altóir,	agus	ba		mhór
candles	wax-GEN	REL	be-IPF	in	use	on	the	altar	and	COP-PST		large

an	lán	coinneal	a	ídítí	sna	teampaill	le linn	Aifrinn
the	great deal	candles-GEN	REL	use-IPF-AUT	in+the	churches	during	mass-GEN

agus	nuair	a	bhíodh	_féilte_	_á_	**gcomóradh.**
and	when	REL	be-IPF	feasts	to+their	celebrate-VBN

'Wax candles were used on the altar and a lot of candles were used in the churches during Mass and when <u>feasts</u> were **being celebrated**.' (Co. *An Mothall sin ort*: 83)

(2)

Lena linn sin,	**beireadh**	_ar_	_an_	_naomhóig_	agus	a	raibh	istigh
during that time	bear-PST	on	the	currach (= type of boat)	and	REL	be-PST	inside

inti,	agus	tógadh	glan	ón	uisce	í	suas	amach	ar	an	bhféar
in-3SGF	and	lift-PST-AUT	clear	from+the	water	it	up	out	on	the	grass

glas,	agus	seo	leo	suas	fé dhéin	tí	an	óil.
green	and	this	with-3PL	up	towards	house-GEN	the-GEN	drink-GEN

'During that time, <u>the currach</u> **was taken hold** <u>of</u> and all that was in it, and it was lifted clear of the water up onto the green grass, and up they went to the pub.' (Mu. *Fiche Bliain ag Fás*: 80)

(3)

"Acht,"	arsa	mise,	"tá	ár	moladh	agus	ár	mbuidheachas	tuillte
but	say-PST	I-EMPH	be-PRS	our	praise	and	our	gratitude	earn-VBA

ag	na	fir	seo,	agus	nach	bhfuil	an	chontabhairt	ann	go
by	the	men	these	and	INT-NEG	be-PRS	the	danger	in-3SGM	that

ndéanfar	_dearmad_	_daobhtha_	cionn is	nach	rabh	an	Ghaedhilg	aca?"
do-FUT-AUT	negligence	to-3PL	because	CONJ-NEG	be-PST	the	Irish	at-3PL

'"But," said I, "these men have earned our praise and gratitude, and isn't there a danger that <u>they</u> **will be <u>forgotten</u>** because they didn't know Irish?"' (Ul. *Saoghal Corrach*: 201)

(4)

Bhí	an	t-eallach	ag	gabháil	thar	an	chrích,	ná	bhí	an
be-PST	the	cattle	at	go-VBN	across	the	boundary	or	be-PST	the

madadh	ag	marbhadh	a	chuid	éanlaithe,	ná	**bhíthear**	_ag_	_goid_
dog	at	kill-VBN	his	share	fowl-GEN	or	be-PST-AUT	at	steal-VBN

a	chuid	mónadh.
his	share	turf-GEN

'The cattle were crossing the boundary, or the dog was killing his fowl, or his turf **was** <u>being stolen</u>.' (Ul. *Dochartach Duibhlionna*: 9)

(5) *Bhí*   *dhá*   *halla* *annsin,* *áit*   *a*   *rachthá*   *isteach* *go*
    be-PST two   halls   there   place   REL   go-COND[for IPF]-2SG   in   CONJ

    ndéantaidhe   <u>*do*</u>   <u>*phas*</u>   <u>*a*</u>   <u>*sgrúdughadh.*</u>
    do-COND[for IPF]-AUT   yout-SG   passport   to   examine-VBN

'There were two halls there, where you went <u>to have your passport examined</u>.' (Ul. *Saoghal Corrach*: 234)

The auxiliary verbs that occur in the autonomous in the database are classified as a separate category. Following the classification of auxiliaries in *Graiméar* (1999: 170ff., 200), and the descriptions of individual verbs in Ó Dónaill (1992), the auxiliary verbs found in the database are *bí*, 'be', as in (4), *féad* 'can', *caith* 'must', and *déan*, 'do', as in (5).

1.1.2 Clause type

The next variable in my classification is clause type. Here the main distinction is between main and subclause. Following *Graiméar* (1999: 261), subclauses are further divided into three groups according to their function as clausal elements in the matrix clause: adverbial, nominal, and relative.[3] The present section deals with the classification of finite subclauses only, non-finite subclauses (containing the passive progressive) are presented in section 1.1.3. A number of conjunctions used to introduce adverbial subclauses are mentioned in *Graiméar* (1999: 279–301); some of the conjunctions that occur most frequently in the present corpus are exemplified below. Most adverbial subclauses are introduced by conjunctions that consist of a combination containing the connective *go*, 'that', or the relative particle *a*, for example, *mar a*, 'like', *cé go*, 'although', *nuair a*, 'when', as in (6), where an instance of the autonomous is used in an adverbial subclause. Sometimes the conjunction is a single word, such as *mar*, 'since, because', as in (7), which includes an autonomous, and *mura*, 'if...not', as in (8), which contains an example of the passive progressive.

As with adverbial subclauses, nominal subclauses are marked in numerous ways, as accounted for in *Graiméar* (1999: 278). The two most frequent types of conjunctions used to introduce nominal subclauses are the conjunctions *go*, 'that', negated *nach*, 'that...not', as in (9), and interrogative particles, such as *cad*, 'what', as in (10).

Relative subclauses are introduced by a relative particle, most often *a/ar* 'who, which', as in (11), or *nach/nár*, 'who, which...not'. The classification of non-finite adverbial, nominal and relative subclauses (containing the passive progressive) will be discussed in the next section.

---

[3] *Graiméar* (1999: 261) distinguishes between adjectival relative clauses and other relative clauses. The first category corresponds to the relative clauses recognised in the present study.

(6) *Nuair*   *a*   **bhéarfaí**   *faoi deara*   *go*   *raibh*   *duine*   *ag*   *déanamh*
    when   REL   give-COND-AUT   under notice   CONJ   be-PST   person   at   do-VBN

    faillí   *ina*   *chuid*   *fómhair*   *agus*   *ag*   *ligean*   *don*   *aimsir*   *bhreá*
    neglect-GEN   in+his   share   harvest-GEN   and   at   let-VBN   to+the   weather   fine

    sleamhnú   *thart*   *gan*   *lá*   *fada*   *a*   *thapú,*   *déarfaí*   *"dá*
    slip-VBN   past   without   day   long   to   grasp quickly-VBN   say-COND-AUT   if

    mbíodh   *soineann*   *go*   *Samhain*   *bheadh*   *breall*   *ar*   *dhuine*   *éigin",*   *mar*
    be-SUBJ-PST   fair weather   until   November   be-COND   arrears   on   person   some   because

    gurb   *"ionann*   *urchar*   *bodaigh*   *i*   *bpoll*   *móna*   *agus*   *oíche*   *fhómhair*
    COP-PRS   same   shot   churl-GEN   in   hole   turf-GEN   and   night   autumn-GEN

    ag   *titim".*
    at   fall-VBN

'When it **was noticed** that somebody was neglecting his harvest, and letting fine weather slip by without availing of a long day, one would say "if there was fair weather until November somebody would be behind with their work", because "the autumn night falls quickly and unexpectedly".' (Co. *An Mothall sin ort*: 92)

(7) *Mar*   *níor*   **facthas**   *riamh*   *sna*   *bólaí*   *sin*   *culaith*   *níos deise*   *ná*
    because   NEG   see-PST-AUT   ever   in+the   parts   that   suit   nice-COMP   than

    an   *chulaith*   *a*   *rinne*   *sé*   *do*   *Shéamaisín.*
    the   suit   REL   do-PST   he   for   Séamaisín

'Because a nicer suit **had** never **been seen** in those parts than the suit he made for Séamaisín.' (Co. *Dúil*: 107)

(8) *Bhí*   *beirt*   *acu*   *suite*   *cois*   *na*   *tine*   *anois*   *gan*   *do*
    be-PST   two   of-3PL   sit-VBA   beside   the-GEN   fire-GEN   now   without   for/of

    chomhrá   *acu*   *ach*   *seanCháit,*   *agus*   *deirim*   *leat,*   *mura*   *raibh*
    conversation   at-3PL   except   old+Cáit   and   say-PRS-1SG   to-2SG   if not   be-PST

    moladh   *á*   **fháil**   *aici,*   *ní*   *lá*   *fós*   *é.*
    praise-VBN   to+its   get-VBN   by-3SGF   COP-PRS-NEG   day   yet   it

'Two of them were sitting beside the fire now and they were talking only about old Cáit, and I'm telling you, she never **had such** praise.' (Mu. *Fiche Bliain ag Fás*: 88)

(9) *Cheap*   *mé*   *féin*   *cúpla*   *babhta*   *go*   **ndearnadh**   *léirmheas*   *mí-thuisceanach*   *ar*
    think-PST   I   -self   couple   time   that   do-PST-AUT   review   misunderstanding   on

    shaothar   *liom*   *ach*   *b'fhada*   *uaim*   *a*   *dhul*   *i*   *bpíobán*   *an*
    work   by-1SG   but   COP-PST+long   from-1SG   to   go-VBN   into   throat   the-GEN

    té   *a*   *rinne*   *an*   *chéad*   *uair*   *eile*   *ar*   *casadh*   *orm*   *é.*
    person   REL   do-PST   the   first   time   other   REL   meet with-PST-AUT   on-1SG   him

'I myself thought a couple of times that work of mine **got** unsympathetic review but I certainly didn't attack the person the next time I met him.' (Co. *Feamainn Bhealtaine*: 146)

(10) *Ní   raibh   a   fhios   againn cad   a   bhí   aige   á   rá.*
    NEG   be-PST   its   knowledge   at-1PL   what   REL   be-PST   by-3SGM   to+its   say-VBN

'We did not know <u>what</u> he was **saying**.' (Mu. *Fiche Bliain ag Fás*: 15)

(11) *Buachaill   is   ea   mise   a   **rugadh**   agus   a   **tógadh***
    boy   COP-PRS   it   I-EMPH   REL   bear-PST-AUT   and   REL   rear-PST-AUT

    thiar   sa   Bhlascaod   Mhór, ...
    west   in+the   Blasket   great

'I am a boy <u>who</u> **was born** and **brought up** over in the Great Blasket, ...' (Mu. *Fiche Bliain ag Fás*: 11)

1.1.3 Subclause structure

The variable subclause structure concerns the passive progressive only. The main distinction is that between finite and non-finite subclauses. Like finite subclauses, non-finite subclauses have adverbial, nominal, or relative function in the matrix clause. Structurally, adverbial non-finite subclauses fall into two main groups. The first group contain those non-finite adverbial subclauses that lack an introductory particle, as in (12), while the second group consists of those that are introduced by *agus*, 'and', (*gan*, 'without', when negated), as in (13).[4] Non-finite adverbial subclauses may also be marked in ways other than the two main types. For example, they may occur as complements of certain verbs, such as the verb of motion *téigh*, 'go', as in (14), or they may be introduced by a conjunction other than *agus*, such as *toisc*, 'because', as in (15).[5] One may note that, as in (15), the auxiliary (the verbal noun *bheith*, 'being') may appear in the passive progressive non-finite clause. Normally, however, it is excluded, as in (12) and (13).

Nominal non-finite subclauses with the passive progressive fall into two main groups. The first group consists of subclauses that function as complements of sensory verbs, as in (16) (Ó Siadhail 1989: 278ff.). The second group of nominal non-finite subclauses consists of clauses that function as subjects of copula clauses, as in (17).

The final group of non-finite subclauses comprises those that have relative function, as in (18). Like the adverbial non-finite subclauses shown above, they lack an introductory particle. This concludes the account of the variables concerning verbs and clauses. In the next section, 1.2, the variables concerning patients and agents are presented.

---

[4] Non-finite adverbial subclauses introduced by *agus*, 'and' are discussed by Ó Siadhail (1989: 284f.) and in *Graiméar* (1999: 284, 291).

[5] Non-finite subclauses introduced by conjunctions other than *agus*, 'and', are discussed in *Graiméar* (1999: 282, 294). Verbal noun complements are discussed in *Graiméar* (1999: 203, 280) and Ó Siadhail (1989: 278ff.).

(12) Seo   linn   arís,   sinn   **á**   **dhalladh**   leis   an   allas,   nó gur   thánamair
this   with-1PL   again   us   at our   blind-VBN   with   the   sweat   until   come-1PL

lasmuigh   dhóibh   arís.
outside   of-3PL   again

'Off we went again, **being blinded** by sweat, until we got beyond them.' (Mu. *Fiche Bliain ag Fás*: 63)

(13) Bhí   an   easóg   faoi   neasacht   fhiche   slat   dó,   í   ag   croitheadh   a
be-PST   the   stoat   under   nearness   twenty   feet   to-3SGM   it   at   wag-VBN   it

heireabaill   le   corp   áthais,   <u>agus</u>   <u>an</u>   <u>cloiginnín</u>   <u>gleoite</u>   <u>sin</u>   <u>**á**</u>   <u>**chrochadh**</u>
tail   with   body   happiness-GEN   and   the   head-DIM   pretty   that   to+its   raise-VBN

<u>agus</u>   <u>**á**</u>   <u>chromadh</u>   <u>aici</u>   <u>go sultmhar</u>   <u>suairc</u>,   amhail   agus   dá   mbeadh
and   to+its   bend-VBN   by-3SGF   cheerfully   cheerful   as   and   if   be-COND

gan   rud   ar bith   a   bheith   ina   croí   ach   carthanas   agus   caoithiúlacht,
without   thing   any   to   be-VBN   in+its   heart   but   friendliness   and   pleasantness

agus   go   mb'fhada   uaithi   mioscais   agus   mailís,   gangaid   agus   goimh.
and   CONJ   COP-PST+long   from+3SGF   hatred   and   malice   bitterness   and   venom

'The stoat was within twenty yards of it, wagging its tail with delight, <u>cheerfully **nodding** that pretty head</u>, as if there was nothing in its heart but friendliness and pleasantness and that it was far from being malicious and venomous.' (Co. *An Mothall sin ort*: 133)

(14) Nuair   a   sheasadh   sé   len   a   bréaga   leis   b'amhala   ba mhó
when   REL   stand-IPF   he   to   its   coax   with-3SGM   COP-PST+thus   great-SUP

a   bhróga   ag   <u>dul</u>   **dhá**   **mbá**.
his   shoes   at   go-VBN   to+their   drown-VBN

'When he stopped to catch his breath, his shoes **sank** further into the clay.'
(Co. *An tSraith ar lár*: 42)

(15) Ag   tagairt   do   Phaid   a   bheifí,   gan   dabht,   <u>toisc</u>   an
at   refer-VBN   to   P.   REL   be-COND-AUT   without   doubt,   because   the-GEN

phinsin   a   bheith   **á**   **tharrac**   aige   féin.
pension-GEN   REL   be-VBN   to+its   draw-VBN   by-3SGM   -self

'One was referring to Paid <u>because</u> he himself was **drawing** the pension.' (Mu. *Na hAird ó thuaidh*: 90)

(16) Níor   <u>chuala</u>   mé   an   t-ainm   sin   **á**   **thabhairt**   ariamh   air.
NEG   hear-PST   I   the   name   that   to+its   give-VBN   ever   on-3SGM

'I never <u>heard</u> it **being called** that.' (Co. *Feamainn Bhealtaine*: 18)

(17)   *Is*   *minic*   *agus*   *is*   *lánmhinic*   *an*   *cheist*   *á*   **chur**   *orm*
      COP-PRS   often   and   COP-PRS   full+often   the   question   to+its   put-VBN   on-1SG

      cad   *é*   *mar*   *shórt*   *duine*   *é*   *an*   *Criothanach,*   *óm*   *chuimhne*
      what   he   like   sort   person-GEN   he   the   C.   from+my   memory

      féin   *air.*
      own   on-3SGM

      'I **am** <u>very often</u> **asked** what sort of person Ó Criothain was, from my own recollection of him.'
      (Mu. *Na hAird ó thuaidh*: 165)

(18)   *Bhí*   *bladhm*   *solais*   *amach*   *tríd*   *an*   *ndoras,*   *boladh*   *cumhra*   *le*
      be-PST   flame   light-GEN   out   through   the   door   smell   sweet-smelling   to

      fáil   *agam*   *agus*   *fuaim*   *ag*   *feoil*   *á*   **róstadh.**
      get-VBN   by-1SG   and   sound   at   meat   at its   roast-VBN

      'There was a gleam of light coming out through the door, I smelt a sweet aroma and heard the sound of meat **roasting**.' (Mu. *Fiche Bliain ag Fás*: 118)

1.2 Patients and agents

The second set of variables referred to in the introduction to this chapter concern the patients and agents (overt as well as implicit) of autonomous and passive progressive clauses. The main aim is to study patients and agents from an

Table 1.2. Variables concerning patients and agents

variable	value	autonomous		passive progressive		
		patient	agent	patient	implicit agent	overt agent
type of overt element	definite NP	yes	no	yes	no	yes
	indefinite NP	yes	no	yes	no	yes
	relative particle	yes	no	yes	no	yes
	clause	yes	no	no	no	no
given vs. new	given	yes	no	yes	no	yes
	new	yes	no	yes	no	yes
recoverability	directly inferable	no	yes	no	yes	no
	pragmatically inferable	no	yes	no	yes	no
	generic	no	yes	no	yes	no
	non-recoverable	no	yes	no	yes	no
continuity	none	yes	yes	yes	yes	yes
	retrospective	yes	yes	yes	yes	yes
	prospective	yes	yes	yes	yes	yes
co-reference with active subject	yes	yes	yes	yes	yes	yes
	no	yes	yes	yes	yes	yes

information packaging perspective. Therefore, the variables included in the investigation have been chosen mainly to measure topicality, following previous surveys of the passive in Irish and other languages presented above, in the Introduction, section 4. The variables concerning patients and agents and the co-occurrence of their values with the autonomous and the passive progressive in my material are displayed in Table 1.2. The five variables displayed in Table 1.2 will be presented in more detail below.

1.2.1 Type of overt element

The first variable, type of overt element, concerns the expression of patients and overt agents as either definite NPs, indefinite NPs, or as an item outside this dichotomy, namely, a relative particle or a clause. Clauses may occur as autonomous patients only. Patients and agents are classified as definite NPs when they appear in one of five forms listed in *Graiméar* (1999: 74f.). Thus, a definite patient or agent may be a noun preceded by the definite article, as in (19), which shows an autonomous patient. A definite patient or agent may also be a name, as in (20), which contains an example of a patient of an autonomous clause. The next type of definite NP consists of a noun preceded by a possessive pronoun, as in (21), which contains an autonomous patient. Further, definite NPs may consist of a noun preceded by *gach*, 'every', as in (22), which includes an example of a passive progressive patient. The final kind of definite NP mentioned in *Graiméar* (1999: 74) is a noun followed by a genitive attribute, as in (23), which shows a passive progressive patient. Finally, apart from the ways of expressing a definite NP listed in *Graiméar* (1999), a definite patient or agent can be a personal pronoun, as is exemplified by the autonomous patient in (24) and the passive progressive agent in (25). As shown in (25), prepositions are inflected in Irish, forming a prepositional pronoun (*agam* = by me).

Following *Graiméar* (1999: 75), patients and agents are classified as indefinite NPs if they do not consist of one of the five structures presented above for definite NPs. A patient or agent is indefinite if it consists of a noun that is not preceded by the article, a possessive pronoun, *gach*, 'every', or is followed by a genitive attribute, as in (26), which shows a passive progressive patient. Apart from NPs, patients and overt agents may be expressed as relative particles. An example of a relative particle acting as a patient of a passive progressive clause is shown in (27). Finally, clauses can occur as patients of the autonomous, as in (28).

(19) Sular   **cuireadh**   <u>an</u> <u>tír</u>   faoi   chuing   na   daoirse   bhí
     before put-PST-AUT   the   country   under yoke   the-GEN slavcry-GEN   be-PST

     saol   sona   suairc   ag   filí   agus ag   lucht   léinn.
     life   happy   pleasant at   poets   and   at   people   learning-GEN

'Before <u>the country</u> **was put** under the yoke of slavery, poets and scholars had a happy and pleasant life.' (Co. *An Mothall sin ort*: 24)

(20) Ba   in   sular   **rugadh**   <u>Newton</u> leis an   tslis mhín a   chur
     COP-PST   that before bear-PST-AUT   Newton to   the chip   fine to   put-VBN

     ar   shaothar   Chopernicus   agus   Ghailileo.
     on   work   Copernicus-GEN   and   Galileo-GEN

'That was before <u>Newton</u> **was born** to complete the work of Copernicus and Galileo.' (Co. *An Mothall sin ort*: 20)

(21) Bhí   seafóid   air   le   dhá   bhliain,   ó   **cailleadh**   <u>a</u>   <u>bhean.</u>
     be-PST   nonsense   on-3SGM   for two   years   since   lose-PST-AUT   his wife

'He had been deranged for two years, since <u>his wife</u> **died**.' (Co. *Dúil*: 148)

(22) Bogann   sí   léi   go mear   agus is   gearr   go   bhfuil   gluaisteáin
     move-PRS   it   with-3SGF quickly   and   COP-PRS   short   until be-PRS   cars

     agus   gach   saghas   carra   ag   imeacht   tharna chéile   ar nós   na   seangán,
     and   every   kind   car-GEN   at   leave-VBN   past each other   like   the   ants

     <u>gach</u>   <u>cúinne</u>   á   chasadh   ag   an   mbus   ar nós   na   gaoithe   agus   fuaim
     every corner   to+its turn   by   the   bus   like   the-GEN   wind-GEN   and   sound

     im   chloigeann   ag   adharca   á   shéideadh   á   gcur   féin   in
     in+my   head   at   horns   to+their blow-VBN   at+their put-VBN   -self in

     iúl   go   rabhadar   ag   teacht—   nach   mór   an   meabhraíocht
     knowledge   CONJ   be-PST-3PL   at   come-VBN   COP-PRS-NEG   big   the   awareness

     a   bhí   ag   na   tiománaithe   iad   féin   do   chosaint   ar   a chéile!
     REL   be-PST   at   the   drivers   them   -self to   protect   on   each other

'It moves on quickly, and soon cars and every kind of motor are passing each other like ants, the bus turning **every corner** like the wind, and the sound in my head of horns being blown letting themselves know that they were coming—aren't the drivers very observant to protect themselves from each other!' (Mu. *Fiche Bliain ag Fás*: 216)

(23) Chloisinn   <u>ainmneacha</u>   <u>na</u>   <u>mórchumadóirí</u>   á   gcur   trína chéile
     hear-IPF   names   the-GEN   great+composers   to+their put-VBN   mixed-up

     aici   ó   am   go   ham.
     by-3SGF   from   time   to   time

'I used to hear her **confusing** <u>the names of the great composers</u> from time to time' (Co. *Feamainn Bhealtaine*: 139)

(24) *Lá ar n-a bhárach*   **cuireadh**   <u>*mé*</u>   *ar*   *teachtaireacht*   *go dtí*   *an*   *teach*   *áirid*
      the next day   put-PST-AUT   me   on   message   to   the   house   particular

      seo;   *agus*   *aindeoin*   *gur*   *imthigh*   *an*   *eagla*   *díom*   *bhí*   *piléar*   *amháin*
      this   and   although   CONJ   leave-PST   the   fear   from-1SG   be-PST   bullet   one

      liom   *in*   *mo*   *phóca*   *i*   *gcás*   *riachtanais.*
      with-1SG   in   my   pocket   in   case   necessity-GEN

      'The next day <u>I</u> **was sent** on an errand to this particular house; and although I was no longer afraid I had a bullet in my pocket in case I should need it.' (Ul. *Rácáil agus Scuabadh*: 70)

(25) *Diaidh ar ndiaidh*   *thuig*   *mé*   *i*   *m'aigne*   *go*   *mb'fhéidir*   *go*   *raibh*
      gradually   understand-PST   I   in   my+mind   CONJ   maybe   CONJ   be-PST

      dearmad   <u>*agam*</u>   *á*   *dhéanamh.*
      mistake   by-1SG   to+its   make-VBN

      'Gradually I realised that maybe <u>I</u> was **making** a mistake.' (Mu. *Mo Scéal féin*: 88)

(26) *Le*   *fada*   *na*   *gcian*   *tá*   <u>*sean-chapaill*</u>   *á*
      with   long [adjective used as noun]   the-GEN   ages-GEN   be-PRS   old+horses   to+their

      gcur   *thar*   *sáile*   *againn.,*
      send-VBN   across   sea   by-1PL

      'For ages we have **been sending** <u>old horses</u> overseas.' (Co. *An Mothall sin ort*: 128)

(27) *Níor*   *dhóigh*   *leat*   *ar*   *chaint*   *an*   *pháipéir*   *go*   *raibh*
      COP-PST-NEG   likely   with-2SG   on   talk   the-GEN   paper-GEN   CONJ   be-PST

      aon   *ní*   *in aon chor*   *ag*   *an*   *mbuíon*   *á*   **dhéanamh**   <u>*nach*</u>   *raibh*
      any   thing   at all   by   the   company   at+its   do-VBN   REL-NEG   be-PST

      acu   *á*   **insint**   *sa*   *pháipéar.*
      by-3PL   to+its   tell-VBN   in+the   paper

      'You would think from the reports in the newspaper that the group wasn't doing anything at all <u>that</u> wasn't **being reported** in the newspaper.' (Mu. *Mo Scéal féin*: 98)

(28) **Dúradh**   <u>*nach*</u>   <u>*raibh*</u>   <u>*an*</u>   <u>*tAire*</u>   <u>*leathshásta*</u>   *ach*   *fear*   *tábhaicht*
      say-PST-AUT   CONJ-NEG   be-PST   the   minister   half+pleased   but   man   importance-GEN

      i   *bhFianna Gael*   *a*   *bhí*   *sa*   **Maoldhomhnach**   *agus*   *bhí*   *mac*   *aige*
      i   Fine Gael   REL   be-PST   in+the   Muldowney   and   be-PST   son   at-3SGM

      in   *a*   *shagart*   *paráiste,*   *fear*   *óigeanta*   *freisin,*   *sa*   *deoise.*
      in   his   priest   parish-GEN   man   youthful   also   in+the   diocese

      'It **was said** <u>that the Minister was not very pleased</u> but Muldowney was an important member of Fine Gael and he had a son who was a parish priest, a youthful man too, in the diocese.' (Co. *An tSraith ar lár*: 151)

1.2.2 Given vs. new

The next variable concerning patients and overt agents is given vs. new. In the present study, an element is classified as given if its referent has been explicitly mentioned before in the same chapter or short story. The patient of the autonomous clause in (29), *féilire*, 'calendar', is mentioned earlier in the text a few paragraphs before, in the sentence given in (30). There is one exception to the criterion for givenness presented above. In the present study, first and second person personal and prepositional pronouns are always classified as given, as in (31) and (32), regardless of whether they have been mentioned previously or not, since they are constantly present in the mind of the writer-reader/speaker-listener (cf. the Introduction, section 3). In (31) a passive progressive first person agent is found; in (32) the patient of the autonomous is a second person pronoun. Patients and agents are classified as new when they refer to a participant that is explicitly mentioned in the chapter or short story for the first time, as the autonomous patient in (33).

(29) | *Sa* | *Rúis* | *níor* | **glacadh** | *leis* | <u>*an*</u> | <u>*bhféilire*</u> | <u>*nua*</u> | *go dtí* | *1918.* |
| --- | --- | --- | --- | --- | --- | --- | --- | --- | --- |
| in+the | Russia | NEG | take-PST-AUT | with | the | calendar | new | until | 1918 |

'In Russia <u>the new calendar</u> **was** not **accepted** until 1918.' (Co. *An Mothall sin ort*: 78)

(30) | <u>*Féilire*</u> | <u>*Ghréagóra*</u> | *a* | **thugtar** | *ar* | *an* | *socrú* | *seo.* |
| --- | --- | --- | --- | --- | --- | --- | --- |
| calendar | Gregory-GEN | REL | give-PRS-AUT | on | the | settlement | this |

'This arrangement **is called** <u>the Gregorian calendar</u>.' (Co. *An Mothall sin ort*: 77)

(31) | *Bhí* | *beirt* | *againn* | *ansan* | *agus* | *sult* | *an* | | *domhain* | <u>*againn*</u> | *á* |
| --- | --- | --- | --- | --- | --- | --- | --- | --- | --- | --- |
| be-PST | two | of-1PL | there | and | fun | the-GEN | | world-GEN | by-1PL | to+its |

bhaint	*as,*		*ach*	*ní*		*ar*	*an*	*gcluiche*	*a*	*bhíomair*
take-VBN	out of-3SGM		but	COP-PRS-NEG		at	the	game	REL	be-PST-1PL

ag	*féachaint*	*ach*	*ar*	*an*	*bhfear*	*agus*	*an*	*strus*	*a*	*chuireadh*	*sé*	*ar*
at	watch-VBN	but	on	the	man	and	the	strain	REL	put-IPF	he	on

a	*mhuineál*	*nuair*	*a*	*bhíodh*	*sé*	*ag*	*glamaíl.*
his	neck	when	REL	be-IPF	he	at	shout-VBN

'There were two of us and <u>we</u> were **enjoying** it enormously, but it wasn't the game we were watching but the man and how he was straining his neck when he was shouting.' (Mu. *Fiche Bliain ag Fás*: 76)

(32) | Fadó, | nuair | ab | | fhusa | daoine | a | chrochadh | ar | bheagán |
|---|---|---|---|---|---|---|---|---|---|
| long ago | when | COP-PRS-REL | | easy-COMP | people | to | hang-VBN | on | little |

siocrach	ná	mar	atá	sé	anois,	dá	ndéanfá		rud	ar bith	as
cause-GEN	than	like	be-PRS	he	now	if	do-COND-2SG		thing	at all	out of

bealach,	déarfaí		leat	go	**crochfaí**		*thú*	chomh	caol
way	say-COND-AUT		to-2SG	CONJ	hang-COND-AUT		you-SG	as	thin

le	cat,...
with	cat

'Long ago when it was easier to hang people for little reason than it is now if you would do anything wrong you would be told that <u>you</u> **would be hanged** like a cat, ...' (Co. *An Mothall sin ort*: 35)

(33) | Ar | ordú | an | | rí | **tugadh** | | <u>comhdháil</u> | le chéile | ag | féachaint |
|---|---|---|---|---|---|---|---|---|---|---|
| on | order | the-GEN | | king-GEN | bring-PST-AUT | | meeting | together | at | see-VBN |

an	bhféadfaí		teacht	ar	an	scéal	a	réiteach
INT	can-COND-AUT		come-VBN	on	the	matter	to	solve-VBN

'On the king's order <u>a meeting</u> **was convened** to see if they could solve the matter.' (Co. *An Mothall sin ort*: 99)

1.2.3 Recoverability

The next variable, recoverability, concerns the way implicit agents, that is, agents that are not overtly expressed in the clause, can be recovered, or identified, by the reader/listener. As mentioned above (the Introduction, section 3) Givón (1979a: 59ff.) states that in agent-less English passives, the agent can be recovered from the preceding or following discourse or from pragmatic knowledge. These two ways to recover implicit agents were found to be relevant to the present study. In addition, based on the analysis of the implicit agents in the present material, two further kinds of recoverability were introduced: generic and non-recoverable. Thus, in the present study, four types of recoverability of implicit agents are distinguished: textually inferable and pragmatically inferable, generic and non-recoverable. The four recoverability types are presented and exemplified below.

A textually inferable agent is recoverable from the preceding or following discourse in the same chapter or short story. For example, the sentence in (34) is preceded by a description of a social gathering. The implicit agent of the auto-nomous *hubhradh*, 'one said', is recoverable from the preceding context and may be identified by the reader as one or several persons among the people present at the previously described gathering. Note that, as in (34), textually inferable implicit agents often refer to a group of people, or one or several members of a group of people. The participant or participants responsible for the action may or may not be explicitly mentioned in the surrounding context.

The next type of implicit agent, the pragmatically inferable ones, are those agents that are recoverable using pragmatic knowledge. In (35) the identification

(34) **Hubhradh**　　　ar ndóigh　go　　rabh　　fáilte　　aige,　　cé　　　nach　　　raibh
　　　say-PST-AUT　　of course　CONJ　be-PST　welcome　at-3SGM　although　CONJ-NEG　be-PST

　　　mórán　duile　　　ag　Peadar a' Mhuilinn　ná　ag　Muintir　Chanann　　ann.
　　　much　desire-GEN　at　Peadar a' Mhuilinn　or　at　family　Canning-GEN　in-3SGM

'**One said** of course that he was welcome, although Peadar a' Mhuilinn and the Cannings did not much like him.' (Ul. *Dochartach Duibhlionna*: 27)

of the type of participant responsible for the action denoted by the autonomous verb form is based on the reader's knowledge of the world.

The third type of implicit agent, generic, occurs in those cases where neither surrounding discourse nor pragmatic knowledge helps the reader identify the agent. Instead, the agent implied is some unspecified person or people in general, as in (36), which contains an implicit autonomous agent.

The fourth category of implicit agents, the non-recoverable category, contains those instances where no agent is logically implied. Many of the implicit agents classified as non-recoverable, especially in the autonomous, occur with verbs that in certain meanings are always used impersonally.[6] I have relied on the definitions in the most comprehensive Irish-English dictionary, Ó Dónaill (1992) to identify these verbs. Two such verbs are *caill*, 'die', lit. 'lose', as in (37), which contains an example of the autonomous, and *taibhrigh*, 'dream', as in (38), which contains an example of the passive progressive. Another example of the non-recoverable category is found in (39). In (39), as opposed to (40), the verb used in the autonomous is not a verb that, in certain meanings, must be used impersonally. However, no agent responsible for the action is logically implied, which is the reason this instance of an autonomous implicit agent has been classified as non-recoverable.

In many instances of the autonomous and (agent-less) passive progressive, there is more than one way to recover the implicit agent. For example, in (40) the agent may be identified as 'the people of the mixed Irish- and English-speaking district of Dingle' from the context in the same sentence. Using pragmatic knowledge, the agent is also identifiable as 'farmers'. Here the textually inferable identification is more precise than the pragmatically inferable one; therefore the agent in (40) is classified as textually inferable in my database.

---

[6] This is related to the "idiosyncratic usages" of certain verbs in the autonomous mentioned in Stenson (1989: 387f.), referred to in the Introduction, section 1. Compare also Ó Corráin (2001), as mentioned in the Introduction, section 3, who discusses the connection between the use of the autonomous and the expression of non-volition on the part of the grammatical subject (i.e. the implicit agent).

(35) —*Ambriathar* *féin,* *arsa* *m'athair,* *go* **bhfuil** *sé* *ráite* *gur*
     Upon my word own say-PST my+father CONJ be-PRS it say-VBA CONJ

     cuireadh *a lán* *daoine* *fé* *dhraíocht* *anso* *fadó,* *agus* *b'fhéidir* *gur*
     put-PST-AUT many people under spell here long ago and maybe CONJ

     cuid *acu* *iad* *sin.*
     some of-3PL they that

     'Upon my word, said my father, it is said that many people **were put** under a spell here long ago, and maybe that those are some of them.' (Mu. *Fiche Bliain ag Fás*: 186)

(36) *Más* *fear* *pinn* *tú* *ní mór* *duit* *bás* *a* *fháil*
     if+COP-PRS man pen-GEN you-SG it is necessary for-2SG death to get-VBN

     sula **dtugtar** *ómós* *nó* *onóir* *duit:* *Seven* *wealthy* *towns* *contend*
     before give-PRS-AUT respect or honour to-2SG

     for *Homer—* *dead,* *through* *which* *the living* *Homer* *begged* *his* *bread.*

     'If you're a penman, you have to die before you **are given** respect and honour: Seven wealthy towns contend for Homer—dead, through which the living Homer begged his bread.' (Co. *An Mothall sin ort*: 23)

(37) *Bhorr* *an* *tOrd* *chomh* *tapa* *sin* *go* *raibh* *seacht* *dtithe* *agus* *fiche*
     grow-PST the order so quickly that CONJ be-PST seven houses and twenty

     acu *i* *bpríomhchathracha* *na* *Fraince* *an* *bhliain* *ar* **cailleadh**
     of-3PL in capital cities the-GEN France-GEN the year REL lose-PST-AUT

     an *naomh* *(1719); agus* *ag* *neartú* *atá* *sé* *ar fud* *an*
     the saint (1719) and at strengthen-VBN be-PRS-REL it throughout the-GEN

     domhain, *ionas go* *bhfuil* *suas* *le* *18,000* *bráthair* *san* *Ord* *anois.*
     world-GEN so that be-PRS up to 18,000 brothers in+the order now

     'The Order grew so quickly that they had twenty-seven houses in the main French cities the year the saint **died** (1719); and it is getting stronger throughout the world so that there are up to 18,000 brothers in the Order now.' (Co. *An Mothall sin ort*: 123)

(38) *B'shin* *iad* *na* *crosa,* *Dia* *linn,* *agus* **gan** **aon** *ní* *eile*
     COP-PST+that they the crosses God with-1PL and without any thing other

     á **thaidhreamh** *dúinn.*
     to+its dream-VBN to-1PL

     'Those were the crosses, God bless us, and we **thought** of nothing else.' (Mu. *Na hAird Ó Thuaidh*: 53)

(39) | Leis | an | anró | a | fuair | sí | an | oidhche | sin | **rinneadh** | í | a |
|------|------|------|------|------|------|------|------|------|------|------|------|
| with | the | hardship | REL | get-PST | she | the | night | that | do-PST-AUT | her | to |

ath-leagadh,	agus	bhí	sí	'na	luighe	'toigh	Nóranna.
re-lay-VBN	and	be-PST	she	in+her	lie-VBN	in house	Nóra-GEN

'Because of the hardship she endured that night she **suffered** a relapse, and she was lying in Nóra's house.' (Ul. *Dochartach Duibhlionna*: 10)

(40) | Feiremeoireacht | is | mó | a | deineadh | riamh | i | gceantar |
|------|------|------|------|------|------|------|------|
| farming | COP-PRS-REL | greatly-COMP | REL | do-PST-AUT | ever | in | district |

bhreac-Ghaeltachta	so	an	Daingin,	ach	amháin	i
mixed Irish- and English-speaking district	this	the-GEN	Dingle-GEN	but	only	in

mBaile Móir	laistiar	agus	i	gcomharsanacht	na	Mín Airde
Baile Mór	on the west side	and	in	neighbourhood	the-GEN	Mín Airde

lastoir.
on the east side

'It was mostly farming that **was carried out** in this mixed Irish- and English-speaking district of Dingle, but only in Baile Mór on the west side and around Mín Airde on the east side.' (Mu. *Na hAird Ó Thuaidh*: 22)

1.2.4 Continuity

There are two variables that concern the continuity of patients and agents (overt as well as implicit) in relation to the immediately neighbouring context: continuity and co-reference with active subject. The latter variable is presented in 1.2.5. Continuity is either retrospective or prospective (compare the studies of continuity accounted for in the Introduction, section 4). In the present classification, retrospective continuity occurs when an agent or patient of an autonomous or passive progressive clause is co-referential with an element that appears earlier in the same sentence or in the preceding sentence. Prospective continuity occurs when an agent or patient of an autonomous or passive progressive clause is co-referential with an element that appears later in the same sentence or in the following sentence. The range of continuity has thus been set at one sentence preceding and one sentence following the sentence containing the autonomous or passive progressive verb form.[7] When there are two or more co-referential elements within the continuity range, only the reference the furthest away (in each direction) from the patient or agent in question is included in the database. Thus there are four types of continuity that will be exemplified below: retrospective in the preceding sentence or within the same sentence, and prospective in the following sentence or within the same sentence. In each case, examples are given of the autonomous as well as the passive progressive. The

---

[7] Compare Risselada (1991) who uses a similar range for his study of discourse cohesiveness, as mentioned in the Introduction, section 3.

(41) | *Cuireadh* | *dhá* | *chéad* | *go leith* | *cóip* | *den* | *Bhíobla,* | *gan* | *aon* | *dá* |
| put-PST-AUT | two | hundred | and a half | copy | of+the | Bible | without | any | two |

| *chóip* | *díobh* | *sa* | *teanga* | *chéanna,* | *faoina* | *bun,* | *gan* | *trácht* | *ar* |
| copy | of-3PL | in+the | language | same | under+its | base | without | mention | on |

| *phíosaí* | *airgid,* | *ar* | *bhréagáin,* | *ná* | *ar* | *a lán* | *rud* | *fánach* | *eile.* |
| pieces | silver-GEN | on | toys | nor | on | many | things-GEN | random | other |

| *Ar éigean* | *a* | **chorrófar** | *as* | *sin* | *arís* | *í.* |
| with difficulty | REL | move-FUT-AUT | from | there | again | it |

'Two hundred copies of the Bible, with no two copies in the same language, were put under <u>its</u> base, not to mention the pieces of silver, toys, and many other things. It is unlikely that <u>it</u> will be moved from there again.' (Co. *An Mothall sin ort*: 59)

(42) | *Ach* | *níor* | *chorraigh* | <u>*an Cárthach,*</u> | *ná* | *aon* | *chuimhneamh* | *aige* | *air.* |
| but | NEG | move-PST | MCCarthy | nor | any | recollection | at-3SGM | on-3SGM |

| *D'imigh* | *stáir* | *eile,* | *ach* | *níorbh* | | *fhada* | *gur* | *chualadar* | *an* |
| go-PST | spell | other | but | COP-NEG-PST | | long | until | hear-PST-3PL | the |

| *trut-trat* | *chúchu* | *aníos;* | | *Paid* | *agus* | *ramsach* | *á* | **bhaint** |
| noise of tramping feet | towards-3PL | up from below | | Paid | and | prancing | to+its | get-VBN |

| *as* | *an* | *ndúidín* | *aige* | *ar* | *a* | *shástacht,* | *agus* | *caipín* | *nua* | *air* | *a* |
| from | the | pipe | by-3SGM | on | his | contentment | and | cap | new | on-3SGM | REL |

| *bhí* | *díreach* | *tar éis* | *teacht* | *ó* | *Mheirice* | <u>*chuige.*</u> |
| be-PST | just | after | come-VBN | from | America | to-3SGM |

'But <u>McCarthy</u> didn't move, nor did he even think of it. Another while passed, and before long, they heard the noise of tramping feet coming towards them from below; it was Paid, **enjoying** his pipe at his ease, with a new cap on <u>him</u> that had just come to <u>him</u> from America.' (Mu. *Na hAird ó Thuaidh*: 58)

first set shows retrospective continuity in the preceding sentence. In (41) the object pronoun *í*, 'it', the patient of the autonomous verb form *corrófar*, 'will be moved', displays retrospective continuity since it is co-referential with the possessive pronoun *a*, 'its', here merged with the preposition *faoi*, 'under', forming *faoina*, 'under its', in the preceding sentence (*faoina*, 'under its', refers to an obelisk). In (42) the prepositional pronoun agent *aige*, 'by him' of the passive progressive *á bhaint*, 'being taken out', refers to *an Cárthach* (a name) in the preceding sentence.

The next type is retrospective continuity in the same sentence. In (43) the patient object pronoun *é*, 'it', of the autonomous *cuireadh*, 'was put', is co-referential with the prepositional pronoun *air*, 'on it', in the same sentence. Both *é* and *air* refer to a piece of papyrus mentioned earlier in the text. In (44) the agent *aige*, 'by him', of the passive progressive *á dhéanamh*, 'being done', is co-referential with the active subject *an buachaill*, 'the boy', mentioned earlier in the same sentence.

(43) *Fritheadh*   *cuid*   *de*   *seo*   *in*   *uaigheanna*   *san*   *Éigipt,*   *go minic*   *lenár*
find-PST-AUT   part   of-3SGM   this   in   graves   in+the   Egypt   often   for+our

linn   *féin,*   *agus*   *an*   *scríbhinn*   *chomh*   *soléite*   <u>*air*</u>   *agus*   *a*   *bhí*
period   own   and   the   writing   as   legible   on-3SGM   and   REL   be-PST

nuair   *a*   **cuireadh**   *sna*   *huaigheanna*   *é*   *na*   *mílte*   *bliain*   *ó shin.*
when   REL   put-PST-AUT   in+the   graves   it   the   thousands   year   ago

'Some of this was found in graves in Egypt, often in our own time, and the writing was as legible <u>on it</u> as it was when <u>it</u> **was put** into the graves thousands of years ago.' (Co. *An Mothall sin ort*: 61)

(44) *Dá bhrí sin,*   <u>*an*</u>   <u>*buachaill*</u>   *a*   *rachadh*   *go*   *Coláiste Cholmáin*   *agus*   *a*
therefore   the   boy   REL   go-COND [for IPF]   to   St. Colmán's College   and   REL

thógfadh   *lóistín*   *sa*   *tsráid*   *dó*   *féin,*   *chaithfeadh*   *sé*
take-COND [for IPF]   lodgings   in+the   street   for-3SGM   -self   must-COND [for IPF]   he

é   *féin*   *a*   *chothú*   *gan*   *puinn*   *rabairne,*   *nó*   *bheadh*
him   -self   to   sustain-VBN   without   not much   extravagance-GEN   or   be-COND

éagóir   <u>*aige*</u>   *á*   **dhéanamh**   *ar*   *an*   *muintir*   *a*   *bheadh*   *sa*
injustice   by-3SGM   to+its   do-VBN   on   the   people   REL   be-COND [for IPF]   in+the

bhaile   *ina dhiaidh,*   *ag*   *obair*   *go crua*   *chun*   *eisean*   *a*   *chur*   *chun*   *cinn.*
home   after him   at   work-VBN   hard   to   him-EMPH   to   put   to   head-GEN

'Because of that, <u>any boy</u> who went to St. Colmán's College and took lodgings in the street for himself, he would have to care for himself without extravagance, or <u>he</u> **would be being** unfair to the people back home who were working hard to support him.' (Mu. *Mo Scéal féin*: 60)

The third type of continuity is prospective continuity in a following sentence. In (45) the patient *an litríocht*, 'the literature', of the autonomous *ceapadh*, 'was composed', is co-referential with the prepositional pronoun *inti*, 'in it' in the following sentence. In (46) prospective continuity is created by the prepositional pronoun *liom*, 'with me' (in *is cuimhin liom*, 'I remember') in the following sentence, since it is co-referential with the agent *agam*, 'by me', of the passive progressive clause.

The last type of continuity is prospective continuity in the same sentence, as in (47) where the patient *galchumhacht agus leictreachas*, 'steam power and electricity', is co-referential with the pronoun *á*, 'them', lit. 'at their', in *á dtiomáint*, 'driving them'. As mentioned above, not only patients and overt agents but also implicit agents have been classified with respect to continuity. In (48) the implicit agents of the autonomous verb forms *cluineadh*, 'was heard', and *tuigeadh*, 'was understood', are co-referential. Based on the context, both may be inferable as 'people in Ireland'. These autonomous verbs thus provide each other with continuity. In (49), the implicit agent of the passive progressive *dá rádh*, 'being said', is co-referential with *muintir Bhaile Átha Cliath*, 'the people of Dublin', in the preceding sentence; it is thus an instance of retrospective continuity.

(45) Is   beag an greann ná an gáire atá   le fáil   *sa*   *litríocht*
COP-PRS little the humour or the laugh be-PRS to find-VBN in+the literature

a   **ceapadh**   *ar feadh* *na*   *seachtú* *haoise*   *déag* *agus* *na*
REL invent-PST-AUT during   the-GEN seventh   century-GEN -teen   and   the-GEN

hochtú *haoise*   *déag.* *An* *brón*   *is*   *mó*   *atá*   *le*
eighth   century-GEN -teen   the   sadness COP-PRS great-COMP be-PRS to

fáil   *inti.*
find-VBN in-3SGF

'Little humour is found in <u>the literature</u> that **was composed** in the seventeenth and eighteenth centuries. Mostly sadness is found <u>in it</u>.' (Co. *An Mothall sin ort*: 95)

(46) Níor mheas   mé an   uair sin   go   raibh   aon   ionadh   rómhór   *agam*
NEG think-PST I   the time that CONJ be-PST any   surprise too+large by-1SG

á   **dhéanamh** *dé*   *féin* *ná*   *den*   *airc*   *a*   *bhí*   *air*   *chun*
to+its do-VBN   of-3SGM -self   nor   of+the   want   REL be-PST on-3SGM for

an   *aráin;*   *ach* *d'fhan*   *an*   *radharc* *i*   *m'aigne,*   *agus* *fanfaidh*
the-GEN bread-GEN but   stay-PST the   sight   in   my+mind   and   stay-FUT

fad   *a*   *mhairfidh* *mé.* Is cuimhin <u>liom</u> *tráthnóna* *éigin* *i*   *gcaitheamh*
as long as REL live-FUT   I   I remember   afternoon   some   in   course

na   *haimsire*   *sin*   *agus* *na*   *daoine* *ag* *rith*   *isteach* *is*   *amach*
the-GEN time-GEN that and   the   people   at   run-VBN in   and   out

agus *iad*   *ag* *caint.*
and   they at   talk-VBN

'I didn't think at the time that <u>I</u> **was** taking much notice of him or his craving for the bread; but the sight stayed in my mind and it will stay for as long as I live. <u>I</u> remember one of those afternoons when the people were running in and out talking.' (Mu. *Mo Scéal féin*: 34)

(47) Nuair a   **cuireadh**   <u>galchumhacht</u> <u>agus</u> <u>leictreachas</u> ag obair   i   dtosach
when   REL put-PST-AUT steam power   and   electricity   at work-VBN in beginning

cheap   *a lán* *go*   *mba*   *draíocht*   *nó* *diabhlaíocht* *a*   *bhí*   *á*
think-PST many   CONJ COP-PST witchcraft or   wizardry   REL be-PST to+their

dtiomáint.
drive-VBN

'When <u>steam power and electricity</u> **were** first **introduced** many thought that <u>they</u> were being driven by magic.' (Co. *An Mothall sin ort*: 20)

(48)
I bhfad	Éireann	sular	**cluineadh**	focal	ar	Fhroebel	nó	ar	Mhontessori,
distant	Ireland-GEN	before	hear-PST-AUT	word	on	Froebel	or	on	Montessori

nó	ar	a	leithéidí,	**tuigeadh**	go cruinn	cén	chiall	a	bhí
or	on	their	likes	understand-PST-AUT	exactly	what	meaning	REL	be-PST

leis	an	seanfhocal:	"An	rud	a	chí	an	leanbh	is	é	a
with	the	old saying	the	thing	REL	see-PRS	the	child	COP-PRS	it	REL

ní	an	leanbh."
do-PRS	the	child

'Long before Froebel or Montessori or the like **had been heard** of, **one understood** exactly the meaning of the old saying: "The child does what the child sees"'. (Co. *An mothall sin ort*: 104)

(49)
Níl	fhios	agam	caidé	an	manadh	a	bhí	ag	*muintir*
be-PRS-NEG	its+knowledge	at-1SG	what	the	attitude	REL	be-PST	at	people

Bhaile Átha Cliath	dúinne	na	bliadhanta	sin.	Acht	tá	fhios
Dublin-GEN	towards-1PL-EMPH	the	years	that	but	be-PRS	its+knowledge

agam	gur	minic	a	chuala	mé	rudaí	mí-ionnraice	**dá**	**rádh**
at-1SG	COP-PRS	often	REL	hear-PST	I	things	dishonest	to+their	say-VBN

leis	a'	Chonnradh.
concerning	the	League (= Gaelic League)

'I don't know what the attitude of <u>Dubliners</u> towards us was in those years. But I do know that I often heard unkind things **being said** about the Gaelic League.' (Ul. *Saoghal Corrach*: 162)

1.2.5 Co-reference with active subject

The variable co-reference with active subject, finally, identifies those patients and agents that are co-referential with a subject of an active clause within the continuity range. As with continuity, only the co-referential element that is furthest away in each direction within the continuity range from the patient or agent in question is considered. Following Risselada (1991), such co-referential elements included in the database have been classified according to whether or not they are the subjects of active clauses. Examples are given below of subjects of active clauses that are co-referential with one each of the five element types under investigation (autonomous patient, autonomous implicit agent, passive progressive patient, passive progressive implicit agent, and passive progressive overt agent), as well as one example of a continuous participant that is co-referential with an element in a function other than active subject. In (50) the passive progressive agent *aige*, 'by him', is co-referential with the subject *fear*, 'a man', earlier in the same sentence. In (51) the implicit agent of the autonomous verb form *ceanglaíodh*, 'was tied', is co-referential with the subject *siad*, 'they', in the active clause *cheap siad*, 'they thought', in the preceding sentence. In (52) the autonomous patient *daoine*, 'people', is co-referential with the active subject

(50) | Bhí | fear | eile | fós | agus | trucail | aige | á | shá | amach |
|---|---|---|---|---|---|---|---|---|---|
| be-PST | man | other | yet | and | trolley | by-3SGM | to+its | push-VBN | out |

roimis,	tinneas	im	cheann	ag	an	bhfothram	a	bhí	aige
before-3SGM	pain	in+my	head	at	the	noise	REL	be-PST	by-3SGM

á	bhaint	amach	as	an	áit.
to+its	take	out	from	the	place

'There was yet another <u>man</u> **pushing** a trolley before him, he was giving me a headache with the noise <u>he</u> was **making**.' (Mu. *Fiche Bliain ag Fás*: 206)

(51) | Nuair | a | bhí | an | tsnáthaid | feistithe | suas | acu | an | dara | babhta |
|---|---|---|---|---|---|---|---|---|---|---|
| when | REL | be-PST | the | needle | fasten-VBA | up | by-3PL | the | second | time |

cheap	siad	go	mb'fhearr	í	a	cheangal	de	loing	agus
think-PST	they	CONJ	COP-PST+good-COMP	it	to	tie-VBN	to	ship	and

í	a	tharraingt	go	Sasana.	Ceanglaíodh	den	ghaltán	Olga	í,	agus
it	to	pull-VBN	to	England	tie-PST-AUT	to+the	steamer	Olga	it	and

bhí	gach	rud	ag	dul	ar aghaidh	ar	sheol	na	bracha	nó gur
be-PST	every	thing	at	go-VBN	forward	on	course	the-GEN	malt-GEN	until

bhain	siad	Bá na Bioscáine	amach.
reach-PST	they	the Biscayne Bay	out

'When they had tied up the needle the second time <u>they</u> decided that it would be best to tie it to a ship and pull it to England. It **was tied** to the steamer Olga, and everything went smoothly until they reached the Bay of Biscay.' (Co. *An Mothall sin ort*: 59) ('the needle' refers to one of the Egyptian pillars known as 'Cleopatra's needles')

(52) | Casfar | daoine | ort | a | chaill | a | misneach | agus | a | ndóchas. |
|---|---|---|---|---|---|---|---|---|---|
| meet-FUT-AUT | people | on-2SG | REL | lose-PST | their | courage | and | their | hope |

Ní	rabh	Éire	riamh	comh	fágtha	is	atá	sí	anois,
NEG	be-PST	Ireland	never	as	helpless	COP-PRS	be-PRS	it	now

adéarfaidh	siad	leat.
say-FUT	they	to-2SG

'You **will meet** <u>people</u> who have lost their courage and hope. Ireland was never as pathetic as it is today, <u>they</u> will tell you.' (Ul. *Saoghal Corrach*: 297)

siad, 'they', in the following sentence. The continuity-creating elements other than active subjects include various items, such as direct objects, adverbials and prepositional objects. An example of the last type is shown in (53), where *den chaiseal seo*, 'of this stone fort', is co-referential with the patient of the autonomous clause in the preceding sentence.

This concludes the presentation of the features that have been studied. In the following three chapters the results of the classification of the autonomous and the passive progressive instances in the database with regard to these features will be presented and discussed.

(53) | Tá | caiseal | ann | a | **rinneadh** | roimh | teacht | na |
|---|---|---|---|---|---|---|---|
| be-PRS | stone fort | there | REL | make-PST-AUT | before | arrival | the-GEN |

Críostaíochta.	Taobh	istigh	den	chaiseal	seo	tá	trí	clocháin
Christianity-GEN	side	inside	of+the	stone fort	this	be-PRS	three	beehive huts

agus	trí	teampaill	bheaga	agus	trí	haltóirí,	gan	trácht	ar	a lán
and	three	chapels	small	and	three	altars	without	mention	on	many

leac	a	bhfuil	cuid	acu	ina	seasamh	agus	cuid	eile,
slabs -GEN	REL	be-PRS	some	of-3PL	in+their	stand-VBN	and	some	other

sínte,	agus	inscríbhinní	orthu	ar fad.
lay flat-VBA	and	inscriptions	on-3PL	entirely

'There is a stone fort there that was built before the arrival of Christianity. Inside this stone fort there are three beehive huts and three small chapels and three altars, not to mention many slabs, some of which are standing and some lying flat and there are inscriptions on all of them.' (Co. *An Mothall sin ort*: 53)

CHAPTER 2

Verbs and clauses

2.1 Introduction

In the present chapter, the results regarding verb and clause type are displayed and discussed. The instances of the autonomous and the passive progressive in the database have been classified according to the type of verb used to form the autonomous and the passive progressive and the clause types in which the constructions occur. The principles of classification and the three variables, verb type, clause type and subclause structure, have been described in 1.1.

One aim of the investigation of verb and clause type is to explore the inherent syntactic differences between the autonomous and the passive progressive and study how these differences are reflected in usage. As regards the variable verb type, a major concern is the distribution of the autonomous across verbs that take direct objects (the categories monotransitive direct and ditransitive) and verbs that do not (the categories monotransitive indirect, intransitive and auxiliary). The question is then whether or not it is an important characteristic of the autonomous, from the language user's point of view, that it can be used with verbs that do not take direct objects. On the other hand, instances of the autonomous of transitive verbs with direct objects (i.e. patients) are of particular interest to the study of patients and agents from an information packaging point of view (dealt with in Chapter 3, and to some extent in Chapter 5). The analysis regarding information packaging focuses on the comparison of the autonomous and the passive progressive with respect to the topicality, or centrality, of patients and agents in the text. The comparison between the autonomous and the passive progressive as regards verb type also concerns the distribution across monotransitive and ditransitive verbs.

When it comes to clause type, the focus is on the comparison of the autonomous and the passive progressive with respect to their distribution across main and subclause. As will be shown later on, the distinction between main and subclause is relevant to the discussion of information packaging, which is the main theme of the following parts of the study (see Chapters 3 and 5).

The final variable, subclause structure, that is, finite vs. non-finite structure,

Table 2.1. Frequency of the autonomous and the passive progressive

	n	%
autonomous	2,956	86%
passive progressive	467	14%
Total	3,423	100%

concerns the passive progressive only, since, as opposed to the autonomous, the passive progressive can be used in non-finite clauses. The aim of the study of subclause structure is to investigate to what extent the possibility of forming non-finite subclauses with the passive progressive is realised in actual usage.

The results regarding verb and clause type will be presented in the following order. First the features that the two constructions have in common, verb type, and clause type will be accounted for. Then the feature that is specific to the passive progressive is presented, namely, subclause structure.

As an introduction to the presentation, the overall frequency of the autonomous and the passive progressive is exhibited in Table 2.1. Table 2.1 shows that the total number of instances of the autonomous and the passive progressive in the database is 3,423. Of these, 2,956 (86%) examples are autonomous and 467 (14%) are passive progressive; the autonomous is thus more than six times as common as the passive progressive.

2.2 Features common to both the autonomous and the passive progressive

2.2.1 Verb type

Verb type is the first variable that is relevant to both the autonomous and the passive progressive. To give a fuller picture in the presentation of the results, examples are given of the verbs most frequently used in each verb type, and their frequencies in the database are stated.

As stated above, any verb type can form the autonomous: monotransitive verbs with direct or indirect objects, ditransitive, as well as intransitive and auxiliary verbs. However, as shown in Table 2.2, the use of the autonomous is mainly confined to the two transitive verb types that take direct objects, monotransitive direct and ditransitive. As mentioned, the passive progressive can only be used with transitive verbs that take direct objects, that is, with mono-transitive direct and ditransitive verbs. As can be seen in Table 2.2, the vast majority, 89% (59% + 30%), of all verbs in the autonomous in the material take direct objects, that is, they are either monotransitive (direct) or ditransitive. The third type of transitive verbs that can be used in the autonomous, monotransitive

Table 2.2. Distribution of the autonomous and the passive progressive across verb type

	mono-transitive, direct		ditransitive		mono-transitive, indirect		intransi-tive		auxiliary		Total	
	n	%	n	%	n	%	n	%	n	%	n	%
autonomous	1,748	59%	896	30%	94	3%	46	2%	172	6%	2,956	100%
passive progressive	378	81%	89	19%	—	—	—	—	—	—	467	100%

$\chi^2 = 40.34$; df = 1; p < 0.05, critical value: 3.84 (calculated on the frequency of monotransitive direct and ditransitive verbs only)

indirect, occurs in only 3% of the instances. As for the remaining verb types, Table 2.2 shows that intransitive verbs are used in only 2% of the instances of the autonomous in the database, while in 6% of the cases the autonomous verb form functions as an auxiliary verb. As mentioned above, the passive progressive is used exclusively with verbs that take direct objects. When it comes to the distribution of transitive verbs across the categories monotransitive (direct) and ditransitive, however, the results indicate that monotransitive verbs are considerably more frequent than ditransitive verbs in both constructions. However, the monotransitive to ditransitive ratio is much higher in the passive progressive than in the autonomous: 4/1 (378/89) in the passive progressive vs. 2/1 (1,748/896) in the autonomous. Thus, around four fifths of the passive progressive verbs that take direct objects are monotransitive, compared to two thirds of the autonomous ones. By far the most common monotransitive verbs in the autonomous are *cuir*, 'put' (218 instances or 12%), as in (1), *abair*, 'say' (106 instances or 6%), and *déan*, 'do, make' (105 instances or 6%). In the passive progressive, the most frequently used monotransitive verbs are *déan*, 'do, make' (58 instances or 15%), as in (2), and *cuir*, 'put' (29 instances or 8%). As for ditransitive verbs, by far the most common verbs in the autonomous are *cas*, in the meaning 'meet with' (178 instances or 20%), as in (3), and *tabhair*, 'give' (166 instances or 19%). In the passive progressive, the most frequent ditransitive verbs are *bain*, 'take'(25 instances or 28%), as in (4), *cuir*, 'put' (20 instances or 22%), and *déan*, 'do, make' (13 instances or 15%).

In the autonomous, there is a second category of monotransitive verbs: monotransitive indirect. As shown in Table 2.2, this verb type is uncommon in the material, represented by only 3% of the instances of the autonomous in the database. The verb *beir*, 'bear' (14 instances or 15%), as in (5), is the only verb of the monotransitive indirect category that occurs more than a few times.

Intransitive verbs constitute the smallest group of verbs used in the autonomous. Only 46 instances (2%) of the autonomous in the material are formed from intransitive verbs. The most common intransitive verbs are *téigh/gabh*, 'go' (9 instances or 20%), as in (6), and *bí*, 'be' (5 instances or 11%), as in (7).

(1)   **Cuirtear**   *isteach*   *i*   *gcoire*   <u>*iad.*</u>
        put-PRS   into   in   cauldron   them

        '<u>They</u> **are put** into a cauldron.' (Co. *Feamainn Bhealtaine*: 118)

(2)   <u>*Dhá*</u>   <u>*chuarán*</u>   <u>*óir*</u>   ***dhá***   ***ndéanamh***   *aige*   *le*   *casúr,*   *ruóg,*
        two   sandal   gold-GEN   to-their   make-VBN   by-3SGM   with   hammer   waxed cord

        meana   *agus*   *seamannaí*   *óir.*
        awl   and   studs   gold-GEN

        'He was **making** <u>two golden sandals</u> with a hammer, cord, awl and golden studs.' (Co. *An tSraith ar lár*: 154)

(3)   *Cupla*   *lá*   *ina dhiaidh sin*   **casadh**   <u>*an*</u>   <u>*tAthair*</u>   <u>*Maitiú*</u>   *orm.*
        couple   day   after that   meet with-PST-AUT   the   father   M.   on-1SG

        'A couple of days after that I **met** <u>Father Matthew</u>.' (Ul. *Saoghal Corrach*: 95)

(4)   *Bhí*   <u>*macalla*</u>   *aige*   *á*   ***bhaint***   *amach*   <u>*as*</u>   <u>*na*</u>   <u>*cuaiseanna*</u>   *anois, ...*
        be-PST   echo   by-3SG-M   to-its   take-VBN   out   from   the   hollows   now

        agus   *nuair*   *a*   *chualaigh*   *a*   *raibh*   *istigh*   *an*   *tiomáint*   *amuigh,*   *níor*
        and   when   REL   hear-PST   REL   be-PST   inside   the   bustle   outside   NEG

        fhan   *fear*   *bean*   *ná*   *páiste*   *ná*   *gur*   *éirigh*   *amach.*
        stay-PST   man   woman   nor   child   but   CONJ   rise-PST   out

        'Now he was **making** the hollows re-echo, ... and when those inside heard the bustle outside, every man, woman and child went out.' (Mu. *Fiche Bliain ag Fás*: 86)

(5)   **Beireadh**   <u>*air*</u>   *taobh*   *amuigh*   *de*   *Dhoire,*   *agus*   *tá*   *cruthughadh*
        catch-PST-AUT   on-3SGM   side   outside   of   Derry   and   be-PRS   proof

        cinnte   *gur*   *spíodóir*   *a*   *bhí*   *ann.*
        certain   CONJ   informer   REL   be-PST   in-3SGM

        '<u>He</u> **was caught** outside Derry, and there is certain proof that he was an informer.' (Ul. *Saoghal Corrach*: 187)

The final verb type is auxiliary with 172 instances (6%). The autonomous occurs in four different auxiliary verbs used in the database (in order of frequency): *bí,* 'be' (72 instances or 42%), as in (8) and (9), *caith,* 'must' (58 instances or 34%), as in (10), *féad,* 'can' (33 instances or 19%), and *déan,* 'do, make' (9 instances or 5%). As in (8) and (9), the vast majority (69/72) of the instances of the auxiliary *bí,* 'be', in the autonomous occur in active progressive clauses. The difference between (8) and (9) is that in (8), the verb used in the active progressive takes a direct object, while in (9), the verb takes an indirect object. Thus, a passive progressive could be used instead of the autonomous and the active progressive in (8), but not in (9). As mentioned in the Introduction, section 2, the use of the active progressive with the auxiliary in the autonomous

(6) **Chuadhthas** go Faithche Caoin— tá 'fhios agat cá bhfuil an
   go-PST-AUT to Faithche Caoin be-PRS its+knowledge at-2SG where be-PRS the

   baile sin— a's b'ann a rannadh an t-iolmhaitheas.
   place that and COP-PST+there REL divide-PST-AUT the wealth

   'They went to Faithche Caoin—you know where that place is—and it was there that the wealth
   was divided.' (Ul. *Crathadh an Phocáin*: 53)

(7) Ní **rabhthar** sásta liom ar chor ar bith as na baramhlacha
   NEG be-PST-AUT pleased with-1SG on way at all from the opinions

   a bhí agam ar "Fháinne" na Féil' Pádruig.
   REL be-PST at-1SG on Ring [title of journal] the-GEN St. Patrick's Day

   'They were not at all pleased with me because of the opinions I expressed in the St Patrick's Day
   issue of the "Fáinne".' (Ul. *Saoghal Corrach*: 258)

(8) **Beithear** _a' cur_ troda go minic air ag iarraidh tabhairt
   be-FUT-AUT at put-VBN fight-GEN often on-3SG-M at attempt give-VBN

   air a' toice lochtach a aisíoc.
   on-3SGM the wealth ill-gotten to repay-VBN

   'People will be forever confronting him, to try to make him pay back the ill-gotten wealth.' (Ul.
   Saoghal Corrach: 87)

(9) Agus dá bhfeicfeá an dóigh a **rabhthar** _a' fanacht_ _leis_
   and if see-COND-2SG the way REL be-PST-AUT at wait-VBN with-3SG

   a' sgéala go rabh sé a' teacht!
   the news CONJ be-PST he at come-VBN

   'And if you could see how **people were** waiting for the news that he was coming!' (Ul. *Saoghal
   Corrach*: 240)

(10) —Is fíor duit é, ar seisean go cráite, ach cad tá le
   COP-PRS true to-2SG it say-PST he-EMPH tormentedly but what be-PRS to

   déanamh? **caithfear** _dul_ ar aghaidh.
   do-VBN must-FUT-AUT go-VBN ahead

   'You're right, said he despondently, but what can we do? **one must** go on.' (Mu. *Fiche Bliain ag
   Fás*: 205)

can be regarded as a progressive passive construction, corresponding to an agent-
less passive progressive clause. In the combination autonomous + active
progressive, as well as in the agent-less passive progressive, the agent is
unspecified and thus demoted in the same way as in the autonomous. This
construction is described in the grammars as a means of avoiding ambiguity
when the grammatical subject as well as (in the case of active progressive) the
direct object/patient are in the third person. Stenson (1981: 154), however,
considers the combination autonomous + active progressive as related to the
simple autonomous in the same way as the (personal) active progressive is

related to the simple active, that is, it may be regarded as a progressive autonomous.[1] A closer look at the instances of the autonomous combined with the active progressive in the present database reveals two things. First, in around half of the instances the passive progressive would not be possible since the verbal nouns phrase does not include a direct object, as in (9), or the direct object is a clause. Second, in many cases where the passive progressive is structurally possible, the context is such that there is only one possible interpretation. In only a small number of instances would the use of the passive progressive have created the risk of ambiguity with regard to the choice of active or passive interpretation. In conclusion, the findings presented above suggest that the choice of this construction is motivated primarily by factors other than to avoid ambiguity. The remaining three clauses occur in periphrastic constructions where the verbal noun phrase is introduced by *le*, 'to' (expressing purpose) and *tar éis*, 'after' (corresponding to a perfect).

To sum up, the results presented above show that there are similarities as well as differences between the autonomous and the passive progressive as regards verb type. The most common verb type in both constructions is monotransitive direct, that is, verbs that take a direct object. While both constructions occur more frequently with monotransitive verbs than with ditransitive verbs, the monotransitive/ditransitive ratio is considerably greater in the passive progressive than in the autonomous, 4/1 (81% to 19%) vs. 2/1 (66% to 34%). The other verb types, available in the autonomous but not in the passive progressive, monotransitive indirect, intransitive and auxiliary, together account for only a small share (11%) of all verbs in the autonomous, 3%, 2% and 6%, respectively.

2.2.2 Clause type

The next category relevant to both constructions under investigation is clause type. Here again there are some inherent restrictions, this time affecting the autonomous. Since the autonomous is a finite verb form, by definition, it can occur in finite clauses only, while the passive progressive can occur also in non-finite clauses.

In the present study, the autonomous and the passive progressive instances have been classified according to whether they occur in main or subclauses. The subclauses in the database have then been classified according to the three functional types of subclause, namely, adverbial, nominal and relative, accounted for above in 1.1.3.

As shown in Table 2.3, in the corpus, the autonomous is more or less equally common in main clauses and subclauses; they account for 47% and 53%, respectively of all instances of the autonomous. Contrary to the autonomous, the passive progressive is much more common in subclauses than in main clauses.

---

[1] Compare Noonan (1994: 289) who refers to this combination as passive progressive impersonal.

Table 2.3. Distribution of the autonomous and the passive progressive across main and subclause

	main clause		subclause		Total	
	n	%	n	%	n	%
autonomous	1,392	47%	1,564	53%	2,956	100%
passive progressive	63	13%	404	87%	467	100%

$\chi^2 = 186.31$, df = 1, p < 0.05, critical value: 3.84

More than four fifths, 87%, of all instances of the passive progressive in my material occur in subclauses. There is thus a considerable difference between the two constructions when it comes to syntactic context: the autonomous is almost as frequent in main clauses as subclauses, whereas the passive progressive occurs mainly in subclauses. Examples of the autonomous and the passive progressive used in main clauses are found in (11) and (12), respectively.

Table 2.4 presents the frequency and distribution of the autonomous and the passive progressive in the three subclause types. Table 2.4 shows that 49% of the instances of the autonomous that occur in subclauses appear in relative clauses. The second most common subclause type is adverbial subclauses, 35%. Only 15% of the subclauses where the autonomous occurs are nominal subclauses. The distribution of the passive progressive across subclause types is in sharp contrast to that of the autonomous. As can be observed in Table 2.4, most passive progressives, 53%, occur in adverbial subclauses. The relative frequency of the passive progressive is considerably lower than that of the autonomous in relative subclauses, 26% vs. 49%. This means that the most frequent subclause type with the autonomous is the least frequent subclause type with the passive progressive. The passive progressive is more common than the autonomous in nominal subclauses, although the difference in relative frequency is less marked than in the other two subclause types, 21% in the passive progressive vs. 15% in the autonomous.

The use of the autonomous and the passive progressive in the three types of subclause is exemplified below. Note that the figures in Table 2.4 include finite as well as non-finite subclauses, but the passive progressive is exemplified below in finite subclauses only. Examples of the passive progressive in non-finite subclauses are given in 2.3 below. Adverbial subclauses are found in (13), which is an example of the autonomous, and (14), which is an example of the passive progressive. For both constructions, most adverbial subclauses are temporal. The use of the autonomous and the passive progressive in nominal subclauses is shown in (15) and (16), respectively. Finally, examples of relative subclauses containing the autonomous and the passive progressive are found in (17) and (18).

(11) **Deirtear** go raibh sé chomh buíoch sin de na héanacha, faoi
say-PRS-AUT CONJ be-PST he so thankful that of the birds under

bheith ag coinneáil chomhluadair leis, gur bheannaigh sé iad agus
be-VBN at keep-VBN company with-3SGM CONJ bless-PST he them and

gur thug sé a mhallacht d'aon duine a dhéanfadh rud as bealach
CONJ give-PST he his curse to+any person REL do-COND thing wrong

orthu, go deo na ndeor.
on-3PL to the end of time

'**It is said** that he was so grateful to the birds, for keeping him company, that he blessed them, and cursed any person who harmed them in any way, to the end of time.' (Co. *Dúil*: 135)

(12) *Sea,* do bhí an aimsir á **caitheamh** agus Máire ag druideam leis
well be-PST the time to+its spend-VBN and Máire at close-VBN with

an sprioclá.
the appointed day

'Yes, time was **passing,** and Máire was approaching the appointed day.' (Mu. *Fiche Bliain ag Fás*: 175)

(13) *"Ba* mhaith liom an ghrian fheiscint," adeir sé, "aon uair
be-COP-COND good with-1SG the sun to+see-VBN say-PRS he one time

amháin eile <u>sula</u> **<u>caillfear</u>** <u>mé.</u>"
one other before lose-FUT-AUT me

'"I would like to see the sun", he says, "one more time <u>before I die</u>".' (Co. *Dúil*: 45)

Table 2.4. Distribution of the autonomous and the passive progressive across subclause type

	adverbial		nominal		relative		Total	
	n	%	n	%	n	%	n	%
autonomous	549	35%	241	15%	774	49%	1,564	99%
passive progressive	215	53%	85	21%	104	26%	404	100%

$\chi^2 = 73.86$, df $= 2$, p < 0.05, critical value: 5.99.

To sum up, the main distinction between the autonomous and the passive progressive as regards clause type is that the autonomous occurs somewhat more frequently in main clauses than in subclauses (47% vs. 53%), whereas the passive progressive is far more common in subclauses than in main clauses (87% vs. 13%). As for type of subclause, one may note that the autonomous occurs most often in relative subclauses (49%). The passive progressive, on the other hand, is most frequently used in adverbial subclauses (53%).

(14) —*Sea,*   *do tharlaigh*   *an*   *scéal*   *go*   *bhfuair*   *an*   *tseanbhean*   *bás*   *an*   *oíche*
      yes   happen-PST   the   story   CONJ   get-PST   the   old+woman   death   the   night

      chéanna,   *agus*   *lá arna mháireach*   <u>*nuair*</u>   <u>*a*</u>   <u>*bhí*</u>   <u>*an*</u>   <u>*corp*</u>   <u>*á*</u>   <u>**ullmhú**</u>
      same   and   the following day   when   REL   be-PST   the   body   to+its   prepare-VBN

      <u>*ag*</u>   <u>*na*</u>   <u>*mná*</u>   <u>*comharsan,*</u>   *do fuair*   *bean*   *acu*   *ailp*   *chruaidh*   *éigin*
      by   the   women   neighbour-GEN   find-PST   woman   of-3PL   lump   hard   some

      casta   *istigh*   *ina*   *cuid*   *gruaige*   *thiar*   *ina*   *cúl,*   *agus*   *cad*   *a*
      twist-VBA   inside   in+her   share   hair-GEN   down   in+her   back   and   what   REL

      bheadh   *ach*   *sparán*   *agus*   *céad*   *punt*   *istigh*   *ann.*
      be-COND   but   purse   and   hundred   pound   inside   there

' —Well, as it happened the old woman died that same night, and the following day <u>when the neighbouring women were **preparing** the body</u>, one of them found a hard lump twisted inside the back of her hair, and what was it but a purse with a hundred pounds in it.' (Mu. *Fiche Bliain ag Fás*: 94)

(15) —*Bhí*   *an*   *rud*   *céanna*   *ormsa,*   *ar*   *seisean,*   *mar*   *is*
      be-PST   the   thing   same   on-1SG-EMPH   say-PST   he-EMPH   because   COP-PRS

      áit   *an-uaigneach*   *é*   *leis,*   *agus*   *is*   *minic*   *a*   *dúirt*
      place   very+spooky   it   with-3SGM   and   COP-PRS   often   REL   say-PST

      m'athair   *liom*   <u>*gur*</u>   <u>**chualathas**</u>   <u>*daoine*</u>   <u>*ag*</u>   <u>*caint*</u>   <u>*thíos*</u>   *ann.*
      my+father   with-1SG   CONJ   here-PST-AUT   people   at   talk   down   there

'I felt the same thing, said he, because it's also a very spooky place, and my father often said to me <u>that people **have been heard** talking down there</u>.' (Mu. *Fiche Bliain ag Fás*: 57)

(16) *Níor*   *dhóigh*   *leat*   *ar*   *chaint*   *an*   *pháipéir*   <u>*go*</u>   <u>*raibh*</u>
      COP-PST-NEG   likely   with-2SG   on   talk   the-GEN   paper-GEN   CONJ   be-PST

      <u>*aon*</u>   <u>*ní*</u>   <u>*in aon chor*</u>   <u>*ag*</u>   <u>*an*</u>   <u>*mbuíon*</u>   <u>*á*</u>   <u>**dhéanamh**</u>   *nach*   *raibh*
      any   thing   at all   by   the   company   at+its   do-VBN   REL-NEG   be-PST

      acu   *á*   *insint*   *sa*   *pháipéar.*
      by-3PL   at+its   tell-VBN   in+the   paper

'You would think from the reports in the newspaper that every single thing <u>that the group **was doing**</u> was being reported in the newspaper.' (Mu. *Mo Scéal féin*: 98)

(17) *Ní*   *raibh*   *cosaint*   *ar bith*   *againne*   *in aghaidh*   *aon*   *rud*   <u>*a*</u>
      NEG   be-PST   defence   any   at-1PL-EMPH   against   any   thing   REL

      <u>**scaoilfí**</u>   <u>*anuas*</u>   <u>*orainn.*</u>
      release-COND-AUT   down   on-1PL

'We had no defence against anything <u>that **might come down** on us</u>.' Co. *Feamainn Bhealtaine*: 23)

(18)

Bhí	*ainm*	*an*	*chosáin*	*chéanna*	*anairde*	*go*	*raibh*	*aeraíocht*
be-PST	name	the-GEN	path-GEN	same	on high	CONJ	be-PST	weirdness

éigin	*ag*	*baint*	*leis,*	*gur*	*cosán*	*é*	<u>*a*</u>	<u>*bhíodh*</u>	<u>*á*</u>	<u>*úsáid*</u>
some	at	concern-VBN	with	COP-PRS	path	it	REL	be-IPF	to+its	use-VBN

<u>*ag*</u>	<u>*an*</u>	<u>*slua*</u>	<u>*sí*</u>	<u>*ina*</u>	<u>*mbóithreoireacht*</u>	<u>*oíche*</u>	*ó*	*pharóiste*	*go*	*paróiste,*
by	the	host	fairy	in+their	walking	night-GEN	from	parish	to	parish

agus	*gur*	*mhór*	*an*	*díth*	*céille*	*dh'éinne*	*a*	*bhí*	*ag*	*canntáil*
and	COP-PRS	great	the	lack	sense-GEN	for+anybody	REL	be-PST	at	take-VBN

an	*bhealaigh*	*orthu*	*san,*	*agus*	*ná*	*rithfeadh*	*leis.*
the	way	on-3PL	those	and	REL-NEG	run-COND	with-3SGM

'That path was reputed to be bewitched, that it was a path <u>that was **used** by the fairies in their night walking from parish to parish</u>, and that it was most unwise for anyone to appropriate their road, and that he wouldn't be successful. (Mu. *Na hAird Ó Thiadh*: 63)

2.3 The variable specific to the passive progressive: subclause structure

As mentioned above, the subclauses containing the passive progressive have been classified according to whether the verb phrase is finite or non-finite. The distribution of adverbial, nominal and relative subclauses across finite and non-finite subclause structure is presented in Table 2.5. As can be seen in Table 2.5, 64% of the subclauses that contain the passive progressive are non-finite. This corresponds to 55% (258/467) of all passive progressive clauses. When it comes to the function of the non-finite subclauses, the highest proportion (84%) of non-finite subclauses is found among the adverbial subclauses, but among the nominal clauses the non-finite proportion is also high (67%). As for relative subclauses that contain the passive progressive, on the other hand, the majority (80%) are finite. In sum, the results suggest that it is an important feature of the passive progressive that it may be used in non-finite subclauses, particularly in adverbial clauses.

The non-finite subclause types will now be presented in more detail, beginning with the adverbial clauses. A little more than half (98/180) of the adverbial non-finite subclauses that contain the passive progressive are introduced by *agus*, 'and', as in (19). The remaining non-finite adverbial subclauses (82/180) lack an introductory particle; they are exemplified in (20) and (21). The difference between the two examples is that (20) contains the matrix clause in the same sentence (*Bhí sí 'na seasamh...*, 'She was standing...'), whereas in (21) the superordinate clause of the subclause *Milseáin á thabhairt...*, 'Sweets being brought...' is found two sentences before the subclause in question: *Righneadóir ab ea Seán Ó Mainnín*, 'Seán Ó Mainnín was a loiterer'. As in (22), most (47/57) nominal non-finite subclauses containing the passive progressive function as

(19) *Bhí   an   easóg   faoi   neasacht fhiche   slat   dó,   í   ag   croitheadh   a*
be-PST the stoat under nearness twenty feet to-3SGM it   at   wag-VBN   it

heireabaill le   corp   áthais,   agus an   cloiginnín gleoite sin á   chrochadh
tail   with body happiness-GEN and the head-DIM   pretty that to+its raise-VBN

agus á   chromadh   aici   go sultmhar suairc,   amhail agus dá   mbeadh
and to+its bend-VBN   by-3SGF cheerfully   cheerful as   and   if   be-COND

gan   rud   ar bith a   bheith   ina   croí   ach carthanas   agus caoithiúlacht,
without thing any   to   be-VBN   in+its heart but friendliness and   pleasantness

agus go   mb'fhada   uaithi   mioscais agus mailís, gangaid agus goimh.
and   CONJ COP-PST+long from+3SGF   hatred   and   malice bitterness and   venom

'The stoat was within twenty yards of him, wagging its tail with delight, <u>cheerfully **nodding** that
pretty head</u>, as if there was nothing in its heart but friendliness and pleasantness and that it was far
from being malicious and venomous.' (Co. *An Mothall sin ort*: 133)

Table 2.5. Distribution of the passive progressives in finite and non-finite
subclauses across subclause type

	adverbial		nominal		relative		Total	
	n	%	n	%	n	%	n	%
finite	35	16%	28	33%	83	80%	146	36%
non-finite	180	84%	57	67%	21	20%	258	64%
Total	215	100%	85	100%	104	100%	404	100%

$\chi^2 = 123.05$, df = 2; p < 0.05, critical value: 5.59.

complements of sensory verbs. Of the remaining ten non-finite nominal subclauses seven are subjects of copula clauses, as in (23). Finally, an example of a
non-finite relative clause is shown in (24).

The results presented above have shown that the passive progressive occurs
more frequently in non-finite than in finite subclauses, and that those non-finite
subclauses are more often adverbial (180/258 = 70%) than nominal (57/258 =
22%) or relative (21/258 = 8%). The question may then be raised as to why the
passive progressive is used so frequently in non-finite subclauses. One important
feature of non-finite clauses is that they are more compact than a finite subclause
with the same meaning and are thus more economical means of expression. That
is often claimed to be the main reason why non-finite subclauses are used (cf., for
instance, Quirk et al. 1985: 995, Biber et al. 1999: 198). Also, non-finite subclauses in my material are often less directly linked than finite subclauses to the
superordinate clause, which, with non-finite subclauses, does not have to be present in the same sentence. The non-finite subclause can be subordinated to either
a main clause several sentences away or to a clause that is only understood from
the context. That feature of the non-finite passive progressive clause could make
it an expedient stylistic device in certain contexts. Possibly, the fact that the

(20) *Bhí   sí   'na   seasamh   ar   bhórd   na   luinge   le   mo thaoibh,*
be-PST she in+her stand-VBN on   board   the-GEN   ship-GEN   with my side

dlaoidheog dá   gruaig dá   slabadh   le   gaoth   na   maidne,
lock   of+her hair   to+its blow-VBN   by   wind   the-GEN   morning-GEN

agus loinnir   i   n-a gruaidhe a   bhéarfadh   solus   don   domhan...
and   radiance in   her cheek   REL bring-COND   light   to+the world

'She was standing on deck by my side, <u>a lock of her hair was **being lifted** up by the morning wind</u>, and there was a radiance in her face that would light up the world…' (Ul. *Saoghal Corrach*: 56)

(21) *Righneadóir   ab   ea   Seán Ó Mainnín,   cuma   an   leathamadáin*
loiterer   COP-PST it   Seán Ó Mainnín   appearance   the-GEN   half-fool-GEN

air,   é   bolgshúileach,   giorraradhairceach.   Téarma   tugtha   ins na   Stáit
on-3SGM   he   pop-eyed   short-sighted   period   spend-VBA   in   the   States

aige   ionas   gur   thug   sé   an   t-am   anall   leis.   Mílseáin
by-3SGM   so that   PRT   give-PST he   the time   from over there with-3SGM   sweets

á   thabhairt   abhaile   go dtís   na   mná   óga   aige   aon   lá   a
to+their bring-VBN   home   to   the   women   young   by-3SGM   any   day   REL

raghadh sé   thar   baile   amach,   ach   n'fheadarsa   ar   chuaigh sé
go-IPF   he   beyond   village out   but   NEG+know-EMPH   INT   go-PST   he

riamh   níos giorra   ná   san   d'éinne   acu,   ach   go   n-íosfadh   cat   ciúin
ever   short-COMP   than   that to+any person   of-3PL   but   CONJ   eat-COND   cat   quiet

fáideog,   mar   a   deirtear.
wick   like   REL   say-PRS-AUT

'Seán Ó Mainnín was a loiterer, he had the appearance of a half-fool, he was pop-eyed and short-sighted. He had spent some time in the States, which left its effect on him. <u>He **used to bring** sweets home to the young women any day he went beyond the village</u>, but I don't know if he ever got closer than that to any of them, although, as they say, you have to watch the quiet ones.' (Mu. *Na hAird ó Thuaidh*: 8)

(22) *Níor   chuala   mé   an   t-ainm   sin   á   thabhairt   ariamh   air.*
NEG   hear-PST   I   the name   that to+its give-VBN   ever   on-3SGM

'I never <u>heard</u> it **being called** that.' (Co. *Feamainn Bhealtaine*: 18)

(23) *Is   cuimhin   liom   go maith an   cheist   sin   a   bheith   á*
COP-PRS recollection with-1SG well   the question   that to   be-VBN   to+its

cur   chugam   féin   go fíormhinic.
put-VBN   to-1SG   -self   very often

'<u>I remember</u> well that question **being put** to me myself very often.' (Mu. *Mo Scéal féin*: 32)

(24) "Is   mímhúinte   an   rud   bheith   ag   breathnú   ar   anam   nochtaithe   _á_
COP-PRS   uncivil   the   thing be-VBN at   look-VBN on   soul   naked-VBA   to+its

shníomh   _le_   _dobrón_   _agus_   _cumha._"
wring-VBN   with   grief   and   sorrow

"'It is uncivil to watch a person **being wrung** with grief and sorrow.'" (Co. _Dúil_: 62)

passive progressive is progressive is of particular relevance to its use in adverbial non-finite clauses, since those often denote an event that is simultaneous to the event expressed in the superordinate clause or describe concomitant circumstances. The use of a non-finite adverbial subclauses may be a means of toning down the events or circumstances mentioned in the subclause (cf. Bäcklund 1984: 179ff.).

2.4 Summary of the results regarding verbs and clauses

Following the research question formulated above (in the Introduction, section 1), I have studied the use of the autonomous and the passive progressive in the material with regard to three formal variables: verb type, clause type and subclause structure. The main purpose was to establish whether there are any major differences between the two constructions as far as those features are concerned. It was shown that such differences exist. The study of verb types showed that although both the autonomous and the passive progressive are most frequently formed from monotransitive verbs that take a direct object (the category monotransitive direct), ditransitive verbs are considerably more common in the autonomous than in the passive progressive. This is the main difference between the two constructions as regards verb type. It was also found that, although monotransitive verbs taking a prepositional object (the category monotransitive indirect) and intransitive verbs can form the autonomous, these verb types are very infrequent in the autonomous in the present corpus. It may then be concluded that this structural difference between the autonomous and the passive progressive is reflected in usage to a very low extent. The study of clause types showed that the distribution of main and subclauses differs greatly between the autonomous and the passive progressive: whereas the autonomous is evenly distributed across main and subclauses, the majority of the passive progressives occur in subclauses. The structural differences between the autonomous and the passive progressive are thus reflected to some extent in the results. As has been mentioned earlier, the autonomous is used in a wider variety of verb types: all verb types can form the autonomous, although, for example, intransitive verbs are seldom found in the autonomous. The passive progressive, on the other hand, can only be formed from transitive verbs that take direct objects. The autonomous is also formed from auxiliary verbs, which is impossible with the passive progressive. However, verbs of the types monotransitive indirect, intransitive, and auxiliary occur in only a small proportion (11%) of the instances of the autonomous in the present material. A feature specific to the passive progressive is that it can be used in non-finite clauses. As shown above, as many as 55% of the instances of the passive progressive in the database occur in non-finite sub-clauses.

All the observed correlations between construction and frequency, verb type, clause type and subclause structure were tried using the chi-square test. Chi-square values were calculated for each quantitative finding (presented in the tables). In one case, namely the distribution of subclause type in the autonomous, some of the expected frequencies were too low (below 5) to allow for a reliable chi-square value. In sum, I have found that there are statistically significant differences between the autonomous and the passive progressive as regards verb and clause type. The importance of the differences accounted for above cannot be fully analysed until we have more information about the patients and agents of the autonomous and the passive progressive, which will be presented in following chapters.

CHAPTER 3

Patients and agents

3.1 Introduction

In the present chapter the classification of patients and agents is discussed with respect to information packaging. As accounted for in Chapter 1, five features have been studied: type of overt element, given vs. new, recoverability, continuity and co-reference with active subject. The first two features concern overt elements, that is, patients of both constructions and overt agents of the passive progressive. The classification according to type of overt element depends on the form in which patients and (overt) agents are expressed. There are three main types, namely, definite/indefinite NP, relative particle and clause. Given vs. new concerns the classification of overt elements according to whether or not they refer to a participant that has been explicitly mentioned previously in the discourse. The third feature, recoverability, is concerned with the reader's ability to identify an implicit agent. In the present study, the implicit agents of the autonomous and passive progressive are classified as recoverable either from the surrounding (usually preceding) discourse, or from the reader's extralinguistic knowledge. In addition, one category of implicit agents has been classified as non-recoverable. The two final features, continuity and co-reference with active subject, apply to overt as well as implicit participants. Continuity has to do with the importance an author gives to a constituent; a constituent with a high degree of continuity is regarded as more central in the discourse than a constituent that has a low degree of continuity. Co-reference with active subject, finally, concerns patients and agents that are co-referential with a subject of an active clause. In every instance of continuity the element that is co-referential with the patient or agent in question that is furthest away within the continuity range (one sentence in each direction) has been classified according to whether or not it is the subject of an active clause. The above-mentioned variables are relevant to the study of information packaging since they concern the way in which the information represented by the autonomous patients and agents is presented in the text and their relationship with elements in neighbouring clauses.

The main aim of the present chapter is to investigate the patients and agents in more detail to be able to compare the autonomous and the passive progressive with regard to topicality, that is, the degree of highlighting given to the patients and agents in the autonomous and the passive progressive clauses at sentence and discourse level in the text. Obviously, the most important of the five features are given vs. new and continuity since they are regarded as measures of topicality. As mentioned in chapter 1, accepting the fact that the most topical element in the clause is usually the subject, it has often been noted that there is a connection between the concept of topicality and the passive. Using the passive is a means to let the non-agent be the topic and thus the most highlighted element in the clause (Givón 1979a: 57). As already presented in the survey of previous research concerning the topicality patterns of the autonomous and passive progressive, Noonan (1994) found that in his material passive progressive (overt) agents and autonomous patients displayed higher topicality than passive progressive patients. His conclusion was then that the autonomous is functionally a passive construction while the passive progressive is not (see the Introduction, section 3). Type, recoverability and co-reference with active subject are connected with the measures of topicality. As noted in the Introduction, definite NPs normally refer to given participants. Further, the classification of type also identifies relative particles, which by necessity are given, and clauses which are unlikely to represent given information. Therefore, the variation across type is relevant when considering the distribution across given and new. Recoverability deals with how the referents of the implicit agents are related to the surrounding context. Only textually inferable agents may refer to a participant that is explicitly mentioned before. Textual inferability may then be regarded as a prerequisite for continuity of implicit agents. The final feature studied identifies co-reference of patients and agents (overt as well as implicit) with subjects of active clauses, which are generally considered highly topical constituents.

The presentation of the results concerning the five variables that deal with patients and agents will be done in three steps. First, the two variables that describe patients and overt agents, that is, type of overt element and given vs. new will be discussed (3.2). Second, the variable dealing with implicit agents only, that is, recoverability will be accounted for (3.3). Third, the variables that concern patients and overt as well as implicit agents, continuity and co-reference with active subject, will be presented (3.4). To conclude the investigation of patients and agents, the instances of the agented and agent-less passive progressive are studied separately and compared (3.5), followed by a summary (3.6).

3.2 Variables pertaining to patients and overt agents

3.2.1 Type of overt element

The first feature to be discussed is type of overt element. This variable concerns mainly the definiteness or indefiniteness of patients and overt agents since most of them are expressed as NPs. Apart from definite and indefinite NPs, patients and overt agents may be expressed as relative particles and (autonomous patients only) clauses. Before presenting examples of the various types of overt element and the results of the classification, the distribution of agented and agent-less passive progressive clauses is displayed in Table 3.1.

As shown in Table 3.1, 62% of the passive progressives in the database are agented. This points to an important difference between the autonomous and the passive progressive: all instances of the autonomous in the database are agent-less, while a majority of the instances of the passive progressive are agented. This difference is relevant to the study of the two constructions from an information packaging perspective since overt agents are more topical than implicit ones simply because they are overtly expressed. As mentioned in the Introduction, section 2, it has been observed that the passive progressive is not a passive construction, although this assumption is based on the use of the passive progressive in Munster in particular (see further Chapter 4 on dialectal variation).

Next follows a presentation of the various types of overt element. Definite NPs are most often expressed as nouns preceded by the definite article, as in (1) where *an biadh*, 'the food', is an example of a patient of a passive progressive clause, and as personal pronouns, as in (2) where *aige*, 'by him', is an example of an overt agent of a passive progressive clause. An example of an indefinite NP passive progressive patient is found in (3). In (4) the autonomous patient is expressed as a relative particle. The final type of overt element, a clause, is exemplified in (5). As explained in Chapter 1, only autonomous patients may be expressed as clauses.

The frequency and distribution of patients and overt agents in the autonomous and the passive progressive across types of overt element are displayed in Table 3.2. As can be seen in Table 3.2, there are differences as well as similarities between the autonomous and the passive progressive. All overt elements appear as NPs in the majority of the instances, but the proportion of NPs varies considerably between the autonomous and the passive progressive. In the autonomous, 71% (44% + 27%) of the patients are expressed as NPs while in the passive progressive 85% (41% + 44%) of the patients and 99% (95% + 4%) of the overt agents are NPs. The variation regarding NP patients and agents can be at least partly explained by the fact that clauses are possible as patients in the autonomous but not in the passive progressive. As regards the distribution of

(1) *Bhí*   *an*   *bhiotáilte* *ag*   *gabháil*   *thart*   *agus*   <u>*an*</u>   <u>*biadh*</u>   **ghá**   **dheánamh**
     be-PST   the   liquor   at   go-VBN   round   and   the   food   to+its   make-VBN

réidh.
ready

'The liquor was going round and <u>the food</u> was **being prepared**.' (Ul. *Dochartach Duibhlionna*: 29)

(2) *Gan*   *dul*   *go*   *Sasana*   *chor ar bith*   *is*   *minic*   *a*   *bheas*
     without   go-VBN   to   England   at all   COP-PRS   often   REL   be-FUT-REL

tú   *in ann*   *creideamh*   *nó*   *polaitíocht*   *duine*   *a*   *thomhas,*   *ar*   *an*   *traen*
you-SG   able   religion   or   politics   person-GEN   to   guess-VBN   on   the   train

nó   *ar*   *an*   *mbus,*   *ón*   *bpáipéar*   *a*   *fheicfeas*   *tú*   *á*
or   on   the   bus   from+the   paper   REL   see-FUT   you-SG   to+its

léamh   <u>*aige.*</u>
read-VBN   by-3SGM

'Without going to England at all you can often guess a person's religion or politics, on the train or on the bus, from the paper that you see <u>him</u> **reading**.' (Co. *An Mothall sin ort*: 68)

(3) *Bhí*   <u>*seanfhear*</u>   *á*   **thórramh**   *thiar*   *i*   *dteach*   *in*   *Eoghanacht*   *nuair*   *a*
     be-PST   old man   to+his   wake-VBN   west   in   house   in   E.   when   REL

tháinigeadar.
come-PST-3PL

'<u>An old man</u> was **being waked** over in a house in Eoghanacht when they came.' (Co. *Feamainn Bhealtaine*: 52)

(4) *Uaigh*   *Tutankhamen,*   <u>*nár*</u>   **fritheadh**   *go dtí*   *lár*   *na*   *bhfichidí*
     grave   T.-GEN   REL-NEG   find-PST-AUT   until   middle   the-GEN   twenties-GEN

de'n   *chéad*   *seo,*   *ba bheag nár*   *bhain*   *sí*   *an*   *t-amharc*   *de*   *na*   *daoine*
of+the   century   this   nearly   take   it   the   vision   from   the   people

a   *d'oscail*   *í.*
REL   open-PST   it

'Tutankhamen's grave, <u>which</u> **was not found** until the mid-twenties of this century, nearly blinded the people who opened it.' (Co. *An Mothall sin ort*: 74)

Table 3.1. Distribution of agented and agent-less passive progressives

	n	%
agented	288	62%
agent-less	179	38%
Total	467	100%

(5) *Seacht scóir   loilíoch   a   fuair   Clann Donnchadha na Céise   ar*
     seven   twenty milch cow REL get-PST Clann Donnchadha na Céise   for

   *Leabhar Bhaile an Mhóta, agus **ceapadh**   go   raibh   sé   saor!*
   The Book of Ballymote   and   think-PST-AUT CONJ be-PST   it   cheap

'Clann Donnchadha na Céise got seven score milch cows for the Book of Ballymote, and **it was thought** that it was cheap! (Co. *An Mothall sin ort*: 60)

Table 3.2. Distribution of types of patient and overt agent in the autonomous and the passive progressive

	definite NP		indefinite NP		relative particle		clause		Total	
	n	%	n	%	n	%	n	%	n	%
autonomous patients	1,164	44%	698	27%	447	17%	313	12%	2,622	100%
pass. progressive patients	192	41%	207	44%	68	15%	-	-	467	100%
pass. prog. overt agents	275	95%	12	4%	1	<1%	-	-	288	99%

χ^2 = 265.87; df = 4; p < 0.05, critical value: 9.49 (excluding clauses)
24 understood autonomous patients are excluded from the classification of type of overt element.

definite and indefinite NPs, the greatest difference is found among passive progressive agents where 95% are definite NPs, compared to 4% indefinite NPs. Passive progressive patients are evenly distributed across definite and indefinite, 41% vs. 44%. As for the autonomous patients, the contrast is greater: 44% definite compared to 27% indefinite expressions. When it comes to relative particles, Table 3.2 shows that the frequency of relative particles as patient is just slightly higher in the autonomous than in the passive progressive, 17% vs.15%. As for passive progressive agents, there is a single instance where the agent is expressed as a relative particle. A clause, finally, is the least frequent type of autonomous patient (12%). To sum up, the results of the classification of type of overt element indicate that the most salient difference between the autonomous and the passive progressive concerns indefinite NPs. Passive progressive patients are more frequently indefinite than autonomous patients, and the vast majority of the passive progressive agents are definite NPs.

3.2.2 Given vs. new

The second variable that deals with patients and overt agents is given vs. new. The classification of patients and agents according to this distinction is one way of comparing the two constructions under investigation as regards the topicality of patients and overt agents. As stated above (1.2), a patient or agent is classified as given if its referent has been explicitly mentioned earlier in the same chapter or short story. An example of a passive progressive overt agent that is given is found in (6). The agent *aige*, 'by him', refers to *Giúdach*, 'a Jew', in the

(6)

Giúdach	_as_	_Bleá Cliath_	_a_	_thug_	_ann_	_iad._	_Uair_	_sa_	_tseachtain_
Jew	from	Dublin	REL	take-PST	there	them	time	in+the	week

bhídís	_á_	_dtaispeáint_	_ar dtús_	_aige_	_agus_	_ní_	_bhíodh_	_ag_	_gabháil_
be-IPF-3PL	to+their	show-VBN	at first	by-3SGM	and	NEG	be-IPF	at	go-VBN

_ag_	_breathnú_	_orthu_	_ach_	_dailtíní_	_óga_	_agus_	_iad_	_ag_	_caitheamh_
at	watch-VBN	on-3PL	except	brats	young	and	they	at	throw-VBN

dairteacha	_agus_	_ag_	_béiciú_	_agus_	_ag_	_pléaráca,_	_nó gur_	_labhair_	_an_
clods	and	at	yell-VBN	and	at	tomfoolery	until	speak-PST	the

sagart	_ón_	_altóir._
priest	from+the	altar

'It was a Jew from Dublin who brought them there. At first he used to show them once a week and only young brats went to see them, throwing clods and yelling and fooling around until the priest spoke from the altar.' (Co. _Dúil_: 60)

(7)

Cairdín	_agus_	_beanseo_	_agus_	_fidil,_	_b'fhéidir,_	_agus_	_máirseanna_	_breátha_
accordion	and	banjo	and	fiddle	maybe	and	marches	fine

_á_	_shéideadh_	_suas_	_orthu._
to+their	blow-VBN	up	on-3PL

'An accordion and a banjo and a fiddle, maybe, and fine marches being played on them.' (Mu. _Na hAird Ó Thuaidh_: 15)

Table 3.3. Distribution of given and new patients and overt agents in the autonomous and the passive progressive

	given		new		Total	
	n	%	n	%	n	%
autonomous patients	1,297	49%	1,349	51%	2,646	100%
passive progressive patients	156	33%	311	67%	467	100%
passive progressive overt agents	246	85%	42	15%	288	100%

χ^2 = 196.96; df = 2; p < 0.05, critical value: 5.99

preceding sentence. The sentence in (7) includes a passive progressive patient whose referent is new in the discourse.

The distribution of patients and agents in the autonomous and the passive progressive across given and new is presented in Table 3.3. As shown in Table 3.3, the autonomous patients are fairly evenly distributed across given and new, 49% vs. 51%. In the passive progressive, on the other hand, the distribution of patients as well as agents is uneven. Two thirds (67%) of the patients are new, that is, their referents appear in the text for the first time, while the vast majority (85%) of the passive progressive agents are given.

To conclude the presentation of the variable given vs. new, the correlation between type of overt element and given vs. new will be examined. The aim is to

Table 3.4. Distribution of given and new patients and overt agents across definite and indefinite NPs in the autonomous and the passive progressive

		definite NP		indefinite NP		Total	
		n	%	n	%	n	%
autonomous patients	given	788	95%	38	5%	826	100%
	new	376	36%	660	64%	1,036	100%
passive progressive patients	given	77	88%	11	13%	88	101%
	new	115	37%	196	63%	311	100%
passive progressive overt agents	given	245	100%	0	0%	245	100%
	new	30	71%	12	29%	42	100%

autonomous patients: $\chi^2 = 685.13$; df = 1; p < 0.05, critical value: 3.84
passive progressive patients: $\chi^2 = 70.13$; df = 1; p < 0.05, critical value: 3.84
Excluded from Table 3.4 are relative particles and clauses, relative particles are naturally always given and clauses are always new.

study whether definite and indefinite NP patients and agents primarily represent given or new information. The correlation between given vs. new and type of overt element in the two constructions under investigation is shown below in Table 3.4. Not surprisingly, there is a strong correlation between definite and given (88%–100%), and this correlation is strongest among passive progressive overt agents. It may also be noted that the majority of indefinite NPs are new and extremely few of the indefinite NPs represent given information. However, the correlation between new and indefinite is not as strong as that between given and definite, especially among passive progressive overt agents (29%, compared to 63–64%).

To sum up, the results regarding patients and overt agents point to great differences between the autonomous and the passive progressive. In the autonomous, where the agent is never overtly expressed, NP patients appear more often as definite than indefinite expressions. Nearly half of them refer to given participants. In the passive progressive, by contrast, overt agents are expressed as definite NPs and represent given information to a considerably higher extent than passive progressive patients. In conclusion, the results indicate that autonomous patients and passive progressive overt agents are more topical than passive progressive patients.

3.3 Recoverability of implicit agents

Recoverability is the variable that concerns implicit agents and how the reader or hearer can identify them. As mentioned above, four types of recoverability are recognised in the present study. Implicit agents may be textually inferable, generic, pragmatically inferable or non-recoverable (as explained in Chapter 1). Usually, the referent of an implicit agent is recoverable from the preceding or, less frequently, following discourse (textually inferable), or from the reader's knowledge of the world (pragmatically inferable). As regards pragmatically inferable agents, it is normally not the individuals responsible for the actions in question that are recoverable but rather the group to which the referents of the implicit agents belong, such as a profession. Finally, when an agent is not identifiable from the context or through the use of extralinguistic knowledge, the agent is classified as either generic, that is, unspecified, or as non-recoverable, that is, the construction occurs in an expression where no agent is logically possible.

Below, examples of the various recoverability types are given, starting with the textually inferable category. Obviously, the degree of exactness in the identification of textually inferable implicit agents varies. An example of the highest exactness is found in (8). The discourse preceding the sentence (8) describes a mother and her daughters clipping wool. The agents of the autonomous *bailíodh*, 'was gathered', are thus individually identified from the context.

In many cases, however, the identifiability of the implicit agent is less exact. Often the agent can be inferred from a geographical reference, as in (9), where *sa chathair*, 'in the city', in the first sentence enables the reader to identify the agent of the autonomous verb form *thabharfaí*, 'would be given', as 'people in the city'. In other cases, the agent is recoverable not from any element that has been mentioned in the preceding sentence, but is understood from the general setting of the text as, for example, 'the people of Connemara', in (10), which is part of an account of expressions in a particular dialect spoken in the Connemara region.

The second recoverability type exemplified is generic, as in (11). The third recoverability type comprises the pragmatically inferable implicit agents, exemplified in (12). Based on his or her knowledge of the world, the reader of (12) can infer the agents of the passive progressive *bhíodh féilte á gcomóradh*, 'feasts were being celebrated', as 'the parishioners/church-goers' etc.

Finally, a group of implicit agents have been classified as non-recoverable. This category consists of instances of the autonomous and the passive progressive where no agent is logically implied.[1] The instances of the non-recoverable category can be divided into two main groups. First, there are instances of verbs that in certain meanings are always used impersonally, such as *cas*, 'meet', lit. 'turn', as in (13). This type occurs almost exclusively in the autonomous. *Cas* is by far the most frequently used verb in the first group of non-recoverable implicit agents (303 instances of the autonomous). The verb most frequently used with non-recoverable implicit agents in the passive progressive is *taibhrigh*, 'dream', with 5 instances (exemplified in Chapter 1, (42)). In contrast, *taibhrigh* occurs only once in the autonomous.

---

[1] Compare the discussion on the use of the autonomous to denote non-volition in Ó Corráin (2001), and the so-called idiosyncratic uses of the autonomous discussed in Stenson (1989). These studies are referred to in the Introduction, section 3.

(8) **Bailíodh**   *an*   *olann.*
gather-PST-AUT   the   wool

'The wool **was gathered**.' (Co. *Dúil*: 102)

(9) **Dúradh**   *liom*   *sa*   *chathair* *seo* *nuair* *a*   *d'inis*   *mé*
say-PST-AUT with-1SG in+the city   this   when   REL tell-PST-AUT I

an   *scéal* *gurbh*   *é*   the creative urge *a*   *bhí*   *ag* *gabháil* *dom*   *an*
the story   COP-PST it   REL be-PST   at   go-VBN to-1SG the

tráth *úd.*   *B'fhéidir* *gurbh* *amhlaidh* *a*   *bhí*   *ach* *níor* *chuimhnigh*
period that maybe   COP-PST like   REL be-PST but   NEG remember-PST

mé *féin* *ar* *a* *leithéid* *d'ainm* *a*   *thabhairt* *air,*   *mar* *ba*   *bheag*
I   self   on its like   of+name to   give-VBN on-3SGM for   COP-PST little

é *m'eolas*   *ar* *an* *urge* *céanna,* *agus* *dá* *gcuimhnínn*   *féin*
it my+knowledge on the urge same   and   if   remember-PST SUBJ-1SG self

ba   *bheag* *an* *chosaint* *dom*   *é.* *Ba*   *bheag* *an* *aird*   *a*
COP-PST little   the defence to-1SG it   COP-PST little   the attention REL

thabharfaí   *orm.*
give-COND-AUT   on-1SG

'I **was told** <u>in this city</u> when I told the story that it was the creative urge that was affecting me at that time. Maybe that was the case but I didn't think of calling it any such thing, for I had little knowledge of that urge, and if I had thought of it, it wouldn't have been much of a defence. **People would have paid** scant attention to me.' (Co. *Feamainn Bhealtaine*: 14)

(10) *Más*   *duine* *socair* *soineanta* *tú*   **déarfar**   *leat*   *gurb*
if+COP-PRS person settled calm   you-SG say-FUT-AUT with-2SG COP-PRS

iad "*na*   *muice* *ciúine* *a* *itheas*   *an* *triosc",* *agus* *má* *tá*
they the   pigs   quiet   REL eat-PRS-REL the hogwash and   if   be-PRS

tú   *tostach* *níl*   *ort*   *ach* "*suan* *na*   *muice*   *bradaí*".
you-SG taciturn be-PRS-NEG on-2SG but   sleep the-GEN pig-GEN thieving

'If you are a calm person you **will be told** that it is "the quiet pigs who get the swill", and if you are taciturn it is said that you are "a sly one".' (Co. *An Mothall sin ort*: 81)

Further, the non-recoverable group contains instances where the verb is used in the autonomous or the passive progressive but does not require these constructions in the current meaning, and the implicit agent does not refer to a participant responsible for the action, as in (14) and (15). The verb *bain*, 'take', as in (14), occurs more frequently than other verbs in this subgroup of the non-recoverable category (58 instances of the autonomous, 3 instances of the passive progressive). In the passive progressive, the verb most frequently used with a non-recoverable implicit agent is *caith*, 'throw, spend', as in (15), with 7 instances.

The distribution of recoverability types of implicit agents in the autonomous

(11) *Airím* *daoine,* *uaireanta,* *ag* *tromaíocht* *ar* *mhuintir* *na* *hÉireann,* *á*
hear-PRS-1SG people sometimes at blame-VBN on people of Ireland at+its

rá, *"dá* **gcuirfí** *Éireannach* *ar* *bhior* *os comhair* *na* *tine*
say-VBN if put-COND-AUT Irishman on spit in front of the-GEN fire-GEN

go *bhfaighfí* *Éireannach* *eile* *a* *chasfadh* *an* *bior."*
CONJ find-COND-AUT Irishman other PRT-REL turn-COND the spit

'I sometimes hear people criticising the Irish, saying, "if an Irishman **was put** on a spit in front of
the fire another Irishman would be found to turn the spit." ' (Mu. *Mo Scéal féin*: 96)

(12) *Coinnle* *céarach* *a* *bhíodh* *in* *úsáid* *ar* *an* *altóir,* *agus* *ba* *mhór*
candles wax-GEN REL be-IPF in use on the altar and COP-PST large

an *lán* *coinneal* *a* *ídítí* *sna* *teampaill* *le linn* *Aifrinn*
the great deal candles-GEN REL use-IPF-AUT in+the churches during mass-GEN

agus *nuair* *a* *bhíodh* *féilte* **á** **gcomóradh.**
and when REL be-IPF feasts to+their celebrate-VBN

'Wax candles were used on the altar and a lot of candles were used in the churches during Mass
and when feasts were **being celebrated**.' (Co. *An Mothall sin ort*: 83)

(13) *Ceann* *de* *na* *rudaí* *is brónaí* *a* **chasfaí** *ort.*
one of the things sad-SUP REL meet-COND-AUT on-2SG

'One of the saddest things you could **come across**.' (Co. *An Mothall sin ort*: 24)

(14) *Nuair* *a* *thánamair* *go dtí* *claí* *na* *páirce* *atá* *ar*
when REL come-PST-1PL to wall the-GEN field-GEN be-PRS-REL on

an *dtaobh* *amuigh* *don* *dtigh,* **baineadh** *geit* *asam.*
the side outside of+the house take-PST-AUT start out of-1SG

'When we came to the wall of the field outside the house, I **was startled**.' (Mu. *Fiche Bliain ag
Fás*: 104)

(15) *Deir* *daoine* *gur* *tuitim* *ó* *sgafall* *a* *rinne* *sé* *nuair* *a*
say-PRS people COP-PRS fall from scaffolding REL do-PST he when REL

bhí *sé* *'na* *stócach,* *gur* **loiteadh** *an* *chloigeann* *aige* *agus*
be-PST he in+his youth so that injure-PST-AUT the head at-3SG and

go *bhfuil* *an* *inchinn* *corrach* *ariamh* *ó shoin* *aige.*
CONJ be-PRS the mind troubled ever since then at-3SGM

'People say that he fell from scaffolding in his youth and that **he injured** his head and that he
hasn't been right since.' (Ul. *Saoghal Corrach*: 90)

and the passive progressive is shown in order of frequency in Table 3.5. As can
be seen in Table 3.5, there is very little variation between the autonomous and the
passive progressive as regards the distribution of implicit agents across the
recoverability types. Implicit agents of both constructions are most frequently

Table 3.5. Recoverability of implicit agents in the autonomous and the passive progressive

	textually inferable		generic		pragmatically inferable		non- recoverable		Total	
	n	%	n	%	n	%	n	%	n	%
autonomous	1,818	62%	347	12%	174	6%	617	21%	2,956	101%
passive progressive	112	63%	13	7%	12	7%	42	23%	179	100%

textually inferable: 62% in the autonomous compared to 63% in the passive progressive. The second most common recoverability type is non-recoverable; 21% of the autonomous agents and 23% of the passive progressive agents belong to this type. There is some variation with respect to the generic recoverability type; the proportion of autonomous implicit agents with generic reference is almost twice as large as that of the passive progressive ones, 12% vs. 7%. Pragmatically inferable, finally, is the least frequent recoverability type; only 6% of the autonomous and 7% of the passive progressive agents belong to this category.

In sum, the results indicate that in the autonomous as well as in the passive progressive, the implicit agents are most often recoverable from the surrounding context, that is, they are textually inferable. These findings can be related to the results of Cornelis' (1997) investigation of the Dutch passive construction.[2] Cornelis (1997: 246) defines the "basic meaning" of the Dutch passive as "process towards a final state, the causer of which should not be identified with" (Cornelis 1997: 246). In Cornelis' (1997: 157) definition, 'to identify with the causer' means to establish a close relationship between the reader/writer and the referent of the implicit agent. Based on her study of different types of text, she finds that there are two central functions of the passive in Dutch: "the passive causer's actions are negatively evaluated, and the passive causer is vague and unspecified" (Cornelis 1997: 181f.). For example, in a collection of soccer reports in Dutch newspapers, Cornelis finds that the passive is used when the agents—implicit agents in particular—refer to the team rather than an individual player. The reason for this is, according to Cornelis (1997: 164), that individuals are more easily identified with. Cornelis' findings regarding the passive construction in Dutch are interesting in relation to the present results concerning implicit agents of autonomous and passive progressive clauses. As mentioned above, my observation is that the majority of the instances of the autonomous and the agent-less passive progressive in the present material, the implicit textually inferable agent refers to a group of people whose members are not individually identified or specified. Taking Cornelis' (1997) findings into account, I suggest that the use of the autonomous and the agent-less passive progressive may be

---

[2] The Dutch passive construction in question consists of an auxiliary verb, *worden*, 'become', and a participle where the patient is the grammatical subject. Optionally, an agent phrase may be added, introduced by the preposition *door*, 'by'. In Cornelis' (1997: 20) material, 87% of the passive clauses are agent-less.

motivated at least partly by the fact that the situation described in the verb involves an agent that it is hard for the reader to identify with since the implicit agent often refers to a group of people rather than to an individual.

3.4 Variables concerning overt as well as implicit patients and agents

3.4.1 Continuity

Continuity is a means of assessing whether or not a patient or agent is co-referential with any element in the immediately surrounding context. Continuity is thus a measure of topicality: the higher the degree of continuity of an element, the more topical or important is its referent in the discourse. In the present study, the range of continuity, that is, the scope of context checked for reference, is restricted to the sentence where the element under investigation occurs and one sentence in each direction. The highest degree of continuity of an element is obtained if it has reference in both directions, that is, in both the preceding and following context. An entity that is not referred to within the continuity range is classified as lacking continuity. In the account below, the main focus is on whether there is continuity or not. Further, when there is continuity, whether it is retrospective, prospective or in both directions. The presentation is done in three steps. First the autonomous and passive progressive patients and passive progressive overt agents that represent new participants are dealt with. Here, obviously, the only possibility is prospective continuity or no continuity. Then the discussion moves on to the patients and overt agents that represent given information. Finally the implicit agents are presented. A passive progressive patient (representing new information) that has no continuity is exemplified in (16). Example (17) contains a new passive progressive overt agent with prospective continuity.

The distribution of patients and overt agents that refer to participants that are new in the discourse is presented in Table 3.6. As can be seen in Table 3.6, the vast majority of elements denoting new participants lack continuity, but there is some variation between the autonomous and the passive progressive. Continuity is especially rare among passive progressive patients; only 6% of them are co-referential with an element in the following discourse within the continuity range. Passive progressive overt agents have the highest relative frequency of continuity, 29%, while the corresponding figure for autonomous patients is 15%. Thus, the greatest contrast is found between patients and overt agents in the passive progressive. Autonomous new patients are continuous to a smaller extent than passive progressive overt agents but to a larger extent than passive progressive patients.

(16) *"Caithfear*   *an*   *poll*   *a*   *dh'fhairsingiú*   *más*   *fonn*   *libh*   *dul*
      must-FUT-AUT   the   hole   to   widen-VBN   if+COP-PRS   wish   with-2PL   go-VBN

      síos   *a thuilleadh,"*   *a*   *dúirt*   *fear*   *na*   *fliúite.*   *Bhí*   *athrú*   *éigin*
      down   more   REL   say-PST   man   the-GEN   flute-GEN   be-PST   change   some

      tagtha   *air*   *siúd*   *anois,*   *díreach*   *fé mar*   *bheadh*   *an*   *t-aethó*   *curtha*
      come-VBA   on-3SGM   that   now   exactly   as if   be-COND   the   crisis   put-VBA

      aige   *dhe,*   *agus*   *bhí*   <u>*orduithe*</u>   *á*   **chur**   *ar*   *dhaoine*
      by-3SGM   of-3SGM   and   be-PST   orders   to+their   put-VBN   on   people

      aige.   *Do tháinig*   *an*   *bheirt*   *aníos,*   *agus*   *baineadh*   *a thuilleadh*   *scraithíní*
      by-3SGM   come-PST   the   two   up   and   take-PST-AUT   more   clods-GEN

      d'uachtar   *na*   *talún.*
      from+top   the-GEN   earth-GEN

' "The hole has to be widened if you want to go further down," said the man with the flute. He had changed somehow now, just as if he had got past the crisis, and he **was giving** <u>orders</u> to people. The two came up, and more clods were taken from the top of the earth.' (Mu. *Na hAird Ó Thuaidh*: 48)

(17) *Nuair*   *a*   *thitfeadh*   *an*   *oíche*   *anuas*   *orthu*   *i gceart,*   *ní*   *bheadh*
      when   REL   fall-COND   the   night   down   on-3PL   right   NEG   be-COND

      de   *chomharthaí*   *agat*   *ansan*   *orthu*   *ach*   *an*   *ghibris,*   *agus*   *an*   *cipín solais*
      of   signs   at-2SG   there   on-3PL   except   the   chattering   and   the   match

      a   *bheadh*   *á*   **lasadh**   <u>*age*</u>   <u>*fear*</u>   *anso*   *agus*   *ansúd*   *chun*   *tine*
      REL   be-COND   to+its   light-VBN   at   a man   here   and   there   for   fire

      a   *chur*   <u>*lena*</u>   *phíp.*
      to   put-VBN   with+his   pipe

'When the night fell properly on them, the only sign you would have of them was the chattering, and the odd match that <u>a man</u> **might light** here and there to light <u>his</u> pipe.' (Mu. *Na hAird Ó Thuaidh*: 145)

The next elements to discuss are the patients and agents whose referents are given in the text. Here there are four possibilities: no continuity, retrospective continuity only, prospective continuity only, and continuity in both directions. The sentences in (18) contain an example of a given passive progressive patient with retrospective continuity. Example (19) contains a given autonomous patient with prospective continuity only. A passive progressive given overt agent that has continuity in both directions is shown in (20). Finally, an example of a given passive progressive patient without continuity, is found in (21).

The distribution of continuity of given patients and agents in the autonomous and the passive progressive is displayed in Table 3.7. Table 3.7 shows first of all that given patients in both constructions, as well as overt agents, are most often continuous: 91% (57% + 27% + 7%) of the passive progressive overt agents, 90% (35% + 46% + 9%) of the autonomous patients and 78% (22% + 47% +

Table 3.6. Continuity of new patients and overt agents in the autonomous and the passive progressive

	prospective continuity		no continuity		Total	
	n	%	n	%	n	%
autonomous patients	205	15%	1,144	85%	1,349	100%
passive progressive patients	18	6%	293	94%	311	100%
passive progressive overt agents	12	29%	30	71%	42	100%

$\chi^2 = 26.69$; df = 2; p < 0.05, critical value: 5.99

8%) of the passive progressive patients display continuity. Retrospective continuity is considerably more frequent than prospective continuity among both autonomous and passive progressive patients as well as passive progressive agents. The main explanation for this is probably that many of the elements that display retrospective continuity are relative particles. As exhibited in table 3.2, 447 (= 34% of the given patients) of the autonomous patients and 68 (= 44% of the given patients) of the passive progressive patients occur as relative particles; of necessity, all of these display retrospective continuity. A closer look at the relative particle reveals that 417 (93%) of the autonomous ones and 58 (85%) of the passive progressive ones display retrospective continuity within the same sentence, which may indicate that they are co-referential with their antecedents only. As for passive progressive overt agents, on the other hand, the picture is different. First, as opposed to patients in the autonomous as well as in the passive progressive, a considerably larger proportion of the given overt agents display continuity in both directions than in one direction, 57%, compared to 34% (27% + 7%) (see Table 3.7). As indicated in Table 3.2, there is only one instance of a passive progressive overt agent expressed as a relative particle in the corpus, co-reference with the antecedent is thus not an explanation for retrospective continuity of this participant category.

A comparison of Table 3.7 and Table 3.6 reveals that, not surprisingly, continuity is considerably more common among given elements than among new elements, 78%–91% vs. 6%–29%. In both cases the greatest contrast is found between passive progressive patients—which display the lowest degree of continuity, and overt agents—which display the highest degree of continuity. Autonomous patients show continuity levels that are between the two extremes.

The final type of element to discuss with regard to continuity is the implicit agent of the autonomous and the passive progressive. Like the given patients and overt agents, the implicit agents can display continuity in three ways: retrospective, prospective and continuity in both directions. Below, the continuity types of implicit agents are exemplified in the order they are presented in Table 3.8. An autonomous agent that has retrospective continuity is exemplified in (22). An example of a passive progressive implicit agent that has prospective continuity is

(18)

—*Ná*	*bac*	*san—*	*is*	*fuiriste*	*dhúinn*	*é*	*sin*	*do*	*leigheas,*
NEG	bother-IPV	that	COP-PRS	easy	for-1PL	it	that	to	remedy-VBN

arsa	*mise,*	*agus*	*seo*	*liom*	*isteach*	*'on*	*tsiopa,*	*agus*	*cheannaíos*
say-PST	I-EMPH	and	this	with-1SG	in	to+the	shop	and	buy-PST-1SG

roinnt	*milseán.*	*Seo*	*linn*	*soir*	*an*	*bóthar*	*ansan*	*agus*	*na*	*milseáin*
some	sweets-GEN	this	with-1PL	eastwards	the	road	then	and	the	sweets

againn	*á*	**chogaint**	*ar*	*ár*	*lándicheall,*	*agus*	*níor*	*dheineamair*
by-1PL	to+their	chew-VBN	on	our	utmost endeavour	and	PRT-NEG	do-PST-1PL

stad	*ná*	*staon*	*nó gur*	*bhaineamair*	*amach*	*Tráigh*	*Fionntrá.*
stop	or	stop	until	take-PST-1PL	out	Beach	F.

'—Don't mind that—it is easy for us to remedy that, said I, and off I went into the shop, and bought <u>some sweets</u>. Then we went along the road, **chewing** the sweets like mad, and we didn't stop until we reached Ventry Beach.' (Mu. *Fiche Bliain ag Fás*: 76)

(19)

"Ar	**báitheadh**	*an*	*t-iomlán*	*aca?"*	*arsa*	*mise.*	*"An*	*t-iomlán*
INT	drown-PST-AUT	the	whole	of-3PL	say-PST	I-EMPH	the	whole

léir	*aca*	*acht*	*triúr,"*	*ar*	*seisean.*
whole	of-3PL	except	three	say-PST	he-EMPH

' "Were <u>all of them</u> **drowned**?" said I. "All of them except three," said he.' (Ul. *Saoghal Corrach*: 183)

shown in (23). The sentences in (24) contains an example of an autonomous agent that has continuity in two directions. An example of an implicit passive progressive agent that has no continuity is shown in (25).

The distribution of continuity of implicit agents in the autonomous and the passive progressive is shown in Table 3.8. As can be seen in Table 3.8, there is very little variation between the autonomous and the passive progressive. The majority of the implicit agents in both constructions lack continuity, 69% and 71%, respectively. In those instances where there is continuity in one direction, the continuous elements are fairly evenly distributed across retrospective and prospective continuity, 12% and 11% vs. 9% and 13%. The least frequent continuity type of implicit agents in the autonomous as well as the passive progressive is continuity in both directions, 8% and 7%.

The results presented above (see Tables 3.6 and 3.7) have shown that a vast majority of the overt elements (patients and overt agents) that refer to given participants in the autonomous and passive progressive display continuity, whereas a minority of the new patients and agents are continuous. As exhibited in Table 3.3, there is great variation as regards the proportions of given and new elements across the items under investigation. While 51% of the autonomous patients and 67% of the passive progressive patients have referents that appear in the text for the first time, 85% of the passive progressive overt agents represent participants that have figured previously in the text. As a consequence, it is not

(20)
Ach	nuair	a	bheadh	*a*	shuipéar	caite	*aige,*	ní
but	when	REL	be-COND	his	supper	spend-VBA	by-3SGM	COP-PRS-NEG

haon	fhonn	fílíochta	ná	réadóireachta	a	bhíodh	ar	*an*	*ainniseoir*
any	desire	poetry-GEN	nor	star-gazing-GEN	REL	be-IPF	on	the	miserable person

bocht,	agus	is	leasmháthair	a	thógfadh	*air*	é	tar éis	a
poor	and	COP-PRS	stepmother	REL	take-COND	on-3SGM	it	after	his

lae.	Ach	bhí	fliúit	stáin	*aige*	a	thairgíodh	sé	*chuige*
day-GEN	but	be-PST	flute	stain-GEN	at-3SGM	REL	draw-IPF	he	to-3SGM

cois	an	iarta,	agus	a	chos	ar	a	leath-ghlúin	aige,	agus
beside	the-GEN	hob-GEN	and	his	foot	on	his	one knee	at-3SGM	and

ní mór ná	go	dtógfadh	sé	na	mairbh	as	uaigh	leis	na	poirt
nearly	CONJ	lift-COND	he	the	dead	out of	grave	with	the	tunes

agus	leis	na	ríleacha	breátha	a	bhíodh	*á*	**sheimint**	*aige*
and	with	the	reels	fine	REL	be-IPF	to+their	play-VBN	by-3SGM

dhuinn.	Seán Ó Maoileoin,	m'athair	críonna,	ar	an	dtaobh	eile	dhe'n	dtine
for-1PL	Seán Ó Maoileoin	my+father	old	on	the	side	other	of+the	fire

agus	iad	araon	ar	gach	re	port,	duine	acu	ar	an	bhfliúit	agus
and	they	both	on	every	other	tune	person	of-3PL	on	the	flute	and

an	fear	eile	ag	portfheadaíol,	agus	nárbh	fhios	cé	acu
the	man	other	at	whistling a tune	and	COP-NEG	knowledge	who	of-3PL

dhe'n	mbeirt	**acu**	dob	fhearr.
of+the	two	of-3PL	COP-PST	better

'But when he had eaten his supper, the poor miserable wretch had no desire for poetry or star-gazing, and only a nasty stepmother would reproach him for that. But he had a tin flute that he would take up beside the hob, with one foot up on his knee, and he would almost raise the dead from the grave with the tunes and with the fine reels that he **played** for us. Seán Ó Maoileoin, my grandfather, on the other side of the fire and both of them playing alternate tunes, one of them on the flute and the other whistling, and one couldn't tell which of them was better.' (Mu. *Na hAird Ó Thuaidh*: 45)

surprising that the patients most often lack continuity, whereas a majority of the passive progressive overt agents are continuous. Implicit agents resemble the patients since they, too, lack continuity in a majority of the instances. Autonomous patients and implicit agents, as well as passive progressive patients and implicit agents all show a similar pattern as regards continuity: a majority of them are discontinuous.

The contrast between the continuity patterns of autonomous patients, passive progressive patients, implicit agents, and overt agents, is illustrated in Table 3.9. Table 3.9 exhibits that the greatest difference between the autonomous and the passive progressive as regards continuity is found among patients: 52% of the autonomous patients are continuous, while the proportion of continuous passive progressive patients is 30%. Implicit agents and passive progressive patients are

(21) | *Ceantar* | *measúil* | *a* | *bhí* | *ann.* | *É* | *chomh* | *measúil* | *sin* | *agus* | *go* |
|---|---|---|---|---|---|---|---|---|---|---|
| district | respectable | REL | be-PST | in-3SGM | it | so | respectable | that | and | so that |

raibh	*an*	*mheasúlacht*	*á*	*phlúchadh.*	*Bhíodh*	*an*	*bia*	*á*	*chiondáil*
be-PST	the	respectability	at+its	smother-VBN	be-IPF	the	food	to+its	ration-VBN

sna	*blianta*	*úd,*	*ach*	*dá*	*n-abraítí*		*liom*	*go*	*raibh*	*an*	*t-aer*
in+the	years	that	but	if	say-PST	SUBJ-AUT	with-1SG	CONJ	be-PST	the	air

féin	*ciondáilte*	*san*	*ascaill*	*úd*	*chreidfinn*		*é.*	*Is*		*cinnte*
self	ration-VBA	in+the	corner	that	believe-COND-1SG		it	COP-PRS		certain

go	*raibh*	*ciondáil*	*déanta*	*ar*	*an*	*suáilceas*	*agus*	*ar*	*an*	*laethúlacht*
CONJ	be-PST	ration	do-VBA	on	the	pleasantness	and	on	the	friendliness

ann.	*ar aon chuma.*
there	at any rate

'It was a respectable district. So respectable that the respectability was smothering it. Food **was
rationed** in those years, but if I had been told that the very air was being rationed in that region I
would have believed it. What is certain is that pleasantness and friendliness had been rationed at
any rate.' (Co. *Feamainn Bhealtaine*: 95)

Table 3.7. Continuity of given patients and overt agents in the autonomous and
the passive progressive

	continuity in both directions		continuity in one direction				no continuity		Total	
			retrospective		prospective					
	n	%	n	%	n	%	n	%	n	%
autonomous patients	453	35%	599	46%	115	9%	130	10%	1,297	100%
pass. prog. patients	35	22%	74	47%	13	8%	34	22%	156	99%
pass. prog. overt agents	140	57%	67	27%	18	7%	21	9%	246	100%

$\chi^2 = 74.26$; df = 6; p < 0.05, critical value: 12.59

the most discontinuous participants, while overt agents are far more often
continuous than any of the other participants. Like the results presented above
concerning given vs. new, these results indicate that the autonomous and the
passive progressive display different topicality patterns. The conclusion is that in
the autonomous, patients are more topical than agents, while in the passive
progressive overt agents are considerably more topical than patients and implicit
agents.

(22) *Lig*   *mé*   *léi,*   *ar eagla*   *go*   *mbuailfeadh*   *sí*   *bóthar* *agus* *go*
let-PST   I   with-3SGF   for fear   CONJ   hit-COND   she   road   and   CONJ

bhfágfadh   *sí* *aonraic* *mé.*   *Shín* *mé* *aici*   *gach* *ar* *iarr*   *sí*
leave-COND   she alone   me   hand-PST I at-3SGF   all   REL ask-PST she

orm,   *gan*   *bacadh*   *lena*   *chomhaireamh,*   *airgead* *a*   **saothraíodh**
on-1SG   without   interfere-VBN   with+its   count-VBN   money   REL earn-PST-AUT

go cruaidh.
hard

'<u>I</u> let her have her way, for fear that she would head off and leave <u>me</u> alone. <u>I</u> gave her everything she asked of <u>me</u>, without bothering to count it, money that **was** hard **earned**.' (Co. *Dúil*: 63)

(23) *Chuaidh* *uair* *fhada* *eile*   *thart;* *agus* *annsin* *mhothuigh* *an* *fear* *a*
go-PST hour long other   by and then hear-PST the man REL

bhí *amuigh* *an* *doras* *dá* **fhoscladh** *a's* *chuala* *sé* *an* *scairt:*
be-PST outside the door to+its open-VBN and hear-PST he the scream

"An *bhfuil* *tú*   *annsin,* *a* *Bhilí?"* *Glór* <u>*an*</u> <u>*tsagairt*</u> *a*
INT be-PRS you-SG there VOC B. voice the-GEN priest-GEN REL

bhí *ann* *a's* *thug* *Bilí* *rúide* *'in* *tosaigh.*
be-PST there and give-PST B. spurt to beginning-GEN

'Another long hour went by, and then the man who was outside heard the door **being opened** and he heard the call: "Are you there, Bilí?" It was <u>the priest</u>'s voice and Bilí made a dash forward.' (Ul. *Crathadh an Phocáin*: 92)

Table 3.8. Distribution of continuity of implicit agents in the autonomous and the passive progressive

	both directions		one direction				none		Total	
			retrospective		prospective					
	n	%	n	%	n	%	n	%	n	%
autonomous	240	8%	354	12%	312	11%	2,050	69%	2,956	100%
passive progressive	12	7%	17	9%	23	13%	127	71%	179	100%

(24) | *Fuair* | *sé* | *an* | *seanduine* | *gránna* | *'na* | *luighe* | *ag* | *saothraoghadh* | *an* |
| --- | --- | --- | --- | --- | --- | --- | --- | --- | --- |
| find-PST | he | the | old man | poor | in+his | lie-VBN | at | labour-VBN | the-GEN |

bháis.	*Thainig*	*an*	*gadaidhe,*	*agus*	*nuair*	*a*	*chonnaic*	*sé*	*gur*
death-GEN	come-PST	an	thief	and	when	REL	see-PST	he	CONJ

h-aithnigheadh	*é*	*bheir*	*sé*	*ar*	*fhorc*	*agus*	*sháith*	*sé*	*i*	*gConchubhar*
recognise-PST-AUT	him	catch-PST	he	on	fork	and	thrust-PST	he	in	Conchubhar

go	*bun*	*na*	*mbionglán*	*í.*	*Thoisigh*	*Conchubhar Óg*	*a*	*chaoineadh*
until	base	the-GEN	prongs-GEN	it	begin-PST	Conchubhar Junior	to	cry-VBN

agus	*a*	*fhiafruighe*	*de'n*	*athair*	*cé*	*a*	*chuir*	*'sa*	*chluiche*	*sin*	*é.*
and	to	ask-VBN	from+the	father	who	REL	put-PST	in+the	trouble	that	him

'He found the poor <u>old man</u> lying in the throes of death. The thief had come, and when he saw that he **had been recognised** he reached for a fork and thrust it into <u>Conchubhar</u> to the base of the prongs. Young Conchubhar began crying and asking <u>his father</u> who had done such a thing to <u>him</u>.' (Ul. *Dochartach Duibhlionna*: 22)

(25) | *Deirim* | *leat,* | *a* | *léitheoir,* | *gur* | *rinceas* | *féin* | *agus* | *Máiréad* | *an* |
| --- | --- | --- | --- | --- | --- | --- | --- | --- | --- |
| say-PRS-1SG | to-2PL | VOC | reader | that | dance-PST-1SG | self | and | M. | the |

lá	*úd*	*agus*	*gur*	*sinne*	*a*	*bhí*	*go sásta.*	*Bhí*	*beirt*	*againn*
day	that	and	that	we-EMPH	REL	be-PST	happy	be-PST	two	of-1PL

suite	*síos*	*anois*	*agus*	*cóta*	*maith*	*allais*	*orainn,*	*cúpla*	*set*	*á*
seated	down	now	and	coat	good	sweat-GEN	on-1PL	couple	set	to+their

rince	*ar*	*an*	*urlár*	*agus*	*sinn*	*ag*	*tabhairt*	*gach*	*ní*	*fé ndeara*
dance-VBN	on	the	floor	and	we	at	give-VBN	every	thing	under notice

I	*gceann*	*tamaill,*	*do bhuail*	*stracaire*	*isteach*	*sa*	*doras,*	*cragadán*
in	end	while-GEN	strike-PST	struggler	into	in+the	door	hardy little man

do	*bhuachaill*	*íseal*	*agus*	*coinneal*	*ina*	*radharc.*
of	boy	short	and	candle	in+his	sight

'I can tell you, reader, that Máiréad and I danced that day and that we were very happy. The two of us were sitting down with a good coat of sweat on us, a couple of sets were **being danced** on the floor and us observing everything. After a while, a straying fellow came in through the door, a broth of a boy with a glint in his eye.' (Mu. *Fiche Bliain ag Fás*: 170)

97

Table 3.9. Continuity of patients and agents in the autonomous and the passive progressive

		autonomous				passive progressive					
		patients		implicit agents		patients		implicit agents		overt agents	
		n	%	n	%	n	%	n	%	n	%
continuity	continuity	1,372	52%	906	31%	140	30%	52	29%	237	82%
	no continuity	1,274	48%	2,050	69%	327	70%	127	71%	51	18%
Total		2,646	100%	2,956	100%	467	100%	179	100%	288	100%
type of continuity	both	453	17%	240	8%	35	7%	12	7%	140	49%
	retrosp. cont.	599	23%	354	12%	74	16%	17	9%	67	23%
	prosp. cont.	320	12%	312	11%	31	7%	23	13%	30	10%
Total		1,372	52%	906	31%	140	30%	52	29%	237	82%

continuity: $\chi^2 = 494.77$; df = 4; p < 0.05, critical value: 9.49
type of continuity: $\chi^2 = 134.87$; df = 8; p < 0.05, critical value: 15.51

3.4.2 Co-reference with active subject

The final variable with regard to patients and agents is co-reference with active subject. The study of this feature concerns those patients and agents that display continuity. Following Risselada (1991), the only syntactic function identified is subject of an active clause. In each instance of the autonomous and the passive progressive where there is continuity of the patient or agent, overt or implicit, the element creating continuity that is furthest away within the continuity range, that is, one sentence in each direction from the agent or patient in question, has been classified with regard to its syntactic function. The main question is then whether there is a tendency for the elements that have been shown previously in this chapter to have the highest topicality to be co-referential with subjects in active clauses in the immediately surrounding discourse to a greater extent than the elements that have been found to be less topical. Based on the results regarding type, given vs. new, and continuity, the hypothesis is that autonomous patients and passive progressive overt agents are co-referential with active subjects more often than the implicit agents and passive progressive patients.

Below, one example is given in turn of an autonomous patient, an autonomous implicit agent, a passive progressive patient, a passive progressive implicit agent, and a passive progressive overt agent, where the element in question is co-referential with an active subject in the same sentence or in the preceding or following sentence. In (26) the autonomous patient *an soitheach*, 'the ship', is co-referential with the active subject *a long*, 'his ship', in the preceding sentence. The agents of the autonomous verb forms *beannuigheadh*, 'one greeted', and *h-iarradh*, 'one asked', in (27) are co-referential with the active subject *siad*,

Table 3.10. Distribution of co-reference with active subject in the autonomous and the passive progressive

	yes		no		Total	
	n	%	n	%	n	%
autonomous patients	464	18%	2,182	82%	2,646	100%
autonomous implicit agents	221	7%	2,735	93%	2,956	100%
passive progressive patients	38	8%	429	92%	467	100%
passive progressive implicit agents	10	6%	169	94%	179	100%
passive progressive overt agents	159	55%	129	45%	288	100%

autonomous: $\chi^2 = 131.65$; df = 1; p < 0.05, critical value: 3.84
passive progressive: $\chi^2 = 264.07$; df = 2; p < 0.05, critical value: 5.99

'they', in the preceding sentence. The sentence in (28) contains a passive progressive patient that is co-referential with the subject of the preceding active clause. In (29) the implicit agent of the passive progressive verb form *á chasadh*, '[being] turned', is co-referential with the active subject *Neidín* in the following sentence. The passive progressive overt agent, *agam*, 'by me', in the second sentence in (30) is co-referential with the subject of the active verb form *gcaithinn*, 'I used to spend' in the preceding sentence.

The distribution of co-reference with active subject of patients and agents is presented in Table 3.10. The results presented in Table 3.10 support the hypothesis formulated above: autonomous patients and passive progressive overt agents are co-referential with subjects of active clauses to a considerably larger extent than the other elements. The most salient finding is that the participant type that has shown the strongest topicality pattern before, passive progressive overt agent, is the participant type that has the highest proportion of co-reference with subjects of active clauses, 55%. Further, patients of autonomous clauses display the second highest relative frequency of co-reference with active subject as continuing element, 18%, which is around twice as high as the implicit agents as well as the passive progressive patients, 6%–8%. In sum, the differences regarding co-reference with active subject tally with the results presented in preceding sections, that is, that the participant types that have been shown to have relatively high topicality, autonomous patients and passive progressive overt agents, are more frequently co-referential with an active subject in the immediately surrounding context than implicit agents whose topicality is lower.

(26) *Bhí*   *a*   *long*   *fá*   *n-a*   *lasta*   *síoda*   *a'*   *tarraingt*   *air,*   *agus*   *dhíolfadh*
       be-PST   his   ship   under   his   load   silk-GEN   at   pull-VBN   on-3SGM   and   pay-COND

       an   *lasta*   *sin*   *a*   *chuid*   *fiach*   *is*   *tuilleadh.*   *Acht*   *caidé*   *tháinig*
       the   load   that   his   share   debts-GEN   and   more   but   what   come-PST

       acht   *oídhche*   *mhilltineach*   *gaoithe*   *móire*   *agus*   **báitheadh**   *an*   *soitheach.*
       but   night   terrible   wind-GEN   great-GEN   and   sink-PST-AUT   the   ship

'His ship carrying a load of silk was approaching him, and that load would pay his debts and more. But what came but a terribly windy night and the ship **sank**.' (Ul. *Saoghal Corrach*: 5)

(27) *Chuala*   *siad*   *coiscéimeanna*   *ar*   *leacacha*   *an*   *dorais*   *anois*   *a's*
       hear-PST   they   footsteps   on   flat stones   the-GEN   door-GEN   now   and

       cé   *thig*   *asteach*   *acht*   *Niall Ó Gallchobhair*   *agus*   *Conall na Luath'.*
       who   come-PRS   into   but   Niall Ó Gallchobhair   and   Conall na Luath'

       Beannuigheadh   *dóibh*   *agus*   **h-iarradh**   *ortha*   *suidhe.*
       greet-PST-AUT   to-3PL   and   ask-PST-AUT   on-3PL   sit-VBN

'**They** heard footsteps on the threshold now and who came in but Niall Ó Gallchobhair and Conall na Luath'. They **were greeted** and **asked** to sit down.' (Ul. *Crathadh an Phocáin*: 56)

(28) *Is*   *í*   *an*   *patrún*   *céanna*   *báid*   *atá*   *á*   **dhéanamh**   *inniu*   *ann*
       COP-PRS   it   the   model   same   boat-GEN   be-PRS-REL   to+its   make-VBN   today   there

       ages   *na*   *Goodwyns*   *sa*   *Leitriúch,*   *agus*   *ag*   *an*   *dá*   *chrannlaoch*   *sa*
       by   the   Goodwyns   in+the   Leitriúch   and   by   the   two   old soldier   in+the

       Ghaeltacht   *thiar,*   *Mícheál Ó Sé an Chuasa*   *agus*   *Mícheál 'ac Gearailt Bhaile na nGall.*
       Irish-speaking area   west   Mícheál Ó Sé an Chuasa   and   Mícheál 'ac Gearailt of Baile na nGall

'It is the same type of boat which the Goodwyns are **building** today in Leitriúch, and the two old soldiers in the west Gaeltacht, Mícheál Ó Sé an Chuasa and Mícheál 'ac Gearailt of Baile na nGall.' (Mu. *Na hAird Ó Thuaidh*: 142)

(29) *Rinne*   *an*   *geata*   *torann*   *binn*   *agus*   *é*   *á*   **chasadh**   *amach.*   *Nuair*
       make-PST   the   gate   noise   melodious   and   it   to+its   turn-VBN   out   when

       a   *bhí*   *Neidín*   *ag*   *gabháil*   *sall*   *go dtí*   *an*   *leath*   *eile,*   *tháinig*
       REL   be-PST   N.   at   go-VBN   across   to   the   side   other   come-PST

       seanghealbhan   *amach*   *as*   *an*   *nead*   *faoi*   *ruathar*   *mór*   *eitill,*   *tar éis*
       old+sparrow   out   from   the   nest   under   rush   great   flight-GEN   after

       péiste   *a*   *roinnt*   *idir*   *éiníní*   *an*   *áil.*
       worm-GEN   to   distribute-VBN   between   birds-DIM   the-GEN   brood-GEN

'The gate made a melodious noise as it was **being opened**. When Neidín was going across to the other side, an old sparrow suddenly flew out from its nest, having divided a worm between the brood.' (Co. *Dúil*: 68)

(30) | *Nach* | *raibh* | *fhios* | *aici* | *féin* | *go* | *gcaithinn* | *an* | *lá* | *thuas* |
| INT-NEG | be-PST | its+knowledge | at-3SGF | -self | CONJ | spend-IPF-1SG | the | day | up |

| *i* | *mo* | *sheomra,* | *fiú* | *lá* | *dá* | *bhreátha,* | *ag* | *léamh* | *Irisleabhair* | *bheannaithe.* |
| in | my | room | even | day | REL | fine | at | read-VBN | journal-GEN | holy |

| *Irisleabhar* | *Phríosúin* | *Sheáin* | *Mhistéil* | *a* | *bhí* | *á* | *léamh* | *agam* | *dáiríre.* |
| journal | prison-GEN | S.-GEN | M.-GEN | REL | be-PST | to+its | read-VBN | by-1SG | in reality |

'Didn't she know that I used to spend the day up in my room, even fine days, reading a holy
Journal. In reality I was **reading** John Mitchell's Prison Journal.' (Co. *Feamainn Bhealtaine*: 96)

3.5 Agented vs. agent-less passive progressives

As shown above, the passive progressive pattern points to highly topical overt
agents, and low topicality of patients and implicit agents, although patients are
tend to be somewhat more topical than implicit agents. These findings raise the
question about the function of the agented vs. the agent-less passive progressive.
In the agented passive progressive the pattern is transparent: the results suggest
that the agented passive progressive is used when the agent phrase refers to a
highly topical element in the text: definite, given, continuous, and co-referential
with a subject of an active clause, while the referents of the patients tend to be
less central in the text: they are somewhat more often indefinite than definite, as
well as most frequently new, discontinuous and seldom co-referential with an
active subject. As for the comparison of patients and implicit agents, however,
the results point to very small differences (not statistically significant). Both
element types seem to be equally low in topicality. To be able to study the topicality patterns of the passive progressive more closely, I compared the results
concerning patients of agented and agent-less passive progressive clauses, as well
as overt and implicit agents, as shown in Table 3.11. The main question is then
whether the contrast with respect to topicality is greater between patients and
implicit in agent-less passive progressive clauses agents than the one observed so
far between them in all passive progressive clauses.

The most salient results presented in Table 3.11 concern differences between,
on the one hand, overt agents and, on the other hand, implicit agents and patients
of agented as well as agent-less passive progressives. These differences are very
similar to those accounted for in previous sections and will therefore not be
commented on further below. When it comes to the comparison of patients of
agented and agent-less passive progressive clauses, Table 3.11 shows that the
major (statistically significant) difference between the two kinds of patients
concerns type of overt element. Patients of agent-less passive progressives are
more often definite than patients of agented passive progressives, 51% vs. 35%.
Conversely, 19% of the patients of agented passive progressive are relative
particles, compared to 7% of the patients of agent-less passive progressive
clauses. As for the variables given vs. new and continuity, there is very little

101

Table 3.11. Patients and agents in agented and agent-less passive progressive clauses

		agented				agent-less			
		patients		overt agents		patients		implicit agents	
		n	%	n	%	n	%	n	%
type of overt element	definite NP	101	35%	275	95%	91	51%	*not*	
	indefinite NP	131	45%	12	4%	76	42%	*applicable*	
	relative particle	56	19%	1	<1%	12	7%		
Total		288	99%	288	99%	179	100%		
given vs. new	given	97	34%	246	85%	59	33%	*not*	
	new	191	66%	42	15%	120	67%	*applicable*	
Total		288	100%	288	100%	179	100%		
continuity	continuity	86	30%	237	82%	54	30%	52	29%
	no continuity	202	70%	51	18%	125	70%	127	71%
Total		288	100%	288	100%	179	100%	179	100%
type of continuity	both directions	14	5%	140	49%	21	12%	12	7%
	retrosp. cont.	56	19%	67	23%	18	10%	17	9%
	prospective cont.	16	6%	30	10%	15	8%	23	13%
Total		86	30%	237	82%	54	30%	52	29%
co-reference with active subject	yes	21	7%	159	55%	17	9%	10	6%
	no	267	93%	129	45%	162	91%	169	94%
Total		288	100%	288	100%	179	100%	179	100%

Since the main concern is to investigate differences between patients of agented and agent-less passive progressive clauses, only the results regarding patients have been tested for statistical significance.
type of overt element: $\chi^2 = 19.21$; df = 2; p < 0.05, critical value: 5.99
continuity type: $\chi^2 = 14.38$; df = 2; p < 0.05, critical value: 5.99

variation between patients. First, approximately the same percentage of the patients in agented than in agent-less passive progressive clauses refer to given participants, 34% (97/288) compared to 33% (59/179). Second, the proportion of continuous patients is 30% of agented as well as agent-less passive progressives. As regards the type of continuity, however, there is some variation (which is statistically significant). While 12% of the patients in agent-less passive progressive clauses display continuity in both directions, only 5% of the patients of agented passive progressives are co-referential with elements in the preceding as well as following context. Further, a closer look at the continuity of patients reveals that all continuous patients that refer to new participants occur in agent-less passive progressives. This may indicate that there is a difference regarding status in discourse between patients of agented and agent-less passive progressive clauses. Finally, when it comes to co-reference with active subject, the results show that patients of agent-less passive progressives are slightly more often co-referential with active subjects than patients of agented passive progressives, 29% vs. 27%.

Considering these findings and the results presented in previous sections, it is hardly surprising that a comparison of patients and implicit agents of agent-less passive progressives indicates that there is virtually no variation with respect to the proportion of continuity, 30% of the patients and 29% of the implicit are continuous. However, as can be seen in Table 3.11, there is some variation between patients and implicit agents of agent-less passive progressive as regards type of continuity. The most common type of continuity among patients is continuity in both directions which is the least common type among implicit agents, 12% vs. 7%. Conversely, prospective continuity is the most frequent continuity type among implicit agents and the least frequent type of continuity among patients, 13% compared to 8%. When it comes to the final variable, co-reference with active subject, the results show that 9% of the patients are co-referential with subjects of active clauses, which is a slightly larger proportion than that of implicit agents, 6%. This difference is not statistically significant.

The results presented above point to an interesting difference between the agent-less passive progressive and the autonomous. On the surface, the two constructions are similar in that the agent is implicit. However, the topicality pattern of the agent-less passive progressive differs from that of the autonomous. As shown above, the contrast between patients and implicit agents in the agent-less passive progressives is considerably smaller than that between patients and implicit agents in autonomous clauses; in the agent-less passive progressive, patients and agents are about equally low in topicality. Thus, it seems that the agent-less passive progressive shares with the autonomous the feature of agent-demotion, but—unlike the autonomous—without promoting the patient.

3.6 Summary

In the present chapter the classification of patients and agents is discussed with respect to information packaging. The five features included in the study are type of overt element, given vs. new, recoverability, continuity and co-reference with active subject. The first two features concern overt elements only, that is, patients of both constructions and overt agents of the passive progressive. The description according to type of overt element depends on the form in which patients and agents are expressed: definite/indefinite NP, relative particle and (as regards patients of autonomous clauses only) clause. Given vs. new is a classification of overt elements according to whether or not they refer to a participant that has been explicitly mentioned previously in the text. The feature recoverability is concerned with the reader's ability to identify an implicit agent: either from the surrounding discourse, or from the reader's extralinguistic knowledge. Continuity has to do with the importance an author gives to a constituent; an element that is mentioned several times is regarded as a constituent with a high degree of continuity and therefore more central in the discourse than a constituent that has a low degree of continuity. Co-reference with active subject, finally, concerns the agents and patients that display continuity. In every instance of continuity the element that is co-referential with the agent or patient in question that is furthest away within the continuity range (one sentence in each direction) has been classified according to whether or not it is the subject of an active clause.

The main aim of the chapter was to investigate the topicality of the patients and agents in the autonomous and passive progressive clauses in the database. As shown in previous research, the topicality of patients and agents, that is, the degree of highlighting they are given in a text, is of relevance for the definition of the function of passive constructions as opposed to active constructions. The distinction is then that in passive constructions patients are more topical than agents, while in active constructions agents are more topical than patients. Noonan (1994) found that in his material, the (overt) agents of passive progressive clauses and the patients of autonomous clauses have higher topicality than the patients of passive progressive clauses. His conclusion was that the autonomous is functionally a passive construction while the passive progressive is not (see the Introduction, section 3). In the present chapter, the two variables primarily concerned with topicality are given vs. new and continuity. To some extent, the type of overt element and the co-reference with active subject may also be regarded as topicality measures, since it has been noted that there is a strong correlation between given and definite, and new and indefinite. Further, Risselada (1991) considers discourse cohesiveness as a topicality measure. Continuity and co-reference with active subject are of particular relevance to the study since they apply to all elements, overt as well as implicit ones, thus enhancing a comparison of the autonomous and the passive progressive. High topicality is indicated by a high proportion of patients and agents expressed as definite NPs, frequent reference to given participants, a high proportion of continuous elements, and high frequency of co-reference with subjects of active clauses.

The results regarding the variables type of overt element, given vs. new, continuity, and co-reference with active subject all point to the same patterns. In the autonomous, patients are more topical than agents, while in the passive progressive, overt agents are more topical than patients as well as implicit agents. Thus, the findings presented above support Noonan's (1994) conclusions.

When it comes to type of overt element, definite NP is the most common expression of autonomous patients and passive progressive overt agents: 44% and 95%. Passive progressive patients, on the other hand, are slightly more often indefinite NPs than definite NPs, 44% vs. 41% (Table 3.2).

As regards the main topicality features, that is, given vs. new, and continuity, it was shown above that 49% of the autonomous patients refer to given participants, while only 33% of the passive progressive patients do. When it comes to passive progressive overt agents, 85% of them refer to a previously explicitly mentioned participant. A pattern similar to the one found with given vs. new is found as regards continuity in that 52% of the autonomous patients are continuous, compared to 30% of the passive progressive ones and 82% of the overt agents. As for implicit agents, in the autonomous as well as in the passive progressive a majority are discontinuous, 31% and 29%, respectively (Table 3.3 and Table 3.9).

A similar pattern appears as regards co-reference with active subject. Most instances of co-reference with the subject of an active clause are found among passive progressive overt agents, 53%. Only 8% of the passive progressive patients and 6% of the implicit agents are co-referential with active subjects. In the autonomous, 18% of the patients are co-referential with active subjects, compared to 7% of the implicit agents (Table 3.10).

When it comes to recoverability, it was shown that implicit agents of the autonomous and the passive progressive are remarkably similar. Most implicit agents, 62% of the autonomous ones and 63% of the passive progressive ones, are recoverable from the text, which in most cases means that they can be identified as some person or persons belonging to a group of people that is explicit or implicit (Table 3.4). It was also shown that 21–23% of the implicit agents do not refer to a logical agent at all: they are non-recoverable. The only difference concerns the generic category: 12% of the autonomous implicit agents compared to 7% of the passive progressive ones belong to this group. Pragmatically inferable agents, that is, the type or class of agent that is recoverable from the reader's knowledge of the world is the least frequent type, 6% and 7%, respectively.

Finally, a comparison of agented and agent-less passive progressives was made. This comparison gave some rather contradictory results. While the contrast with respect to topicality is considerable in the agented passive progressive (that is, the same pattern as shown throughout), the same contrast was not found in the agent-less passive progressive clauses (Table 3.10). Further, patients of agent-less passive progressives are more often definite NPs than patients of agented ones, 51% vs. 35%, and equally often given as well as continuous. Patients of agent-less passive progressives, however, are more often continuous in both directions than patients of agented passive progressive as well as implicit agents, 12% compared to 5% and 7%. Finally, there is very little variation between patients of agented and agent-less passive progressives as regards co-reference with active subject, 7% compared to 9%.

In sum, the findings presented in the present chapter indicate that the contrast between the autonomous and the passive progressive with regard to the topicality of patients and agents is considerable. The results suggest that the patients of autonomous clauses refer to participants that are more topical, or central, in the text than agents, while in the passive progressive, overt agents refer to participants that are more topical than the participants that occur as patients and implicit agents. Since the vast majority of passive progressives in the database are agented, it may be concluded that the passive progressive is primarily used when the patient is less topical than the agent, although there is some evidence that in agent-less passive progressives patients are more topical than the implicit agents.

CHAPTER 4

Dialectal variation

4.1 Introduction

A secondary aim of the present study is to investigate dialectal variation in the use of the autonomous and the passive progressive (see the Introduction). In the present chapter the results of the classification of the features regarding verbs, clauses, patients and agents in the Connacht, Munster and Ulster texts are compared. As described in the Introduction, section 4, the present corpus contains 11 texts, totalling around 600,000 words evenly distributed across the three dialects. In the corpus, the Connacht dialect is represented by 4 texts by 4 authors, Munster by 3 texts by 3 authors, and Ulster by 4 texts by 3 authors. Before presenting the results, I will give a brief introduction to the dialects of Irish.

There are three main dialects of Irish: Connacht, Munster and Ulster, named after the province where each dialect is spoken. There is variation among them especially in phonology, the inflection of nouns and verbs, in vocabulary and also to some extent in syntax. In writing, the dialects began to emerge in the 17th century, after the demise of the Irish Bardic schools, where a highly standardised literary language had been maintained. In the 1940s and 1950s, work towards a new written standard led to the publication of an official spelling norm (1945) and an official grammar (1958). The official grammar contains mainly recommended nominal and verbal inflections. Most published studies of the dialects focus on a description of the phonology and morphology of the language spoken in some limited area. I have not found any comparative studies of the autonomous and the passive progressive in the dialects of relevance to the present investigation (but see the discussion on the passive progressive in the Munster dialect in Ó Siadhail (1989), as accounted for in the Introduction, sections 3–4).[1]

The account below is organised as follows. After a presentation of the overall distribution of the autonomous and the passive progressive in the dialects (Table 4.1), the results regarding verbs and clauses are presented (Tables 4.2–4.3), followed by those regarding patients and agents (Tables 4.5–4.9). In addition to

---

[1] For a general description of the Irish language and the main dialects, see, for example, Greene 1977, Mac Eoin 1993, Ó Dochartaigh 1992, Ó Murchú 1985, Ó Rahilly 1976, Ó Siadhail 1989.

the discussion of the tables, comparisons are made of the autonomous and the passive progressive and of patients and agents within each of the two constructions. The results presented in the tables as well as the comparisons have been tested for statistical significance. In the tables showing the results concerning the passive progressive (4.3, 4.7–4.9), one or more expected frequencies for Ulster are below five, thus yielding unreliable test results. In these cases, the figures for Connacht and Munster only have been tested.

The frequency of the autonomous and the passive progressive across dialects in the database is shown in Table 4.1. Table 4.1 exhibits that the autonomous and the passive progressive taken together are fairly evenly distributed over the dialects, but there is considerable variation between the dialects as regards the frequency and distribution of each construction, the passive progressive in particular. As indicated, the variation in Table 4.1 is statistically significant. Beginning with the passive progressive where the greatest variation occurs, the results show that the vast majority of passive progressives (73%) occur in the Munster texts. A significantly smaller proportion (22%) is found in the Connacht material, and the Ulster material contains only 5% (24 instances) of the passive progressives in the corpus. As for the autonomous, Table 4.1 shows that its relative frequency is uneven in the three dialects, though not at all to the same extent as the passive progressive; 38% and 39% of the instances of the autonomous occur in the Connacht and Ulster texts, respectively, while a significantly smaller proportion (23%) is found in the Munster material.

In sum, there is considerable variation among the dialects as regards the relative frequency of the autonomous and the passive progressive. This variation is illustrated by the autonomous to passive progressive ratio. In Connacht it is 11/1, Munster 2/1, and Ulster 48/1. In the whole material the autonomous to passive progressive ratio is 6/1. The more frequent use of the passive progressive in Munster than in the other dialects has been pointed out in previous research. As mentioned in the Introduction, section 2, Ó Siadhail (1989: 298) remarks that in Munster the passive progressive has, to some extent at least, replaced the active progressive. The passive progressive has thus, according to Ó Siadhail, ceased to function as a passive construction in this dialect. The higher frequency of the passive progressive in the Munster material than in the Connacht and Ulster texts in the corpus might be seen as a validation of that claim. Obviously, this claim applies to the agented passive only, although Ó Siadhail (1989) does not mention this explicitly. Other scholars have commented on the passive progressive in Munster dialect. For example, Greene (1979: 134) considers the agented passive in the Munster dialect as "passive in structure" but "active in meaning".[2] This is in line also with the conclusions drawn by Noonan (1994) that

---

[2] For a similar observation, see Sjoestedt-Jonval (1938: 155).

Table 4.1. Frequency and distribution of the autonomous and the passive progressive across dialects

	autonomous		passive progressive		Total	
	n	%	n	%	n	%
Connacht	1,109	38%	102	22%	1,211	35%
Munster	687	23%	341	73%	1,028	30%
Ulster	1,160	39%	24	5%	1,184	35%
Total	2,956	100%	467	100%	3,423	100%

$\chi^2 = 496.35$; df = 2; p < 0.05, critical value: 5.99

the passive progressive is passive in form only (see the Introduction, section 3); Noonan (1994) does not discuss dialectal variation, however. It should be pointed out that due to the predominance of instances of the passive progressive from Munster texts in the present database, the results presented in Chapters 2 and 3 reflect Munster use of the passive progressive to a great extent, rather than Connacht and Ulster use. Therefore, it cannot be ruled out that the passive progressive is used differently in the Connnacht and Ulster dialects, as suggested by, for instance, Ó Siadhail (1989). The comparison of topicality features of the patients and agents of the passive progressive between, on the one hand, Munster, and, on the other, Connacht and Ulster is thus of particular interest when one takes into account the observations made by Ó Siadhail (1989), Greene (1979) and Noonan (1994) (although Noonan does not claim that the active function of the passive progressive is specific to Munster use). Further, the comparison of the passive progressive in the three dialects is especially interesting, as the use of the passive progressive in Connacht and Ulster is not discussed in any of the studies I have found. After this introduction, the results regarding verbs and clauses, and patients and agents in the three dialects will be presented.

4.2 Verbs and clauses

The first set of variables concerns verbs and clauses. In the following, the use of the autonomous and the passive progressive in the dialects will be compared, beginning with the autonomous. In addition, the autonomous and the passive progressive in each dialect will be compared. The distribution of the autonomous across verb and clause type in the three dialects is shown in Table 4.2. As can be seen in Table 4.2, there is variation among the dialects as regards the distribution of the autonomous across verb and clause type. As indicated, the differences observed are statistically significant. The greatest contrast is found concerning verb type between Connacht, on the one hand, and Munster and Ulster, on the

Table 4.2. Features of the autonomous as regards verbs and clauses in the three dialects

		Connacht		Munster		Ulster	
		n	%	n	%	n	%
verb type	monotransitive direct	700	63%	388	56%	660	57%
	ditransitive	310	28%	231	34%	355	31%
	monotransitive indirect	22	2%	25	4%	47	4%
	intransitive	13	1%	10	1%	23	2%
	auxiliary	64	6%	33	5%	75	6%
Total		1,109	100%	687	100%	1,160	100%
clause type	main clause	441	40%	297	43%	654	56%
	subclause	668	60%	390	57%	506	44%
Total		1,109	100%	687	100%	1,160	100%
subclause type	adverbial	228	34%	144	37%	177	35%
	nominal	91	14%	52	13%	98	19%
	relative	349	52%	194	50%	231	46%
Total		668	100%	390	100%	506	100%

verb type: $\chi^2 = 22.06$; df = 8; p < 0.05, critical value: 15.51
main vs. subclause: $\chi^2 = 68.16$; df = 2; p < 0.05, critical value: 5.99
subclause type: $\chi^2 = 10.71$; df = 4; p < 0.05, critical value: 9.49

other. Connacht displays a somewhat higher proportion of monotranstive (direct) verbs, 63%, compared to 56% in Munster and Ulster, and conversely, a somewhat lower proportion of ditransitive verbs, 28%, compared to 34% in Munster and 31% in Ulster. When it comes to clause type, Table 4.2 shows that there is dialectal variation in particular between, on the one hand, Connacht and Munster and, on the other hand, Ulster. In Connacht and Munster a slight minority of the instances of the autonomous occur in main clauses, 40% and 43%, respectively, while in Ulster the majority of the instances of the autonomous are found in main clauses, 56%. There is also some variation among the dialects concerning the distribution across adverbial, nominal and relative subclause function. While the relative frequency of adverbial subclauses is fairly similar in the three dialects, there are differences with respect to the distribution of nominal and relative subclauses. The greatest contrast is found between Ulster and the other two dialects: the proportion of nominal subclauses is higher in Ulster than in Connacht and Munster, 19% vs. 14% and 13%, respectively. Conversely, the proportion of relative subclauses is slightly lower in the Ulster texts than in the Connacht and Munster ones, 46% vs. 52% and 50%, respectively.

Another issue worth commenting on concerns the use of the autonomous combined with the active progressive to form a construction very similar to the agent-less passive progressive: both constructions are progressive and lack an explicit agent (see the Introduction, section 2, and 2.2.1). As mentioned in 2.2.1,

(1) | *Agus* | *go díreach* | *tráthnóna* | *amháin* | *eadar* | *an* | *dá* | *Lá Samhna* | *rith* | *an* |
|---|---|---|---|---|---|---|---|---|---|
| and | indeed | afternoon | one | between | the | two | All Hallows | run-PST | the |

scéal	*thríd*	*na*	*bailte*	*go*	*raibh*	*sean-Bhrian*	*an*	*Toighe*	*Móir*
news	through	the	villages	CONJ	be-PST	old+Brian	the-GEN	house-GEN	big-GEN

'na	*luighe*	*le*	*bás,*	*nach*	**rabhthar**	<u>*ag*</u>	<u>*súil*</u>	<u>*le*</u>	<u>*n-a*</u>
in+this	lie-VBN	to	death	CONJ-NEG	be-PST-AUT	at	expectation-VBN	with	his

<u>*bhiseach,*</u>	*a's*	*gur*	*cuireadh*	*teachtaire*	*ar lorg*	*an*	*tsagairt*
recovery	and	CONJ	send-PST-AUT	messenger	looking for	the-GEN	priest-GEN

óig	*a*	*bhí*	*i ndiaidh a*	*theacht*	*'un*	*na*	*h-áite.*
young-GEN	REL	be-PST	after	his come-VBN	to	the-GEN	place-GEN

'And indeed one afternoon during the Halloween period the news spread through the villages that old Brian of the Big House lay dying, that <u>he wasn't</u> **expected** <u>to recover,</u> and that the young priest who had just come to the place had been sent for.' (Ul. *Crathadh an Phocáin*: 91)

(2) | *Bhí* | *sé* | *ag* | *amharc* | *suas* | *ar* | *a'* | *bhreitheamh* | *mar* | *bhéadh* | *a* | *chroidhe* |
|---|---|---|---|---|---|---|---|---|---|---|---|
| be-PST | he | at | look-VBN | up | on | the | judge | like | be-COND | his | heart |

a'	*creathnughadh*	*roimhe*	<u>*na*</u>	<u>*ceisteannaí*</u>	*a*	**bhíthear**	<u>*a*</u>	<u>*chur*</u>	*air.*
at	tremble-VBN	before	the	questions	REL	be-PRS-AUT	to	put-VBN	on-3SGM

'He was looking up at the judge as though his heart was trembling before <u>the questions</u> that **were** <u>being put</u> to him.' (Ul. *Saoghal Corrach*: 37)

around half of the instances of the autonomous combined with the active progressive in the database occur where the passive progressive could not have been used, either because there is no direct object in the verbal noun phrase or because the direct object is expressed as a clause, as in (1). In the remaining instances the use of the passive progressive is possible, since the verbal noun phrase takes a direct object, as in (2). A closer look at the distribution of the autonomous used with the active progressive shows that 70% (48/69) of these occur in Ulster texts.[3] The more frequent use of the autonomous with an active progressive may reflect the observed reluctance to use the passive progressive in the Ulster dialect in the corpus. One may also note that the number of instances of this construction is twice the number of passive progressives in the Ulster material (48 vs. 24 instances).

The results regarding verb and clause type in the passive progressive in the three dialects are shown in Table 4.3. The figures in Table 4.3 suggest that there is some variation among the dialects as regards verbs and clauses in the passive progressive. A comparison of the use of the passive progressive in the three dialects is somewhat difficult due to the extremely varying frequency of the construction, especially the very small number of instances in the Ulster texts in the corpus. As indicated, statistically significant differences are found between

---

[3] The number of instances in the Connacht and Munster texts is 19 and 3, respectively.

Table 4.3. Features of the passive progressive as regards verbs and clauses in the three dialects

		Connacht		Munster		Ulster	
		n	%	n	%	n	%
verb type	monotransitive direct	91	89%	264	77%	23	96%
	ditransitive	11	11%	77	23%	1	4%
Total		102	100%	341	100%	24	100%
clause type	main clause	17	17%	41	12%	5	21%
	subclause	85	83%	300	88%	19	79%
Total		102	100%	341	100%	24	100%
subclause type	adverbial	34	40%	171	57%	10	53%
	nominal	22	26%	55	18%	8	42%
	relative	29	34%	74	25%	1	5%
Total		85	100%	300	100%	19	100%
subclause structure	finite	37	44%	104	35%	5	26%
	non-finite	48	56%	196	65%	14	74%
Total		85	100%	300	100%	19	100%
non-finite subclause type	adverbial	23	48%	149	76%	8	57%
	nominal	17	35%	34	17%	6	43%
	relative	8	17%	13	7%	0	0%
Total		48	100%	196	100%	14	100%

verb type (Connacht and Munster): $\chi^2 = 6.86$; df = 1; $p < 0.05$, critical value: 3.84
subclause type (Connacht and Munster): $\chi^2 = 7.69$; df = 2; $p < 0.05$, critical value: 5.99

Connacht ant Munster as regards verb type, subclause type and non-finite subclause type. Although no valid conclusions may be drawn regarding the passive progressive in the Ulster material because the instances are so few, it may be noted that the results for Ulster do not diverge in any major way from the overall tendencies observed in the whole material.

Beginning with the variable verb type, Table 4.3 shows that considerably more passive progressives are formed from monotransitive verbs in Connacht than in Munster texts, 89% vs. 77%. In the Ulster material, all but one out of 24 instances of the passive progressive are formed from monotransitive verbs. Turning to clause type, there is some variation as regards the distribution of the passive progressive across main and subclause. Munster shows the highest proportion of passive progressives in subclauses, 88%, compared to 83% in Connacht and 79% (19/24) in the Ulster material. In the Connacht as well as the Munster texts, a higher proportion of the subclauses containing the passive progressive are adverbial than nominal and relative. However, the proportion of adverbial subclauses is considerably higher in Munster, 57%, than in Connacht, 40%. Conversely, the relative frequency of passive progressives in nominal and relative subclauses is higher in Connacht, 26% and 34%, respectively, than in the Munster texts, 18% and 25%, respectively. In the Ulster texts, 53% (10/19) of the subclauses are adverbial, 42% (8/19) are nominal, and one (5%) relative. As for subclause structure, variation among the dialects is great. The smallest proportion of non-finite subclauses containing the passive progressive is found in the Connacht material, 56% (48/85); the corresponding figure for Munster is 65% (196/300). The Ulster texts display the largest proportion of non-finite subclauses containing the passive progressive, 74% (14 of 19 instances). When it comes to the type of non-finite subclause, it is striking that in the Munster texts, 76% (149/196) of the non-finite subclauses are adverbial, compared to 48% (23/48) in Connacht and 57% (8/14) in Ulster. Conversely, while 17% (34/196) of the non-finite subclauses in the Munster material are nominal, the corresponding figures for Connacht and Ulster are considerably higher, 35% (17/48) and 43% (6/14), respectively. As regards the least frequent type of non-finite subclause, one may note that in the Connacht material 17% (8/48) of the instances of the passive progressive that occur in non-finite subclauses are found in relative subclauses, while the corresponding figure for Munster is only 7% (13/196). No instances of the passive progressive in the Ulster material are found in a relative non-finite subclause. To sum up, the greatest variation as regards verbs and clauses concerns the distribution of the instances of the passive progressive across type of subclause, non-finite subclauses in particular. Munster is characterised by the highest proportion of adverbial subclauses, finite (57%) as well as non-finite (76%). In the other dialects the distribution is more even.

A comparison of Tables 4.2 (autonomous) and 4.3 (passive progressive) indicates that in the three dialects there is the same contrast between the autonomous and the passive progressive as regards the distribution across monotransitive (direct) and ditransitive verbs, and across main and subclause. In all dialects, the proportion of monotransitive verbs is considerably larger in the passive progressive than in the autonomous, and the autonomous occurs more frequently in main clauses than the passive progressive. The differences are statistically significant (except for the variable subclause type in Ulster, where one expected frequency is below five).[4]

Next follows the presentation of the results regarding the features discussed in Chapter 3 relating to patients and agents. As in earlier sections, the autonomous and the passive progressive will be presented in separate sections, starting with the autonomous.

---

[4] Results of the chi-square test are the following. Connacht, verb type: $\chi^2 = 17.88$, Connacht, clause type $\chi^2 = 21.19$, subclause type: $\chi^2 = 27.90$ (df = 2; critical value: 5.99); Munster, verb type: $\chi^2 = 21.92$, Munster, clause type: $\chi^2 = 100.57$, Munster, subclause type: $\chi^2 = 45.16$ (df = 2; critical value: 5.99); Ulster, verb type: $\chi^2 = 9.88$, Ulster, clause type: $\chi^2 = 12.04$. Unless otherwise stated, df = 1; p < 0.05, critical value: 3.84.

4.3 Patients and agents

As in Chapter 3, the results concerning each of the five elements investigated in connection with patients and agents are presented in a separate table, beginning with the autonomous patients.

4.3.1 The autonomous

The results regarding the patients of autonomous clauses are shown in Table 4.4. As can be seen in Table 4.4, there is some variation between the dialects with regard to all three features. As indicated, all results are statistically significant, except those concerning type of continuity. When it comes to the first variable, type of overt element, the figures indicate that the greatest difference concerns the proportion of definite NPs. The highest proportion of definite NP patients is found in Ulster, 49%, compared to 39% in Connacht and 45% in Munster. Conversely, Connacht has the highest relative frequency of indefinite NP patients, 29%, compared to 25% in Munster and 26% in Ulster. As for given vs. new, a slight majority of the patients of autonomous clauses in the Connacht and Ulster texts refer to new participants, 51% and 53%, respectively. As for Munster, however, a slight majority of the autonomous patients, 54%, refer to given elements. Table 4.4 also shows that autonomous patients in Munster texts are the most continuous ones in the corpus, 57% of them display continuity compared to 53% in the Connacht material and 48% in the Ulster material. One may also note that 21% of the patients of autonomous clauses display continuity in both directions, the highest degree of continuity, compared to 16% in Connacht and Ulster. Finally, the results indicate that around the same proportion of autonomous patients in the three dialects, 17%–19%, are co-referential with subjects of active clauses.

In conclusion, the most salient dialectal differences shown in Table 4.4 point to a pattern: in the Munster material autonomous patients refer to elements that have been explicitly mentioned previously in the text, and display continuity (especially continuity in both directions) more frequently than in the rest of the corpus. This suggests that patients in the autonomous clauses in the Munster texts are marginally more topical than those in the Connacht and Ulster material in the corpus.

Next, the results regarding the recoverability and continuity of autonomous implicit agents are discussed, as shown in Table 4.5. Table 4.5 indicates that there is variation across dialect as regards implicit agents of the autonomous. The results of the chi-square tests indicate that the differences are statistically significant. As for the first variable, recoverability, the figures in Table 4.5 point to dialectal variation regarding the generic recoverability type (unspecified reference) in particular. Considerably more autonomous implicit agents in the Connacht texts (19%) are generic than in Munster (7%) and Ulster (8%).

Table 4.4. Features of the autonomous patients in the three dialects

		Connacht		Munster		Ulster	
		n	%	n	%	n	%
type of overt element	definite	390	39%	277	45%	497	49%
	indefinite	284	29%	155	25%	259	26%
	relative particle	198	20%	109	18%	140	14%
	clause	122	12%	74	12%	117	12%
Total		994	100%	615	100%	1,013	101%
given vs. new overt element	given	489	49%	332	54%	476	47%
	new	519	51%	287	46%	543	53%
Total		1,008	100%	619	100%	1,019	100%
continuity	continuity	533	53%	353	57%	486	48%
	no continuity	475	47%	266	43%	533	52%
Total		1,008	100%	619	100%	1,019	100%
type of continuity	retrospective cont.	256	25%	145	23%	198	19%
	prospective cont.	120	12%	77	12%	123	12%
	both directions	157	16%	131	21%	165	16%
Total		533	53%	353	56%	486	47%
co-reference with active subject	yes	168	17%	104	17%	192	19%
	no	840	83%	515	83%	827	81%
Total		1,008	100%	619	100%	1,019	100%

type: $\chi^2 = 24.68$; df = 6; p < 0.05, critical value: 12.6
given vs. new: $\chi^2 = 7.55$; df = 2; p < 0.05, critical value: 5.99
continuity: $\chi^2 = 14.12$; df = 2; p < 0.05, critical value: 5.99
24 understood patients are excluded from the classification of type: Connacht 14, Munster 4, Ulster 6.

Further, the relative frequency of textually inferable agents is higher in the Munster material, 68%, than in Ulster, 61%, and, especially, Connacht, 58%. The non-recoverable implicit agents, on the other hand, are more or less equally frequent in all dialects. As for continuity, the most notable difference is found between Connacht and Ulster, on the one hand, and Munster, on the other. More autonomous agents are discontinuous in the Connacht and Ulster texts (71%) than in the Munster texts (65%). There is little variation as regards the final variable, co-reference with active subject. In the Ulster texts, 9% of the autonomous agents are co-referential with subjects of an active clause in the surrounding discourse, compared to 7% and 6% in the Munster and Connacht material, respectively.

As shown in Table 4.5, there are fairly small differences as regards the distribution of autonomous implicit agents across recoverability types. There is considerable variation, however, in another aspect in connection with recoverability. In general, no clear patterns of variation between the dialects can be observed (cf. Appendix). As regards autonomous clauses with non-recoverable implicit agents, however, there are considerable differences between

Table 4.5. Features of the autonomous implicit agents in the three dialects

		Connacht		Munster		Ulster	
		n	%	n	%	n	%
recoverability	textually inferable	642	58%	464	68%	712	61%
	non-recoverable	195	18%	149	22%	273	24%
	generic	208	19%	45	7%	94	8%
	pragmatically inferable	64	6%	29	4%	81	7%
Total		1,109	101%	687	101%	1,160	100%
continuity	continuity	325	29%	242	35%	339	29%
	no continuity	784	71%	445	65%	821	71%
Total		1,109	100%	687	100%	1,160	100%
type of continuity	retrospective continuity	126	11%	92	13%	136	12%
	prospective continuity	129	12%	85	12%	98	8%
	both directions	70	6%	65	9%	105	9%
Total		325	29%	242	34%	339	29%
co-reference with active subject	yes	64	6%	51	7%	106	9%
	no	1,045	94%	636	93%	1,054	91%
Total		1,109	100%	687	100%	1,160	100%

recoverability: $\chi^2 = 97.29$; df = 6; p < 0.05, critical value: 12.59
continuity: $\chi^2 = 8.82$; df = 2; p < 0.05, critical value: 5.99
continuity type: $\chi^2 = 11.41$; df = 4; p < 0.05, critical value: 9.49
co-reference with active subject: $\chi^2 = 9.30$; df = 2; p < 0.05, critical value: 5.99

the dialects concerning the verbs used. By far the most common verb with a non-recoverable agent in Connacht as well as in Ulster is *cas*, almost exclusively used in the meaning 'meet', as in (3). In the Ulster and Connacht texts, 43% (118/273) and 31% (61/195), respectively, of the autonomous verb forms in the non-recoverable category are formed from the verb *cas*, compared to only 7% (11/149) in the Munster material in the corpus. In the Munster texts, on the other hand, the most frequently used verb in the non-recoverable category is *tuig* in the meaning 'realise', as in (4); 32% (48/149) of the Munster non-recoverable agents are instances of *tuig*, compared with 4% (8/195) of the Connacht ones and none of the Ulster ones. The second most common verb is *bain*, 'take', which is used in 18% (27/149) of the instances in the non-recoverable category in the Munster material, occurring in expressions like *baineadh geit as*, 'he was startled', literally 'a start was taken out of him', as in (5). In contrast, only 4% (8/195) of the non-recoverable agents found in the Connacht texts and 8% (23/273) of the Ulster ones are instances of this verb. In Connacht and Ulster the second most common verb is *feic* in the meaning 'seem', as in (6), which is used in 12% (24/195) of the instances in Connacht and 12% (34/273) of the instances of the autonomous with non-recoverable agent in the Ulster texts, while it does not occur at all in the Munster texts. The verb *caill*, 'lose', used impersonally in the meaning 'die', as in (7), is the third most frequently used verb in the Connacht

(3)   *Bliadhain is fiche*   *a*   *bhí*   *mé*   *nuair*   *a*   **casadh**   *orm*   *í.*
     twenty-one   REL   be-PST   I   when   REL   meet-PST-AUT   on-1SG   her

     I was twenty-one when I **met** her. (Ul. *Dochartach Duibhlionna*: 8)

(4)   *Is*   *gearr*   *gur*   **tuigeadh**   *dom*   *go*   *bhfeaca*
     COP-PRS   short   until   understand-PST-AUT   to-1SG   until   see-PST-1SG

     naomhóg   *ag*   *déanamh*   *isteach*   *ar*   *an*   *gcaladh.*
     currach (= type of boat)   at   make-VBN   into   on   the   harbour

     'I soon **realised** that I saw a currach proceeding into the harbour.' (Mu. *Fiche Bliain ag Fás*: 95)

(5)   *Nuair*   *a*   *thánamair*   *go dtí*   *claí*   *na*   *páirce*   *atá*   *ar*   *an*
     when   REL   come-PST-1PL   to   wall   the-GEN   field-GEN   be-PRS-REL   on   the

     dtaobh   *amuigh*   *don*   *dtigh,*   **baineadh**   *geit*   *asam.*
     side   outside   of+the   house   take-PST-AUT   start   out of-1SG

     'When we came to the wall of the field outside the house, I **was startled**.' (Mu. *Fiche Bliain ag Fás*: 104)

(6)   **Tchíthear**   *damh*   *féin*   *nach*   *bhfuil*   *Séimín*   *comh*   *staidéartha*
     see-PRS-AUT   to-1SG   -self   CONJ-NEG   be-PRS   Séimín   as   sensible

     leat-sa.
     with-2SG-EMPH

     'It **seems** to me that Séimín isn't as sensible as you.' (Ul. *Crathadh and Phocáin*: 62)

(7)   *Go deimhin*   *sílim*   *gur*   **cailleadh**   *an*   *bheirt*   *an*   *bhliain*   *chéanna.*
     indeed   think-PRS-1SG   CONJ   lose-PST-AUT   the   two   the   year   same

     'Indeed I think that the two **died** the same year.' (Co. *Feamainn Bhealtaine*: 17)

material, occurring in 11% (21/195) of the instances of the autonomous in the non-recoverable category. In the Munster and Ulster material, on the other hand, it belongs to the less frequently used verbs: 4% (6/149) in Munster, and 2% (6/273) in Ulster. Finally, one may note that all the most frequently used verbs in the non-recoverable category mentioned above belong to the group of verbs that in certain meanings are always used impersonally.[5] There is some dialectal variation as regards the distribution of this type of verb in the autonomous. In Ulster the portion of verbs of this type is 58% (159/273) of all instances of the autonomous in the non-recoverable category, whereas in the Connacht material the corresponding figure is 44% (86/195), and in the Munster material 39% (58/149).

To sum up, the greatest variation between the dialects concerning autonomous implicit agents is found in the distribution across the recoverability types. In particular, Connacht exhibits a pattern that is somewhat different from that of

---

[5] This applies mostly to verbs used in the autonomous; only a few verbs occurring in the database are used impersonally in the (agent-less) passive progressive.

Munster and Ulster, especially as regards the category generic; this category is more than twice as common in the Connacht texts as in the Munster and Ulster texts. It was also pointed out that there is variation between the dialects as regards the verbs used when no agent is logically implied (the non-recoverable category).

As shown in Chapter 3, there is great contrast between patients and implicit agents of autonomous clauses as regards the topicality features: patients were found to be considerably more topical than implicit agents. To be able to evaluate whether that contrast exists in all three dialects, Tables 4.4 (patients) and 4.5 (implicit agents) were compared. This comparison revealed that in all dialects there are statistically significant differences between the patients and implicit agents of the autonomous clauses (except for continuity type in the Ulster texts): patients are considerably more often continuous than implicit agents, and patients are more often than implicit agents co-referential with a subject of an active clause in the neighbouring discourse.[6] Thus, patients are considerably more topical than implicit agents in autonomous clauses in all three dialects.

4.3.2 The passive progressive

As an introduction to the discussion of the variables regarding patients and agents of passive progressive clauses, the distribution of agented and agent-less passive progressives in the three dialects is shown in Table 4.6. There is considerable variation among the dialects in the distribution of agented and agent-less passive progressives.[7] As indicated in Table 4.6, this variation is statistically significant. Most instances of the passive progressive in the Munster material are agented, 73%, compared to 36% of those in the Connacht material and only 8% (2/24) of the Ulster ones.[8] The higher relative frequency of agented passive progressives in the Munster material indicate that in that dialect the passive progressive is not mainly used to demote the agent. This supports the claim mentioned above that the (agented) passive progressive is used as an active progressive in that dialect. The question may be raised whether there are further results suggesting that the

---

[6] Results of the chi-square test are the following. Connacht, continuity: $\chi^2 = 121.72$, continuity type: $\chi^2 = 29.20$ (df = 2, critical value: 5.99), co-reference with active subject: $\chi^2 = 64.24$; Munster, continuity: $\chi^2 = 62.40$, continuity type: $\chi^2 = 14.26$ (df = 2, critical value: 5.99), co-reference with active subject: $\chi^2 = 27.38$; Ulster, continuity: $\chi^2 = 78.66$, co-reference with active subject: $\chi^2 = 43.27$. Unless otherwise stated, df = 1; p < 0.05, critical value: 3.84.

[7] As mentioned in the Introduction, section 2, one feature of the Munster dialect is that the overt agent often precedes the verbal noun phrase. The position of the overt agent has not been considered in the study. However, it may be noted that in the vast majority of the agented passive progressives from Munster texts in the database, the agent appears before the verbal noun phrase, in contrast with the order in the two other dialects (see the Introduction, section 2).

[8] Compare Ó Searcaigh (1954: 48), who states that the agent is often not mentioned in the passive progressive.

118

Table 4.6. Agented and agent-less instances of the passive progressive in the three dialects

	Connacht		Munster		Ulster	
	n	%	n	%	n	%
agented	37	36%	249	73%	2	8%
agent-less	65	64%	92	27%	22	92%
Total	102	100%	341	100%	24	100%

$\chi^2 = 75.30$; df = 2; p < 0.05, critical value: 5.99

passive progressive is assigned active force in the Munster dialect as opposed to the Connacht and Ulster dialects. Of interest for this discussion are the features that concern information packaging, that is, definite vs. indefinite, given vs. new, continuity and co-reference with an active subject, which will be discussed below (cf. Chapter 3).

The first element to discuss is the passive progressive patient; the distribution across dialects of features connected with passive progressive patients is shown in Table 4.7. Again, the very small number of instances of the passive progressive in the Ulster texts makes a comparison of the Ulster results with those of Connacht and Munster difficult (cf. Table 4.3). None of the differences displayed in Table 4.7 are statistically significant. When it comes to type, the greatest contrast concerns the distribution across definite and indefinite NPs. The largest proportion of the patients of passive progressive clauses are expressed as definite NPs in Connacht (45%) and Ulster (15/24 = 63%), while in Munster, passive progressive patients are most often expressed as indefinite NPs (46%). As for given vs. new, Munster and Ulster patients refer more frequently to new elements than those in the Connacht texts, 68% and 71% (17/24) vs. 62%. Next, as regards continuity, Table 4.7 shows that the patients of passive progressive clauses in Munster and Ulster texts are more often discontinuous, 70% and 83% (20/24), than the patients in the Connacht material in the corpus, 66%. Further, in the Munster material, only 6% of the passive progressive patients display continuity in both directions compared to 13% in the Connacht material. In the Ulster material, there is only one continuous patient (4%) of a passive progressive clause. These results suggest that the passive progressive patients in the Connacht texts are more topical than those in the Munster texts since they are expressed as definite NPs, refer to a given participant and are more often continuous. As regards co-reference with an active subject, the final variable, the results in Table 4.7 show that there is some variation between the dialects. In the Munster texts, 9% (32/341) of the passive progressive patients are co-referential with subjects of active clauses in the immediately surrounding context. The corresponding figures for Connacht and Ulster are somewhat lower, 5% (5/102) and 4% (1/24), respectively.

Table 4.7. Features of the passive progressive patients in the three dialects

		Connacht		Munster		Ulster	
		n	%	n	%	n	%
type of overt element	definite	46	45%	131	38%	15	63%
	indefinite	42	41%	157	46%	8	33%
	relative particle	14	14%	53	16%	1	4%
Total		102	100%	341	100%	24	100%
given vs. new overt element	given	39	38%	110	32%	7	29%
	new	63	62%	231	68%	17	71%
Total		102	100%	341	100%	24	100%
continuity	continuity	35	34%	101	30%	4	17%
	no continuity	67	66%	240	70%	20	83%
Total		102	100%	341	100%	24	100%
type of continuity	retrospective cont.	16	16%	55	16%	3	13%
	prospective cont.	6	6%	25	7%	0	0%
	both directions	13	13%	21	6%	1	4%
Total		35	35%	101	29%	4	17%
co-reference with active subject	yes	5	5%	32	9%	1	4%
	no	97	95%	309	91%	23	96%
Total		102	100%	341	100%	24	100%

In sum, the results concerning patients of the passive progressive clauses point to certain differences in topicality patterns between, in particular, Connacht and Munster. The number of passive progressive patients in the Ulster texts is too low (24 instances) for any valid conclusions to be drawn. Possibly, patients of passive progressive clauses are somewhat more topical in the Connacht material compared to the ones in the Munster and Ulster material. However, none of the observed differences are statistically significant.

Next follows a summary of the results of the classification of the passive progressive implicit agents in the three dialects as shown in Table 4.8. As exhibited in Table 4.8, there is some variation between the dialects concerning passive progressive implicit agents, but none of the differences is statistically significant. When it comes to the first variable, recoverability, the results show that more implicit agents in the Munster and Connacht texts are textually inferable, 70% (64/92) and 60% (39/65), respectively, than in the Ulster texts, 41% (9/22). More notably, as many as 50% (11/22) of the implicit agents in the Ulster material are non-recoverable, compared to 26% (24/92) of the Munster ones and only 11% (7/65) of the Connacht ones. Further, the generic recoverability type is considerably more common in Connacht, 17% (11/65), than in Munster and Ulster, 2% (2/92) and 0 instances, respectively. The pragmatic recoverability type is also very infrequent in the Munster material, 2% (2/92), and more common in the Connacht material, 12% (8/65). With regard to continuity there is less variation. Connacht agents are more discontinuous, 78%

Table 4.8. Features of the passive progressive implicit agents in the three dialects

		Connacht		Munster		Ulster	
		n	%	n	%	n	%
recoverability of	textually inferable	39	60%	64	70%	9	41%
implicit agents	non-recoverable	7	11%	24	26%	11	50%
	generic	11	17%	2	2%	0	0%
	pragmatically inferable	8	12%	2	2%	2	9%
Total		65	100%	92	100%	22	100%
continuity	continuity	14	22%	29	32%	9	41%
	no continuity	51	78%	63	68%	13	59%
Total		65	100%	92	100%	22	100%
type of continuity	retrospective cont.	4	6%	11	12%	2	9%
	prospective cont.	8	12%	10	11%	5	23%
	both directions	2	3%	8	9%	2	9%
Total		14	22%	29	32%	9	41%
co-reference with	yes	3	5%	7	8%	0	0%
active subject	no	62	95%	85	92%	22	100%
Total		65	100%	92	100%	22	100%

(51/65), than the Munster ones, 68% (63/92). While it is difficult to draw any conclusions regarding the implicit agents in the Ulster texts due to their small number, it may be worth noting that the proportion of discontinuous agents is lower, 59% (13/22), in the Ulster material than in the Connacht and Munster texts. As regards the final variable, co-reference with active subject, Munster displays a larger proportion of co-reference with subjects of active clauses than Connacht and Ulster, 8% (7/92) vs. 5% (3/65) and 0 instances.

To sum up, the results presented above suggest that implicit agents in agent-less passive progressive clauses in the Munster material are somewhat more topical than those in Connacht texts since a larger proportion of them are con-tinuous and co-referential with a subject of an active clause. However, none of the differences tested is statistically significant.

A comparison of Tables 4.7 (patients) and 4.8 (implicit agents) indicates that in the three dialects there is very little contrast between passive progressive patients and implicit agents (there are no statistically significant differences). Thus, it seems that in all three dialects patients and implicit agents of passive progressive clauses are equally low in topicality.

Next follow the results regarding the passive progressive overt agents. The distribution of the passive progressive overt agents across topicality features in the three dialects is shown in Table 4.9. Table 4.9 shows that there are some dialectal differences concerning passive progressive overt agents. The only sta-tistically significant difference, however, concerns given vs. new in Connacht and Munster. Due to the extremely small number of passive progressive overt agents in the Ulster texts (2 instances) they will not be further dealt with in the

Table 4.9. Features of the passive progressive overt agents in the three dialects

		Connacht		Munster		Ulster	
		n	%	n	%	n	%
type of overt element	definite	34	92%	240	96%	1	50%
	indefinite	2	5%	9	4%	1	50%
	relative particle	1	3%	0	0%	0	0%
Total		37	100%	249	100%	2	100%
given vs. new overt element	given	26	70%	219	88%	1	50%
	new	11	30%	30	12%	1	50%
Total		37	100%	249	100%	2	100%
continuity	continuity	28	76%	208	84%	1	50%
	no continuity	9	24%	41	16%	1	50%
Total		37	100%	249	100%	2	100%
type of continuity	retrospective cont.	7	19%	60	24%	0	0%
	prospective cont.	6	16%	24	10%	0	0%
	both directions	15	41%	124	50%	1	50%
Total		28	76%	208	84%	1	50%
co-reference with active subject	yes	15	41%	143	57%	1	50%
	no	22	59%	106	43%	1	50%
Total		37	100%	249	100%	2	100%

given vs. new (Connacht and Munster): $\chi^2 = 8.20$; df $= 1$; p < 0.05, critical value: 3.84

account below. Beginning with the variable verb type, the results do not point to any major differences between Connacht and Munster. Regarding overt agents, they are somewhat more often definite in the Munster texts, 96% (240/249), than in the Connacht texts, 92% (34/37). Further, a larger proportion of the Munster overt agents are given, 88% (219/249), than those in the Connacht texts, 70% (26/37). As for continuity, the overt agents are continuous to a larger extent in the Munster material than in the Connacht material, 84% (208/249) compared to 76% (28/37). Finally, Table 4.9 suggests that there is great variation between Connacht and Munster as regards the final variable, co-reference with active subject. The majority of the overt agents of passive progressive clauses in the Munster texts are co-referential with a subject of an active clause in the surrounding context, 57% (143/249), while the corresponding figure for Connacht is 41% (15/37).

In sum, the results presented in Table 4.9 indicate that in the Munster texts the passive progressive is used with overt agents that are slightly more topical than is the case in the Connacht texts. There are only two instances of agented passive progressives in the Ulster part of the database, which is too few to draw any conclusions from about the topicality of passive progressive overt agents in Ulster texts. The main conclusion is that the same pattern as regards topicality found in the main database is found in the Connacht as well as the Munster texts, that is, overt agents are highly topical, considerably more topical than passive progressive patients, and, in particular, implicit agents.

A comparison between Tables 4.7 (patients) and 4.9 (overt agents) reveals that in the Connacht and, in particular, Munster texts there is a great contrast between overt agents and patients of the passive progressive: overt agents of passive progressive clauses in Connacht and Munster are considerably more topical than patients. The extremely small number of overt agents (two instances) in the Ulster material does not allow for a valid comparison between patients and overt agents to be made. All the differences regarding Munster as well as most of the differences concerning Connacht are statistically significant.[9] Similarly, the comparison of the results regarding overt and implicit agents (Tables 4.9 and 4.8, respectively) indicates that the topicality of overt agents is considerably greater than that of implicit agents in Connacht as well as in Munster, and the greatest contrast is found in the Munster material. Again, no valid conclusion regarding Ulster may be drawn due to the small number of instances in the corpus. All the differences except those related to continuity type (and the Ulster results) are statistically significant.[10]

4.4 Summary

In conclusion, the most salient differences between the three dialects concern the use of the passive progressive in the Munster texts of the corpus as opposed to the Connacht and Ulster material. First, it has been shown that the passive progressive occurs considerably more often in the Munster texts in the corpus than in the Connacht and, above all, the Ulster ones; 73% of the instances of the passive progressives in the database occur in the Munster material, compared to 22% in Connacht and only 5% in Ulster. Second, the results point to considerable dialectal differences as regards the distribution of agented and agent-less passive progressives. While 73% of the Munster passive progressives are agented, the corresponding figures for Connacht and Ulster are 36% and 8% (23 instances), respectively. It should also be pointed out that the extremely low frequency of the passive progressive in the Ulster texts is an interesting result of this investigation. As mentioned above, the relatively higher frequency of the passive progressive in Munster dialects has been noted in, for example, Greene (1979) and Ó Siadhail (1989), while the infrequent use of the passive progressive in Ulster observed in the present corpus does not seem to have attracted much scholarly attention.

As for the frequency of the autonomous, the results presented above show that there is variation in frequency between the dialects, although not as considerable

---

[9] Results of the chi-square test are the following. Connacht: given vs. new: $\chi^2 = 11.19$, continuity: $\chi^2 = 18.74$, co-reference with active subject: $\chi^2 = 28.00$; Munster: type: $\chi^2 = 207.68$ (df = 2, critical value: 5.99), given vs. new: $\chi^2 = 180.96$, continuity: $\chi^2 = 167.71$, continuity type: $\chi^2 = 41.30$ (df = 2, critical value: 5.99), co-reference with active subject: $\chi^2 = 159.23$. Unless otherwise stated, df = 1; p>0.05, critical value 3.84.
[10] Results of the chi-square test are the following. Connacht, continuity: $\chi^2 = 28.53$, co-reference with active subject: $\chi^2 = 20.94$; Munster, continuity: $\chi^2 = 85.74$, co-reference with active subject: $\chi^2 = 67.68$. Unless otherwise stated, df = 1; p < 0.05, critical value: 3.84.

as that regarding the passive progressive: 39% of the instances of the autonomous in the database are found in the Ulster texts, 38% in the Connacht material, while the smallest portion, 23%, is found in the Munster texts.

As regards verbs and clauses, the results point to some variation among the dialects, but in no case is the variation between the dialects greater than that between the autonomous and the passive progressive within each dialect. The same conclusion may be drawn when it comes to the results of the classification of patients and agent. My results suggest that the three dialects display basically the same contrast between the use of the autonomous and the passive progressive as regards the topicality of those participants chosen to act as patients and agents, namely, that the autonomous is used when the patient is considerably more topical, or central, in the discourse than the agent. In the passive progressive the pattern is the opposite: in my material, the passive progressive is used mainly with agents that are more central in the text than the patients. However, the results also suggest that the contrast with regard to topicality between the autonomous and the passive progressive is greater in the Munster texts than those from Connacht and Ulster.

CHAPTER 5

The autonomous and the passive progressive from a contextual perspective: a closer look

5.1 Introduction

The purpose of the present chapter is to further explore the functions of the autonomous and the passive progressive in context. I return here to the research question formulated in the Introduction (section 1), namely, what differences in use are there between the autonomous and the passive progressive? So far, the autonomous and the passive progressive have been studied from two angles. In Chapter 2, syntactic characteristics of the constructions were discussed. Chapter 3 was devoted to the autonomous and the passive progressive in relation to information packaging, including topicality features of patients and agents. In the present chapter, the autonomous and the passive progressive are further analysed and compared with regard to their textual functions. For the purpose of this analysis, a subset was selected from the main corpus containing 293 instances of the autonomous and 308 instances of the passive progressive, 601 instances in total (approximately 18% of the total number of instances in the main corpus) of the autonomous and the passive progressive. The subset is described in more detail in section 5.2 below. Based on the findings presented and discussed in previous chapters, the analysis involves two aspects of the autonomous and the passive progressive in context; one aspect relates to clauses and their functions, the other aspect concerns patients and agents. For clarity, below follows a brief overview of the results discussed in Chapters 2 and 3, highlighting the findings that are relevant to the present chapter. The findings accounted for in Chapter 2 are summarised in Table 5.1, and a summary of the results presented in Chapter 3 is displayed in Table 5.2.[1]

---

[1] Unless indicated, the differences are statistically significant according to the results of the chi-square test.

Table 5.1. Overview of features of the autonomous and the passive progressive

	autonomous	passive progressive
frequency	2,956 (86%)	467 (14%)
verb type	monotransitive direct 1,748 (59%) ditransitive 896 (30%) monotransitive indirect 94 (3%) intransitive 46 (2%) auxiliary 172 (6%)	monotransitive direct 378 (81%) ditransitive 89 (19%) *only transitive verbs that take direct* *objects can form the passive* *progressive*
clause type	main clause 1,392 (47%) subclause 1,564 (53%)	main clause 63 (13%) subclause 404 (87%)
subclause structure	*only finite clauses are possible*	finite 146 (36%) non-finite 258 (64%)

The most important results in Table 5.1 point to significant variation between the autonomous and the passive progressive concerning frequency, distribution of transitive verbs across ditransitive and monotransitive (direct), and clause type. First, there is a marked difference in frequency between the two constructions: the autonomous is approximately six times (2,956/467) more common than the passive progressive. Next, as pointed out in Chapter 2, the distribution of verbs taking direct objects across the monotransitive (direct) and ditransitive categories varies between the autonomous and the passive progressive. The ratio between monotransitive verbs that take direct objects (the most common verb type in both constructions) and ditransitive verbs is twice as high in the passive progressive, four to one (378/89), as in the autonomous, where the corresponding ratio is two to one (1,748/896). Moving on to the distribution of the autonomous and the passive progressive across different clause types, it is striking that whereas 47% of the autonomous examples in the database occur in main clauses, the corresponding figure for the passive progressive is only 13%. As regards variation within the passive progressive, Table 5.1 shows that 64% of the subclauses containing the passive progressive are non-finite, thus, no fewer than 55% (258/467) of the instances of the passive progressive in the corpus occur in non-finite subclauses. For the purpose of the analysis of the autonomous and the passive progressive in context, the most salient difference between them concerns their distribution across main and subclauses: the autonomous is evenly distributed across main and subclause while the passive progressive occurs most often in subclauses. As will be shown below (5.1.1), this contrast is relevant to the study of information packaging.

In Chapter 3 the focus shifted from a comparison of the autonomous and the passive progressive to a comparative study of patients, overt agents (passive progressive only, since all instances of the autonomous in the corpus are agent-less) and implicit agents, in all, five different elements. A summary of the results presented in Chapter 3 is found in Table 5.2.

Table 5.2. Overview of features of patients, overt agents and implicit agents of the autonomous and the passive progressive

	patients		overt agents	implicit agents	
	autonomous patients	passive progressive patients	passive progressive overt agents	autonomous implicit agents	passive progressive implicit agents
no. of instances	2,646	467	288	2,956	179
type of overt element					
definite NP	1,164 (44%)	192 (41%)	275 (95%)	*not*	*not*
indefinite NP	698 (27%)	207 (44%)	12 (4%)	*applicable*	*applicable*
relative particle	447 (17%)	68 (15%)	1 (<1%)		
clause	313 (12%) (understood 24 (1%))	—	—		
given vs. new overt element					
given	1,297 (49%)	156 (33%)	246 (85%)	*not*	*not*
new	1,349 (51%)	311 (67%)	42 (15%)	*applicable*	*applicable*
recoverability of implicit agents					
generic	*not*	*not*	*not*	347 (12%)	13 (7%)
non-recoverable	*applicable*	*applicable*	*applicable*	617 (21%)	42 (23%)
textually inferable				1,818 (62%)	112 (63%)
pragmatically inferable				174 (6%)	12 (7%)
continuity					
continuity	1,372 (52%)	140 (30%)	237 (82%)	906 (31%)	52 (29%)
no continuity	1,274 (48%)	327 (70%)	51 (18%)	2,050 (69%)	127 (71%)
co-reference with active subject					
yes	464 (18%)	38 (8%)	159 (55%)	221 (7%)	10 (6%)
no	2,182 (82%)	429 (92%)	129 (45%)	2,735 (93%)	169 (94%)

Differences regarding recoverability of implicit agents are not statistically significant.

According to Table 5.2, there are significant differences between patients and agents in both constructions as regards features associated with information packaging, which point to a general difference between the two constructions in this respect. The most distinct pattern is found among overt passive progressive agents. As regards the main topicality features (given vs. new, and continuity), passive progressive overt agents are used differently from patients and implicit agents of both the autonomous and the passive progressive. The vast majority of them refer to given elements (85%), and display continuity, that is, are linked by explicit reference to the immediately preceding and/or following context (82%). The other extreme with respect to topicality is the passive progressive patient: passive progressive patients most often refer to new participants (67%) and are discontinuous (70%). In addition, the proportion of the passive progressive overt agents (55%) that are co-referential with a subject of an active clause within the continuity range is considerably larger than that of the passive progressive patients (8%). These results indicate that in the passive progressive, patients have low topicality, whereas overt agents are highly topical. Autonomous patients display medium topicality; they are more often given (49%) and continuous (52%) than the passive progressive patients (33% and 30%, respectively). Further, autonomous patients are co-referential with a subject of an active clause more than twice as often as passive progressive patients (18% compared to 8%). Finally, Table 5.2 shows that in the autonomous, as well as the passive progressive, implicit agents display low topicality since they are most often discontinuous (69% and 71%, respectively). Moreover, the smallest proportion of elements co-referential with a subject of an active clause is found among the implicit agents of both constructions (7% in the autonomous and 6% in the passive progressive), which is a further indication of their low topicality. In conclusion, these figures suggest that the autonomous is used with patients referring to participants that are topical, or central, in the text to a greater extent than the passive progressive.

After this brief summary of the results from Chapters 2 and 3, I will discuss the three discourse features that are relevant to the analysis in the present chapter, namely, text function in relation to the eventline, personal perspective, and level of participation.

5.1.1 Text function in relation to the eventline

The discourse functions of clauses with regard to the type of information they contain have been widely studied (see, for example, Givón 1979b, Hopper and Thompson 1980, Tomlin 1987, Haiman and Thompson 1988, and Abraham, Givón and Thompson 1995). A distinction often made is that between foregrounding and backgrounding.[2] In addition, it has frequently been noted that main and subclauses play different roles in text. Main clauses are generally associated with sequential ordering of events, or foregrounded information. In other words, material that builds up the main trail of events, the eventline, in a narrative text tends to be expressed in main clauses. Conversely, subclauses are generally associated with information that is not sequentially ordered, that is, supporting material, or backgrounded information. It has been pointed out that due to its supporting and commenting function, backgrounded information often denotes happenings simultaneous to actions on the eventline (Hopper 1979: 214). Further, it has been observed that verbs used to denote backgrounded events are often durative and occur in imperfective clauses. Moreover, they are largely found in subclauses. Hopper (1979: 215), for example, remarks that foregrounded events are usually (but not exclusively) expressed by punctual verbs, since

---

[2] See Hopper (1979: 215f.) for a detailed definition of foregrounded vs. backgrounded information.

"the sequencing of these clauses usually imposes the constraint that a foregrounded event is contingent on the completion of a prior event".

Several studies have shown, however, that there is no absolute correlation between, on the one hand, main clause structure and foregrounding, and, on the other hand, subclause structure and backgrounding. The same goes for other features that are often correlated with foregrounded vs. backgrounded information, such as punctual vs. durative, new vs. given. Findings presented by, for example, Hopper (1979), Givón (1987), Thompson (1987a), and Matthiessen and Thompson (1988) suggest that there is a need to modify the 'clear-cut' distinction between foregrounding and backgrounding as regards features such as main vs. subclause, punctual vs. durative and new vs. given. However, these findings do not in any substantive way challenge the view that it is primarily main clauses that are used to encode information as part of the eventline of a text. This may be illustrated by the results presented by Thompson (1987a). She has studied the correlation between subclauses and temporal sequencing in two passages of English narrative text. After selecting the subclauses in her material, Thompson determined which clauses denoted actions on the eventline (time line in Thompson's terminology), that is, the "predicates [that] named a punctual event that followed the previous sequenced event and preceded the following sequenced event" (Thompson 1987a: 442). The results of her analysis indicate that a vast majority (89%) of the subordinated clauses contain information that is not part of the temporal sequence. Further, Thompson found that the remaining subclauses (11%), that is, those that denote actions that are part of the eventline, always "do some other discourse work" in addition to keeping the temporal sequence of the narrative (Thompson 1987a: 445f.). Thompson's analysis reveals that the additional discourse function of subclauses that express sequentially ordered information is, for example, to code simultaneity, or to relate the following clause to the temporal sequence. An example of the latter function is *When he finished grooming Josh, Nim turned to Stephanie and her family and repeatedly signed "PLAY"*. (Thompson 1987a: 447). This sentence concludes a descriptive passage that is off the eventline. The subclause (*when he...*) then works as the link between the eventline that was interrupted by the descriptive passage, and the main clause, whose two predicates (*turned* and *signed*) are part of the temporal sequence. In conclusion, Thompson's (1987a) findings suggest that, first, in relation to the eventline, main clauses are used more often than subclauses to build up the temporal sequence of a narrative text, and second, that subclauses are not excluded from expressing sequentially ordered events, but when they do, they perform additional functions.

Returning to the present study, it seems fair to conclude that the investigation of the autonomous and the passive progressive in context should include the feature sequential ordering of events as well as an analysis of supporting clauses. As discussed above, previous research suggests that the distinction between information that is sequentially ordered and information that supports, expands, etc., the eventline is related to the distinction between main and subclause as well as that between punctuality and durativity. The relevance to the present study is therefore that there is significant variation between the autonomous and the passive progressive as regards their distribution across main and subclauses, as well as an inherent difference between the two constructions concerning punctuality and durativity (compare Chapter 2 and Table 5.1).

5.1.2 Personal perspective

The second concept that is relevant to the discussion of discourse function is that of perspective.[3] Perspective is the result of the speaker's or writer's choice of point of view. The basic idea is that a point of view is chosen for every utterance. The choice of point of view has consequences for the discourse function of each statement. In one study dealing with perspective, Sanders and Spooren (1997) discuss what they term subjectivity. In their analysis, there are two kinds of subjectivity. The first type, subjectification, occurs when there is an explicit connection between the information expressed in an utterance and the speaker, as in *I believe Jan is in Paris,* and *Surely, Jan is in Paris* (Sanders and Spooren 1997: 85). The marker of subjectification is in the first example *I believe*, an example of what Sanders and Spooren (1997: 106) label 'I-embedding', that is, clauses that "explicitly embed the speaker's thoughts, beliefs or opinions".[4] In the second example, subjectification is established by the use of the disjunct *surely*, an "evaluative reflection", that indicates the speaker's comment on the value of what is said (Sanders and Spooren 1997: 91). Other linguistic markers of subjectification mentioned by Sanders and Spooren (1997: 91) are modality (as in *Jan must be in Paris*), conditionals (as in *If Marie is well informed, Jan is in Paris*), and predictions (as in *Jan will stay in Paris*). The other type of subjectivity, perspectivization, occurs when a statement is explicitly linked to a subject other than the speaker, as in *Marie believes Jan is in Paris* (Sanders and Spooren 1997: 85). Here subjectivity is created by the use of the verb of cognition *believe* that explicitly links the content of the subordinated clause to *Marie* (Sanders and Spooren 1997: 89). Perspectivization can also be established by the use of direct quotation and verbs of utterance, such as *tell, say*, etc. (Sanders and Spooren 1997: 89). In Sanders and Spooren's analysis, subjectivity indicates the presence of an explicit subject of consciousness, that is, "the subject, either the speaker or the character in the discourse, to whom the responsibility for the information is attributed" (1997: 87). Subjectification occurs when the speaker is the subject of consciousness, whereas perspectivization involves a subject of consciousness other than the speaker, such as *Marie* in the example *Marie believes Jan is in Paris* above. In the sentence *Jan*

---

[3] The terminology in this field varies considerably among scholars and studies. For an overview of some research studies, see Sanders and Spooren (1997) and Smith (2002).

[4] Sanders and Spooren (1997: 106f.) point out that "[i]n I-embeddings, subjectification and [the second type of subjectivity] perspectivization, seem to merge", where perspectivization is "overruled" by subjectification.

is going to Paris, on the other hand, there is no subject of consciousness to which the propositional content is explicitly linked, that is, this sentence does not display subjectivity.

In the present study, the variable personal perspective has been included. As explained in more detail below (5.2), this variable corresponds roughly to subjectivity as defined by Sanders and Spooren (1987).

5.1.3 Level of participation

To be able to make a more detailed comparative analysis of the function of the autonomous and the passive progressive in a text, I introduced one further variable, namely, level of participation. Like given vs. new and continuity, level of participation is a topicality measure but it is meant to be a more detailed measure of topicality than continuity and given vs. new. Level of participation measures the degree of centrality of agents, overt as well as implicit, and patients in terms of text level. The higher the text level where a participant appears, the higher is its level of participation and the more central, or topical, is the participant in the text. In the present study, 'text' denotes a short story or a chapter of a novel, the maximum range considered (the same range used for the classification of given vs. new in Chapter 3). Three levels of participation in text are recognised: sentence, passage and story. The highest level of participation, story-level participation, occurs when the referent is mentioned repeatedly in the text as a whole. Passage-level participation, the intermediate level of participation, occurs when the referent appears in more than one sentence but only within one passage or part of a text (chapter/short story). The lowest level of participation, sentence-level participation, has two sub-categories: single occurrence and multiple occurrences within the same sentence. The aim of the classification of level of participation is to study the topicality of patients and agents in more detail, so that the differences between the autonomous and the passive progressive as regards topicality of patients and agents that were accounted for in Chapter 3 may be further explored.

In the following, I will discuss the autonomous and the passive progressive in context based on a study of a selection of instances from the main database. First I will give an account of the material used and the classification criteria considered.

5.2 Material and principles of classification

For the study of the information packaging of the autonomous and the passive progressive in more detail a subset of instances was selected from the main database, since limited time resources prevented an investigation of all instances in the main database. The subset contains 293 instances of the autonomous and 308 instances of the passive progressive, in total 601 instances. These instances were systematically selected from the main database in the following way. From the autonomous part of the main database every tenth instance was selected. Since the number of instances of the passive progressive is considerably smaller than that of the autonomous, a larger proportion of the passive progressive instances in the database were included in the study. Every third instance of the passive progressive in the main database was excluded, thus leaving two thirds of the instances in the subset.

As has already been accounted for (5.1), two variables based on previous studies were selected for the subset analysis, namely, text function in relation to the eventline and personal perspective. A third variable was added, namely, level of participation, which is intended as a more detailed measure of topicality than continuity and given vs. new. The variables are exemplified and discussed in more detail below.

First, each autonomous and passive progressive clause was classified according to whether or not it expresses an event that is part of a sequentially ordered chain of events, that is, an event that takes place after an action expressed in the preceding discourse and/or before an action expressed in the following discourse. An example of this classification is found in (1), where the autonomous verbs *cuireadh*, 'one put', and *tugadh*, 'one took', denote actions that are parts of an eventline.

In many cases the classification of eventline events is not completely straightforward. For example, many chapters or short stories in the corpus (the text range considered in the investigation of the autonomous and the passive progressive in context, cf. 5.1) contain more than one eventline; an eventline may be embedded, for example, in another temporally sequenced chain of events, in a non-narrative passage, or in direct speech. In other instances, the eventline is interrupted by, for example, a descriptive passage. Further, the number of events that are part of a sequentially ordered chain varies considerably; minimally, an eventline consists of two events.

The clauses that do not describe actions or happenings as part of an eventline contain material that supports the eventline in different ways. Based on the results of a preliminary analysis of these clauses in the subset, five supporting functions are recognised:

– to summarise or conclude an event or events described in the preceding (or, in some cases, following) discourse;
– to explain an event or events described in the preceding discourse;
– to refer to the result or effect of an event or events described in the preceding discourse;
– to describe a setting or background for events described in the surrounding discourse;
– to modify a previously mentioned element or elements.

(1) **Cuireadh** *i málaí í agus* **tugadh** *abhaile í.*
    put-PST-AUT in bags it and take-PST-AUT homewards it

'It **was put** into bags and **taken** home.' (Co. *Dúil*: 102)

(2) *Ní* **fhacthas** *domh go rabh éagcóir ar bith á dhéanamh orm.*
    NEG see-PST-AUT to-1SG CONJ be-PST injustice any to+its do-VBN on-1SG

'It didn't **seem** to me that I was being wronged at all.' (Ul. *Saoghal Corrach*: 137)[5]

(3) *Glór a scanraigh mé féin go minic, ach ar ndóigh, ní bhíodh aon*
    voice REL frighten-PST me -self often but of course NEG be-IPF any

    bhaint ró-mhór aige linne. Ní raibh aon Ghaeilge
    connection too+big at-3SGM with-1PL-EMPH NEG be-PST any Irish

    aige agus ní **thugtaí,** *an tráth úd, aon ordú dúinne i*
    at-3SGM and NEG give-IPF-AUT the time that any order to-1PL-EMPH in

    mBéarla, mar an té a thugadh orduithe dúinne ní bhíodh
    English for the person REL give-IPF orders to-1PL-EMPH NEG be-IPF

    gá ar bith aige leis mar Bhéarla.
    need at all at-3SGM with-3SGM like English

'A voice that often frightened me, of course, but he didn't have much to do with us. He didn't know any Irish and, at that time, no orders **were given** to us in English, for the one who gave us orders had no need for English.' (Co. *Feamainn Bhealtaine*: 129)

A number of clauses perform functions not matching the descriptions above, so a further category, 'other', was added to the classification.

Examples of the supporting functions are given below. In (2), an example is given of a clause that concludes the events described in the preceding discourse. In (3), an example is found of a clause whose function is to explain events described in the preceding context. The autonomous clause *ní thugtaí...*, 'used not to be given...', explains the clause *ní bhíodh aon bhaint ró-mhór aige linne*, 'he wouldn't have much to do with us' in the preceding sentence. The passive progressive clause in (4) expresses the situation resulting from events mentioned in the preceding discourse. In (5), the passive progressive is used to describe a setting or background for the events mentioned in the preceding sentence. The last supporting function listed above, that of modifying an element, is exemplified in (6). The passive progressive clause *á róstadh*, 'being roasted', modifies the immediately preceding element *feoil*, 'meat'. Finally, a number of supporting clauses perform other functions than the ones listed above. One of the more common functions in the category 'other' is to present new information, as in (7).

---

[5] Normally one would here expect *á déanamh*, since *á* refers to the feminine noun *éagcóir*, instead of *á dhéanamh* which indicates that the referent is masculine.

(4)
Bhí	*sé*	*á*	**chrochadh**	*amach*	*chun*	*farraige*	*leis*	*an*	*sruth.*
be-PST	it	to+its	carry-VBN	out	to	sea-GEN	by	the	current

'It was **being carried** out to sea by the current.' (Co. *Dúil*: 24)

(5)
Chuireas	*féin*	*tine*	*síos*	*agus*	*chuas*		*amach*	*ag*	*triall*	*ar*
put-PST-1SG	-self	fire	down	and	go-PST-1SG		out	at	travel-VBN	on

uisce	*go dtí*	*an*	*tobar.*	*Anois*	*a*	*bhí*	*fionnóga*	*an*	*lae*	*ag*
water	to	the	well	now	REL	be-PST	dawn rays	the-GEN	day-GEN	at

oscailt	*thoir;*	*an*	*ghealach*	*ina*	*luí*	*laistiar*	*do*	*sna Feo*	*agus*
open-VBN	in the east	the	moon	in+its	set-VBN	on the west	of	the Feo	and

dath	*dearg*	*na*	*gréine*	*ag*	*ardú*	*os cionn*	*na*	*gCruacha Dubha*
colour	red	the-GEN	sun-GEN	at	raise-VBN	above	the-GEN	Cruacha Dubha-GEN

agus	*mar*	*sin*	*anoir*	*thar*	*Bá an Daingin;*	*solas*	*na*	*hoíche*	*á*
and	like	that	from the east	across	Dingle Bay	light	the-GEN	night	to+its

mhúchadh	*ag*	*solas*	*an*	*lae.*
extinguish	by	light	the-GEN	day-GEN

'I set a fire and went for water to the well. Now the first rays of dawn were appearing in the east, the moon was setting west of the Feo and the red colour of the sun was rising above the Cruacha Dubha and from the east across Dingle Bay; the light of night was **being extinguished** by the light of day.' (Mu. *Fiche Bliain ag Fás*: 110)

(6)
Bhí	*bladhm*	*solais*	*amach*	*tríd*	*an*	*ndoras,*	*boladh*	*cumhra*	*le*
be-PST	flame	light-GEN	out	through	the	door	smell	sweet-smelling	to

fáil	*agam*	*agus*	*fuaim*	*ag*	*feoil*	*á*	**róstadh.**
get-VBN	by-1SG	and	sound	at	meat	at its	roast-VBN

'There was a gleam of light coming out through the door, I smelt a sweet aroma and heard the sound of meat **roasting**.' (Mu. *Fiche Bliain ag Fás*: 118)

The next feature related to context that has been analysed is personal perspective, that is, explicit links between the content of the autonomous or passive progressive clause and a subject of consciousness. The subject of consciousness is the author or some character in the discourse to whom the clause in question is linked. The notion and classification of personal perspective in the present study is based on Sanders and Spooren's (1997: 86) definition of subjectivity, as described in 5.1.2. In the present study, I apply a core part of Sander and Spooren's (1987) methodology, since their concept of subjectivity may be of relevance to the comparison of the autonomous and the passive progressive. However, my analysis does not strictly adhere to the theoretical framework of their study (which is not corpus-based and deals mainly with modals). Therefore, the term subjectivity is not fully adequate in the present context, which is why I decided to use the term personal perspective instead of subjectivity. The clauses in the subset are classified with respect to personal

(7) | Is | ansan | a | chonac | Paddy | suite | thíos | ar | charraig, | *a* | *phíp* |
|---|---|---|---|---|---|---|---|---|---|---|
| COP-PRS | then | REL | see-PST-1SG | Paddy | sit-VBA | down | on | rock | his | pipe |

aige	*á*	*líonadh*	agus	é	ag	féachaint	uaidh	in airde	agus	ag
by-3SGM	to+its	fill-VBN	and	he	at	looks-VBN	from	up	and	at

leamhgháirí.
faint smile-VBN

'Then I saw Paddy seated on a rock, **filling his pipe** and looking around and smiling.' (Mu. *Fiche Bliain ag Fás*: 103)

(8) | *Do chloisinn* | anois is arís | foscread | *á* | **ligint** | aici, | agus |
|---|---|---|---|---|---|---|
| hear-IPF-1SG | now and then | occasional+scream | to+its | let out-VBN | by-3SGF | and |

fé mar	a	bhí	sí	ag	imeacht	uaim,	bhí	an
according as	REL	be-PST	she	at	go away-VBN	from-1SG	be-PST	the

bhéiceach	ag	dul	i	laige,	nó gur	thiteas	i	dtromshuan.
yelling	at	go-VBN	into	weakness	until	fall-PST-1SG	into	heavy+sleep

'Now and then I heard her **letting out** an occasional scream, and as she was going away from me, the yelling was getting weaker, until I fell into a heavy sleep.' (Mu. *Fiche Bliain ag Fás*: 19)

perspective according to the following principles. First, it is determined whether there is an explicit link that creates personal perspective or not. Then, in those cases where a personal perspective is identified, it is determined whether the participant linked to the information in the sentence in question (the subject of consciousness in Sanders and Spooren's terminology) is the speaker, that is, the author, or a character in the text. Finally, the linguistic marker that is used to establish the link is classified. Following Sanders and Spooren (1997), the following categories of linguistic markers are recognised:

– direct speech;
– verb of perception, such as, *feic*, 'see', *clois*, 'hear';
– verb of cognition, such as, *ceap*, 'think', *meas*, 'estimate';
– verb of utterance, such as, *abair*, 'say', *inis*, 'tell';
– disjuncts that reflect the attitude of the subject of consciousness towards the truth value of the propositional content of the clause, such as *b'fhéidir*, 'maybe'.

Examples of sentences displaying a personal perspective are found below. An example where the subject of consciousness is the author is found in (8), and examples where the subject of consciousness is a character in the text are found in (9)–(12). In (9) a personal perspective is expressed by the use of direct speech that explicitly binds the utterance to a specific person. In (10), a personal perspective is established by the verb of perception *chuala*, 'heard', which links the author to the information contained in the passive progressive clause. In (11),

(9)   *"Caithfear*   *a'*   *dligheadh*   *a*   *choimhlíonadh.*   *Gearr*   *punta*   *feola*
     must-FUT-AUT   the   law   to   fulfil-VBN   cut   pound   flesh-GEN

     as   *taoibh*   *an*   *fhir*   *seo,"*   <u>*ar*</u>   <u>*seisean*</u>   *leis*   *an*   *Údas.*
     from   side   the-GEN   man-GEN   this   say-PST   he-EMPH   to   the   Jew

' "The law **must** be complied with. Cut a pound of flesh from the side of this man," <u>he said</u> to the Jew.' (Ul. *Saoghal Corrach*: 6)

(10)   *Chreathnaigh*   *an*   *gasúr*   *ó*   *cheann*   *go*   *cos*   *agus*   *tháinig*   *fonn*   *tréan*
      tremble-PST   the   boy   from   head   to   foot   and   come-PST   desire   strong

      caoineacháin   *air*   *nuair*   *a*   <u>*chuala*</u>   *sé*   *a*   *mháthair*   *á*   ***maslú.***
      crying-GEN   on-3SGM   when   REL   hear-PST   she   his   mother   to+her   insult-VBN

'The boy trembled from head to foot and he felt like bursting into tears when he <u>heard</u> his mother **being insulted.**' (Co. *Dúil*: 69)

the linguistic marker of personal perspective is the verb of cognition *mheas siad*, 'they thought'. The autonomous clause in (12) is explicitly linked to a subject of consciousness through the use of the verb of utterance *inis*, 'tell'. Finally, in (13), the disjunct *b'fhéidir*, 'maybe', is used to link the autonomous clause to a subject of consciousness, in this case the author, reflecting the author's assessment of the truth value of the content of the autonomous clause, and thus creating a personal perspective. When there is no explicit connection of the kind described above between the proposition and the author or some other subject of consciousness, as in (14), the clause is classified as not expressing a personal perspective.

The final feature investigated in the subset is the level of participation of patients and agents. As explained in 5.1.3, level of participation is a topicality measure based on the centrality of a participant in the text. As pointed out above, level of participation concerns patients and overt as well as implicit agents. The three levels of participation that are recognised are related to sentence, passage or story. Sentence-level participation is further divided into single occurrence and multiple occurrences. The lowest level of participation is single-occurrence sentence-level participation, which occurs when the element referred to by the patient or agent appears only once in the text. An example of sentence-level participation involving a single occurrence is found in (15), multiple-occurrence sentence-level participation is displayed in (16).[6] The patient of the passive progressive clause in (15), *aithris*, 'imitation', does not occur outside the passive progressive clause. In (16) the implicit agent of the passive progressive in the first clause has the same reference as the implicit agent of *clos*, 'hear', in the final clause of (16), that is, "the inhabitants of the places where '*Fáilte Uí Cheallaigh*' is not heard". The intermediate level of participation comprises instances where the patient or agent is mentioned either in more than one sentence, or is the topic

---

[6] When no actor is logically implied, as in instances of implicit agents that have been classified as non-recoverable, the agent is classified as displaying single-occurrence level of participation.

(11)

Mheas	*siad*	*go*	*bhféadfaidís*	*iad*	*féin*	*a*	*chosaint*	*ar*	*an*
think-PST	they	CONJ	can-COND-3PL	them	-self	to	protect-VBN	on	the

bhfeallaire	*ach*	*gan*	*aon*	*eolas*	*a*	*thabhairt*	*d'aon* *duine*	*ar*	*an*	*ngnó*
betrayer	if	without	any	information	to	give-VBN	to+any one	on	the	business

ach	*eolas*	*nach*	**bhféadfaí**	*a*	*dhíol,*	*eolas*	*nach*
but	information	REL-NEG	can-COND-AUT	to	sell-VBN	information	REL-NEG

mbeadh	*aon*	*tairbhe*	*don*	*namhaid*	*ann,*	*agus*	*dá bhrí sin,*	*nach*
be-COND	any	benefit	for+the	enemy	in-3SGM	and	therefore	REL-NEG

gceannófaí	*ó*	*aon* *duine.*
buy-COND-AUT	from	any one

'<u>They thought</u> that they could defend themselves from the traitor if they didn't give anyone information about the matter except information that **one couldn't** sell, information that was of no use to the enemy, and therefore wouldn't be bought from anyone.' (Mu. *Mo Scéal féin*: 96)

(12)

I gcionn	*chupla*	*lá*	*fuair*	*mé*	*sgéala*	*uatha*	*ag*	<u>*innse*</u>	*domh*	*go*
at the end of	couple	day	get-PST	I	news	from-3PL	at	tell-VBN	to-1SG	CONJ

bhfuair	*siad*	*mo*	*leitir*	*agus*	*go*	**gcuirfidhe**	*"fé bhrághaid*	*an*
get-PST	they	my	letter	and	CONJ	put-COND-AUT	in front of	the-GEN

Choiste	*í".*
Committee-GEN	it

'After a couple of days I got a message from them <u>informing</u> me that they had received my letter and that it **would be referred** "to the Committee". (Ul. *Saoghal Corrach*: 273)

(13)

Má	*ghní*	*tú*	*mórán*	*comhráidh*	<u>*b'fhéidir*</u>	*go*
if	make-PRS	you-SG	much	conversation-GEN	maybe	CONJ

dtabharfaí	*geabaire*	*ort;*	*má*	*fhanann*	*tú*	*'do*	*thost*
call-COND-AUT	chatterbox	on-2SG	if	stay-PRS	you-SG	in+your	silence

<u>*b'fhéidir*</u>	*go*	**dtabharfaí**	*smutaidhe*	*nó*	*béal*	*gan*	*smid*	*ort.*
maybe	CONJ	call-COND-AUT	sulky person	or	mouth	without	syllable	on-2SG

'If you talk a lot <u>maybe</u> you **would be called** a chatterbox; if you keep quiet <u>maybe</u> you **would be called** a sulky person or an unsociable person.' (Ul. *Rácáil agus Scuabadh*: 26)

(14)

Acht	*caidé*	*tháinig*	*acht*	*oidhche*	*mhilltineach*	*gaoithe*	*móire*	*agus*
but	what	come-PST	but	night	terrible	wind-GEN	great-GEN	and

báitheadh	<u>*an*</u> <u>*soitheach.*</u>
sink-PST-AUT	the ship

'But what came but a terribly windy night <u>and the ship **was sunk**</u>.' (Ul. *Saoghal Corrach*: 5)

of an entire passage, as in (17). The patient of the autonomous in (17), *an tAthair Maitiú*, 'Father Matthew', occurs in the text following the sentence containing the autonomous verb form under investigation, as well as in other places in the

(15)

Eisean	féin,	is		minic	**aithris**	á		**dhéanamh**	aige		ar
he-EMPH	-self	COP-PRS		often	imitation	to+its		make-VBN	by-3SGM		on

shaothar	na	nGréagach.
works	the-GEN	Greeks-GEN

'He himself often **imitates** Greek works.' (Co. *An Mothall sin ort*: 28)

(16)

Áiteacha	nach	gcluinfeá		"Fáilte Uí Cheallaigh"		á
places	REL-NEG	hear-COND-2SG		Ó Ceallaigh's welcome (= a generous welcome)		to+its

lua		go brách	is		mion	minic	"chomh	fial	le	Fionn",	nó
mention-VBN		never	COP-PRS		very	often	as		generous	as	F.	or

"chomh	flaithiúil	leis	na	Fianna",	le	_clos_	iontu.
as	generous	as	the	F.	to	hear-VBN	in-3PL

'Places where you would never hear **people say** "Ó Ceallaigh's welcome", you can very often <u>hear</u> "as generous as Fionn", or "as generous as the Fianna".' (Co. *An Mothall sin ort*: 11)

(17)

Cupla	lá	'na dhiaidh sin	**casadh**		_an_	_tAthair_	_Maitiú_	orm.
couple	day	after that	meet with-PST-AUT		the	father	M.	on-1SG

Bhí	cuma	air	nach	raibh	sé	sásta	liom.
be-PST	appearance	on-3SGM	CONJ-NEG	be-PST	he	pleased	with-1SG

'A couple of days after that I **met** <u>Father Matthew</u>. <u>He</u> looked as if <u>he</u> was not pleased with me.' (Ul. *Saoghal Corrach*: 95)

(18)

D'ardaigh	sí	a	ceann	agus	bhreathnaigh	sí	go fiáin	ar	an	tseanmháthair
raise-PST	she	her	head	and	look-PST	she	fiercely	on	the	grandmother

ag	a	raibh	_an_	_leanbh_	á	**chóiriú**	thall	le cois	na	tine.
by	REL	be-PST	the	infant	to+its	dress-VBN	over there	beside	the-GEN	fire-GEN

'She raised her head and looked fiercely at the grandmother who was **dressing** <u>the infant</u> beside the fire.' (Co. *Dúil*: 37)

passage. The highest level of participation, story-level participation, is assigned, for example, to a central character of a text, as in (18), where the patient, *an leanbh*, 'the infant', is one of the three main characters in the short story. As is clear from the above, level of participation is related to continuity—they are both topicality measures—but level of participation differs from continuity in that it takes into account not only explicit but also implicit references, as well as a wider context than the immediately surrounding sentences.

The remainder of the present chapter will be devoted to a presentation and discussion of the results of the analysis of the subset with regard to the features mentioned above. The features clause type and continuity will also be considered since, as was explained above (5.1), they are related to sequential ordering, the supporting function of clauses, and the level of participation of patients and agents.

5.3 Results of the subset analysis

5.3.1 Text function in relation to the eventline

As mentioned in the preceding section, the first part of the analysis of the subset instances was to determine whether the events expressed in the autonomous or the passive progressive clauses are sequentially ordered, that is, actions that are part of the eventline of a narrative, or whether they contain supporting material. The frequency and distribution of the autonomous and the passive progressive across sequential ordering and supporting functions is shown in Table 5.3. Also included in Table 5.3 is their distribution across main and subclause since the contrast between main and subclause is relevant for the function of clauses in discourse (see 5.1.1). There is statistically significant variation between the autonomous and the passive progressive as regards the distribution of clauses across text function in relation to the eventline, as well as across main and subclause. As can be seen in Table 5.3, the majority of clauses in both constructions in the subset contain material that fulfils supporting functions. However, while one quarter, 24%, of the autonomous clauses are part of a sequentially ordered chain of events, only 4% of the passive progressive clauses occur in such a chain. Table 5.3 also shows that there are differences between the two constructions as regards distribution across main and subclause. The overall proportion of main clauses in the subset is 47% in the autonomous and 14% in the passive progressive, (which corresponds well to the distribution of the autonomous and the passive progressive across main and subclause in the main database, 47% and 13%, respectively). Not surprisingly, the majority (83%) of the autonomous eventline clauses are main clauses, whereas a considerably smaller proportion (36%) of those that contain supporting material are main clauses. This is in line with previous research on the discourse functions of main and subclauses, as accounted for in 5.1.1. In the passive progressive, on the other hand, 82% of the eventline clauses, as well as 86% of those containing supporting material are subclauses. Finally, it appears from these figures that the relative frequency of main clauses that fulfil supporting functions is more than twice as high in the autonomous as in the passive progressive, 36% vs. 14%.

Examples of eventline clauses are presented and commented upon below. The results of the classification of supporting clauses are presented and discussed in the following section. As shown in Table 5.3, autonomous eventline clauses are typically main clauses, as in (19); only 12 of them, 17%, are subclauses, as in (20). In (20) the sequentially ordered event is expressed in the adverbial subclause *go dtí go dtainigtheas fhad le Ceallaigh*, 'until it was Ceallaigh's turn'.

Table 5.3. Distribution of autonomous and passive progressive clauses across text function in relation to the eventline. Frequency and distribution across clause type.

	autonomous		passive progressive	
	n	%	n	%
sequentially ordered events	70	24%	11	4%
main clause	58	(83%)	2	(18%)
subclause	12	(17%)	9	(82%)
supporting functions	223	76%	297	96%
main clause	81	(36%)	41	(14%)
subclause	142	(64%)	256	(86%)
total	293	100%	308	100%

sequentially ordered events vs. supporting functions: $\chi^2 = 53.16$; df = 1; p < 0.05, critical value: 3.84
supporting functions, main vs. subclause: $\chi^2 = 35.97$; df = 1; p < 0.05, critical value: 3.84

In (21) the eventline action is expressed in a (non-finite) subclause governed by a verb of perception whose subject is the speaker.[7]

In sum, the most salient finding presented in Table 5.3 is that more than six times as many autonomous clauses as passive progressive ones, 24% vs. 4%, express events as part of the eventline. Thus, the majority of autonomous as well as passive progressive clauses contain supporting material; 96% of the passive progressive clauses have supporting functions, compared to 76% of the autonomous clauses. Further, the distribution of main and subclauses across text function varies between the constructions. In the autonomous there is a marked difference between clauses denoting actions as part of an eventline and those that are off the eventline as regards clause type; whereas 83% of the eventline clauses are main clauses, only 36% of the off-eventline clauses are main clauses. In the passive progressive, on the other hand, the difference is not that great: 18% of the eventline clauses and 14% of the off-eventline clauses are main clauses. As predicted, then, these results reflect the correlation pointed out in previous studies (see 5.1.1) between, on the one hand, punctuality, main clause, and fore-grounded information, and, on the other hand, durativity, subclause and back-grounded information. The next section presents and discusses the results concerning the supporting functions of off-eventline clauses in the subset.

---

[7] Eight of the nine passive progressive clauses that express sequentially ordered events occur in nominal subclauses, where the sequentially ordered event is expressed as a complement of a verb of perception, such as *mothaigh*, 'feel', 'hear', in (19). The eventline action is described through the eyes of the speaker and reflects his attitude towards it. (19) is thus an example of personal perspective, as described in 5.1.2 and 5.2. For further discussion of this type of explicit connection, see 5.3.3 below.

(19) **_Deineadh_** _an_ _cnag_ _arís_ _ar_ _an_ _ndoras_ _go feargach,_ _do bhris_ _ar_
make-PST-AUT the knock again on the door angrily break-PST on

_an_ _bhfoighne_ _sa_ _deireadh_ _aici,_ _d'oscail_ _sí_ _an_ _doras,_ _agus_ _cé_
the patience in+the end at-3SGF open-PST she the door and who

bheadh _ann_ _ach_ _an_ _sagart._
be-COND there but the priest

'**There was** an angry knock on the door again, she lost her patience eventually, opened the door, and who was there if not the priest.' (Mu. *Fiche Bliain ag Fás*: 16)

(20) _D'ól_ _acha'n_ _dhuine_ _é_ _go fonnmhar,_ _go dtí_ _go_ **_dtainigtheas_** _fhad le_
drink-PST every person it eagerly until CONJ come-PST-AUT as far as

Ceallaigh.
Ceallaigh

'Everybody drank it eagerly, until it was Ceallaigh's turn.' (Ul. *Dochartach Duibhlionna*: 27)

(21) _Seal_ _mór_ _fada,_ _dar_ _liom,_ _a_ _b'éigean_ _damh_ _fanacht_
period great long it seemed to-1SG REL COP-PST+necessity for-1SG wait-VBN

sul ar _mhothuigh_ _mé_ _trup_ _na_ _mboltaí_ **_dá_** **_mbaint._**
before hear-PST I noise the-GEN bolts-GEN to+their open-VBN

'I had to wait a long while, it seemed to me, before I heard the sound of the bolts **being opened**.' (Ul. *Dochartach Duibhlionna*: 16)

5.3.1.1 Classification of clauses containing supporting material

Table 5.3 showed that 76% of the autonomous clauses and 96% of the passive progressive clauses contain supporting material. As mentioned in 5.2, five supporting functions are recognised. The clauses classified as performing other functions than those five were defined as belonging to the category 'other'. The distribution of autonomous and passive progressive clauses across supporting functions is presented in Table 5.4. Comparing the results regarding the autonomous and the passive progressive in Table 5.4, one finds that the distribution across the supporting functions varies to some extent between the two constructions. The most salient differences between the autonomous and the passive progressive concern the functions to explain an event or events, to modify an element, and to describe a setting. The first of these functions, to explain an event or events, is the most common supporting function in both constructions (not counting the category other in the passive progressive) but the proportion is larger in the autonomous than in the passive progressive; 30% of the autonomous supporting clauses fulfil this function compared to 20% of the passive progressive ones. As regards clauses used to modify an element, this function is almost twice as common among autonomous supporting clauses than among passive

Table 5.4. Distribution of the autonomous and the passive progressive across supporting functions

	autonomous		passive progressive	
	n	%	n	%
to explain an event or events described in the preceding discourse	68	30%	58	20%
to modify a previously mentioned element or elements	50	22%	36	12%
to refer to the result or effect of an event or events described in the preceding discourse	38	17%	42	14%
to summarise or conclude an event or events described in the surrounding discourse	31	14%	47	16%
to describe a setting or background for events described in the surrounding discourse	1	<1%	52	18%
other	35	16%	62	21%
Total	223	99%	297	101%

$\chi^2 = 53.70$; df = 5; p < 0.05, critical value: 11.07

progressive clauses, 22% compared to 12%. Finally, the greatest difference between the two constructions is found in the frequency of clauses describing a setting. As can be seen in Table 5.4, 18% of the passive progressive supporting clauses are used to describe a setting, while there is only one instance (< 1%) of this function among the autonomous supporting clauses. Table 5.4 also shows that a number of autonomous as well as passive progressive clauses perform functions other than the five main ones identified in this classification: 16% of the autonomous supporting clauses and 21% of the passive progressive ones perform functions that belong to the category 'other'. Without having fully analysed these instances, the observation may be made that one of the most common functions in this category is the one exemplified in (7) above, to add information. This function is almost twice as common in the passive progressive as in the autonomous.

5.3.2 Personal perspective

The next variable to consider is personal perspective, that is, the presence or absence of explicit links between the information contained in an autonomous or passive progressive clause and the speaker or some participant other than the speaker (as accounted for in 5.1.2). The explicit links in question are, among others, verbs of utterance and cognition, direct quotation, and disjuncts that reflect the speaker's assessment of the truth value of the proposition in question, such as *b'fhéidir*, 'maybe'. (The various means of creating a personal perspective and their frequencies in the subset were discussed in 5.2). On the basis of the presence of one such linguistic marker between the clause content and participant to whom the contents of the clause is attributed—the subject of consciousness—the sentences containing the autonomous and the passive progressive in the subset have been categorised depending on whether they express a personal perspective or not. The frequency of autonomous and passive progressive clauses where a personal perspective is expressed, as well as where no personal perspective is expressed, is presented in Table 5.5. As can be seen in Table 5.5, the majority of autonomous as well as passive progressive clauses do not display a personal perspective. Around one third of the clauses in the subset, 31% of the autonomous ones and 33% of the passive progressive ones, are explicitly linked to a subject of consciousness. There is thus very little variation between the two constructions in this respect.

Next follows the distribution of clauses that display a personal perspective across type of linked participant, as presented in Table 5.6. According to Table 5.6, the subject of consciousness explicitly linked to the clause content is in most instances of both constructions a character in the text. However, the proportion is considerably higher in the autonomous than in the passive progressive, 74% vs. 53%, a difference which is statistically significant. Conversely, it may be noted that in as many as 47% of the instances of the passive progressive where there is a personal perspective, the subject of consciousness is the author of the text. In the autonomous, the corresponding figure is only 26%. Thus, the passive progressive is used when actions are seen through the eyes of the author to a significantly larger extent than the autonomous.

As described in 5.2, the clauses that display a personal perspective have been classified according to the linguistic marker used to establish the link to the subject of consciousness. The distribution of linguistic markers of personal perspective is presented in Table 5.7. Table 5.7 shows that there are considerable differences between the autonomous and the passive progressive as regards the way in which a personal perspective is created. In the autonomous, direct speech is the most frequent linguistic marker; it is used in 54% of the cases of personal perspective involving the autonomous, but only in 25% of the passive progressive ones. The most frequent type of marker in the passive progressive is a verb of perception, occurring in 50% of the passive progressive clauses that are explicitly linked to a subject of consciousness. In contrast, there is only one instance of an autonomous clause being linked by the use of a verb of perception. The figures in Table 5.7 also indicate that verbs of utterance, as well as disjuncts, occur more frequently with the autonomous, 17% and 8% respectively, than with the passive progressive, 8% and 1% (one instance), respectively. When it comes to the remaining way of creating a personal perspective, namely by using a verb of cognition, one may note that the relative frequency of verbs of cognition is fairly similar in the two constructions, 20% in the autonomous, and somewhat lower, 16%, in the passive progressive.

Table 5.5. Distribution of autonomous and passive progressive across clauses that display a personal perspective and those that do not

	autonomous		passive progressive	
	n	%	n	%
personal perspective	90	31%	102	33%
no personal perspective	203	69%	206	67%
Total	293	100%	308	100%

Table 5.6. Distribution of autonomous and passive progressive clauses displaying a personal perspective across subject of consciousness

	autonomous		passive progressive	
	n	%	n	%
author[a]	23	26%	48	47%
other	67	74%	54	53%
Total	90	100%	102	100%

$\chi^2 = 9.49$; df = 1; p < 0.05, critical value: 3.84
[a]In two instances, the subject of consciousness is not the author but the fictitious narrator of the text.

Table 5.7. Distribution of autonomous and passive progressive clauses that display a personal perspective across linguistic markers

	autonomous		passive progressive	
	n	%	n	%
direct speech	49	54%	26	25%
verb of perception	1	1%	51	50%
verb of cognition	18	20%	16	16%
verb of utterance	15	17%	8	8%
disjuncts	7	8%	1	1%
Total	90	100%	102	100%

$\chi^2 = 61.37$; df = 4; p < 0.05, critical value: 9.49

In conclusion, the results concerning personal perspective suggest that there is very little variation between the autonomous and the passive progressive as regards their tendency to be used in clauses that are explicitly linked to some subject of consciousness. It was also shown that there is variation between the constructions as regards the nature of the subject of consciousness. In 74% of the autonomous clauses explicitly linked to a subject of consciousness this subject of consciousness is some person in the text. In the passive progressive, however, in 53% of the cases the subject of consciousness is the author. As for the ways in which a personal perspective is established, on the other hand, there is considerable variation between the two constructions. In the autonomous, the most frequent linguistic marker of a personal perspective is direct speech (54%), while a verb of perception is the most commonly used marker (50%) with the passive progressive.

5.3.4 Level of participation

After the presentation of the results regarding the function of autonomous and passive progressive clauses in the texts and the presence or absence of a personal perspective, I now turn to the final variable, the level of participation of patients and agents. As discussed in 5.1.3, this variable measures topicality but in a slightly different way compared to the primary topicality features discussed in Chapter 3, continuity and given vs. new. Level of participation concerns the whole text (chapter or short story), thus, a wider range of material compared to the analysis of continuity and given vs. new. As mentioned above, three levels of participation are recognised: sentence, passage and story. Sentence-level participation comprises participation of two kinds, single occurrence, that is, the referent is only mentioned once in the text, and multiple occurrences which applies when the referent is mentioned more than once in a given sentence (but not elsewhere in the text). Passage-level participation is assigned to patients and agents whose referent is mentioned in more than one sentence but only within the same passage or part of the text. Finally, story-level participation occurs when the referent of the patient or agent is mentioned in several places throughout a text. The frequency and distribution of the autonomous and passive progressive patients and agents across the four categories of participation are displayed in Table 5.8. Table 5.8 shows that there is great variation among elements as regards the variable level of participation. As indicated, there is considerable variation within the autonomous, within the passive progressive, as well as between the constructions. For example, the relative frequency of patients and agents that display participation at the single-occurrence sentence level only (that is, these elements occur once only in the text) ranges from 9% among passive progressive overt agents to 71% among autonomous agents. A comparison between the autonomous and the passive progressive reveals two distinct patterns. In the autonomous, patients have higher relative frequency than agents at all levels except at the single-occurrence sentence level, the difference ranges from 14 to 17 percentage points. As regards single-occurrence sentence-level participation, the relative frequency of autonomous implicit agents is considerably higher, 71%, than that of autonomous patients, 34%. In short, these results suggest that in the autonomous clauses in the subset, patients are central in the text to a larger extent than implicit agents, that is, the patients refer to participants that are more topical than those referred to by the implicit agents. This pattern is similar to the one found in Chapter 3 (see, for example, Table 5.2).

Table 5.8. Distribution of autonomous and passive progressive patients and agents across levels of participation

	autonomous				passive progressive					
	patients		implicit agents		patients		implicit agents		overt agents	
	n	%	n	%	n	%	n	%	n	%
sentence-level part., single occurrence	93	34%	207	71%	188	61%	71	62%	18	9%
sentence-level part., multiple occurrences	50	19%	15	5%	52	17%	10	9%	27	14%
passage-level participation	103	38%	62	21%	54	18%	25	22%	73	38%
story-level participation	24	9%	9	3%	14	5%	9	8%	75	39%
total	270	100%	293	100%	308	101%	115	101%	193	100%

autonomous: $\chi^2 = 78.36$; df = 3; p < 0.05, critical value: 7.81
passive progressive: $\chi^2 = 197.25$; df = 6; p < 0.05, critical value: 12.59

In the passive progressive, the pattern is different. The overt agents are more frequent than the patients at higher levels of participation. Most prominently, while 39% of the overt agents display story-level participation, only 5% of the patients do. Conversely, as single occurrences at sentence-level, passive progressive patients are considerably more frequent than overt agents, 61% vs. 9%. Thus, the figures in Table 5.8 suggest that in the subset, passive progressive overt agents are more topical, or central, than passive progressive patients. As for passive progressive implicit agents, they seem to be very similar to the patients with regard to level of participation. Only one example of each level of participation is given below; more examples are found in 5.2 above.

Below, examples are given of the element type that has the highest relative frequency of the level of participation in question. An example of an autonomous implicit agent displaying single-occurrence sentence-level participation is shown in (22). The autonomous patient in (23) displays multiple-occurrence sentence-level participation. The intermediate level of participation, passage-level, is exemplified in (24), which contains a passive progressive overt agent that is co-referential with participants within the same sentence as well as in neighbouring sentences. The final example, (25), contains an instance of a passive progressive overt agent that displays story-level participation. The 'I' in (25) is the narrator and main character of the novel.

To present the results concerning level of participation in a way that makes comparisons between elements and constructions easier, the average level of participation (with one decimal) was calculated for each of the five elements, that is, patients and implicit agents in both constructions, and overt agents in the

(22)

Dhá	mhí	roimhe	sin	bhí	plód	mór	éan	ag	maireachtaint
two	month	before-3SGM	that	be-PST	flock	large	birds-GEN	at	live-VBN

sa	gcuan;	éanacha	de	gach	saghas	dá	bhfeictear	ag
in+the	harbour	birds	of	every	kind	of those who	see-PRS-AUT	at

neadú	i	bhfarragáin	aille.
nest-VBN	in	ledge	cliff-GEN

'Two months before that there was a large flock of birds living in the haven; birds of every kind that can **be seen** nesting on a cliff ledge.' (Co. *Dúil*: 18)

(23)

Ach	nuair	a	chuaigh	mé	isteach	sa	Choláiste	agus	chuir	mé
but	when	REL	go-PST	I	into	in+the	College	and	put-PST	I

aithne	ar	bhuachaillí	a	tógadh	in	áiteanna	eile,	agus	nuair
acquaintance	on	boys	REL	raise-PST-AUT	in	places	other	and	when

a	fuair	mé	nach	raibh	aon	fhocal	Gaeilge	acu,	bhí
REL	find-PST	I	CONJ-NEG	be-PST	any	word	Irish-GEN	at-3PL	be-PST

ionadh	agus	alltacht	orm.
surprise	and	astonishment	on-1SG

'But when I went to the College and I got to know <u>boys who</u> **were brought up** in other places, and when I found out that <u>they</u> didn't know a word of Irish, I was shocked and horrified.' (Mu. *Mo Scéal féin*: 87)

passive progressive.[8] Patients and agents included in the analysis were given the value 0 when their referent appears only once in the text (single occurrence); the value 1 was assigned to patients and agents that are referred to more than once in the given sentence but not elsewhere in the text (multiple occurrences). The value 2 or 3 is given to a participant according to the level, that is, passage or story, where its referent occurs in the text outside the sentence in question. The average values for level of participation of patients and agents are shown in Table 5.9. According to Table 5.9, the average level of participation varies considerably among the patients and agents of the autonomous and the passive progressive, displaying basically the same pattern as 5.8. The highest average value, 2.1, is found among passive progressive overt agents, while autonomous agents display the lowest value, 0.6. These values suggest that the most topical of the five elements in question is the passive progressive overt agent, and the least topical element is the autonomous implicit agent. A comparison between patients and agents within each construction shows that in the autonomous, patients display

---

[8] The average level of participation was calculated as follows: ((0 multiplied by the number of elements with single-occurrence sentence-level participation) + (1 multiplied by the number of elements with multiple-occurrence sentence-level participation) + (2 multiplied by the number of elements with passage-level participation) + (3 multiplied by the number of elements with story-level participation)) / total number of elements. For example, the calculation of the average level of participation of autonomous patients looks like this: ((93 x 0) + (50 x 1) + (103 x 2) + (24 x 3)) = 328/270 = 1.2.

(24) *Sheas*   *sé*   *ansin*   *agus*   *bhreathnaigh*   *sé*   *síos*   *go faiteach*   *ar*   *thriúr*   *fear,*
    stand-PST   it   there   and   look-PST   it   down   fearfully   at   three   men-GEN

    a   *bhí*   *ag*   *obair*   *go deifreach*   *ar*   *bhruach*   *na*   *haille.*   *Bhí*
    REL   be-PST   at   work-VBN   hurriedly   on   edge   the-GEN   cliff-GEN   be-PST

    bun   *téada*   *ceangailte*   *acu*   *de*   *mhodhlaer*   *mór*   *cloiche*   *eibhir*
    end   rope-GEN   tie-VBA   by-3PL   to   boulder   great   stone-GEN   granite-GEN

    agus   *eiris*   *déanta*   *den*   *cheann*   *faoi*   *ascaill*   *an*   *fhir*   *ba hairde*
    and   strap   make-VBA   of+the   one   under   armpit   the-GEN   man-GEN   tall-SUP

    Bhí   *mála*   *beag*   *donn*   *ceangailte*   *dá*   *chrios*   *ag*   *an*   *bhfear*   *céanna.*
    be-PST   bag   small   brown   tie-VBA   to+his   belt   by   the   man   same

    Nuair   *a*   *chonaic*   *an*   *seabhac*   *go*   *raibh*   *an*   *fear*   *ard*   *á*   *ligean*
    when   REL   see-PST   the   hawk   CONJ   be-PST   the   man   tall   to+his   let-VBN

    síos   *le*   *taobh*   *na*   *haille*   *ag*   *an*   *mbeirt*   *eile,*   *go dtí*   *tulán*
    down   along   side   the-GEN   cliff-GEN   by   the   two   other   to   ledge

    beag   *caol*   *a*   *bhí*   *cothrom*   *le*   *tulán*   *na*   *nide*   *agus*
    small   narrow   REL   be-PST   level   with   ledge   the-GEN   nest-GEN   and

    scathamh   *fánach*   *soir*   *uaidh,*   *bhí*   *sé*   *cinnte*   *go*   *raibh*
    distance   casual   eastward   from-3SGM   be-PST   it   certain   CONJ   be-PST

    lucht   *na*   *téada*   *ag*   *iarraidh*   *é*   *a*   *scrios.*
    people   the-GEN   rope-GEN   at   attempt-VBN   it   to   destroy-VBN

'The hawk remained still there and looked down fearfully on three men who were working hurriedly at the edge of the cliff. They had tied one end of a rope to a large granite boulder and its other end in a loop under the arms of the tallest man. This same man had a small brown bag tied to his belt. When the hawk saw that the tall man was **being lowered** down the side of the cliff by the other two to a small narrow ledge that was level with the ledge where the nest was, just a little way away from it, it was certain that the people with the rope were trying to destroy it.' (Co. *Dúil*: 21)

(25) *Bhíos*   *ansan*   *ar*   *mo*   *shástacht*   *agus*   *mé*   *ag*   *féachaint*   *tríd*   *an*
    be-PST-1SG   there   on   my   contentment   and   I   at   look-VBN   through   the

    leabhar,   *ach*   *deirimse*   *leat*   *ná*   *raibh*   *dearúd*   *agam*
    book   but   say-PRS-1SG-EMPH   to-2SG   CONJ-NEG   be-PST   negligence   by-1SG

    á   *dhéanamh*   *ar*   *an*   *mbéal,*   *go*   *raibh*   *sé*   *lán*   *i gcónaí.*
    to+its   do-VBN   on   the   mouth   CONJ   be-PST   it   full   always

'I was there at my ease, looking through the book, and I can tell you that I wasn't **forgetting** my mouth, it was always full.' (Mu. *Fiche Bliain ag Fás*: 12)

an average level of participation that is twice as high, 1.2, as that of agents, 0.6. In the passive progressive, on the other hand, overt agents have nearly three times as high an average level of participation, 2.1, as patients have, 0.7. Implicit agents display an average level of participation that is only slightly higher, 0.8, than that of patients in the passive progressive, but considerably lower than that

Table 5.9. Average level of participation of autonomous and passive progressive patients and agents

	autonomous	passive progressive
patients	1.2	0.7
implicit agents	0.6	0.8
overt agents	-	2.1

of overt agents, 2.1. The results displayed in Table 5.9 and 5.8 point to an important difference in use between the autonomous and the passive progressive. In the autonomous, patients are more topical than agents, whereas in the passive progressive, agents are more topical than patients. It is of course hardly surprising that autonomous agents are less topical than patients since they are always implicit. More interesting perhaps are the results concerning passive progressive implicit agents, which do not suggest that they differ in any major way from the passive progressive patients as regards level of participation. These results tally well with the findings presented and discussed in 3.5 regarding the comparison of the agented and agent-less passive progressives in the main database.

In sum, the results suggest that the autonomous is used to a large extent to denote events involving patients that are more central to the narrative than the agents. In contrast, the agented passive progressive seems to be used largely to express actions where the participant that is given the role of agent is significantly more central in the text than the participant with the role of patient. When it comes to the agent-less passive progressive, however, the results are less easily interpreted since the difference in average level of participation between implicit patients and agents in the passive progressive is so small, 0.8 vs. 0.7. The difference in topicality patterns between the autonomous and the passive progressive was suggested also in Chapter 3, but the results of the classification of level of participation show a more distinct variation than the earlier results concerning given vs. new and continuity.

This concludes the presentations of the results. In the next section (5.4), some of the findings are discussed in more detail.

5.4 Discussion

Some of the findings presented above have particular implications for the understanding of the differences in use between the autonomous and the passive progressive. In the present discussion three aspects will be considered. First, the results regarding text function in relation to the eventline and personal perspective are related to contrast between perfective and imperfective aspect. Second, possible non-aspectual functions of the passive progressive will be considered. Third, the results concerning level of topicality are discussed in relation to the passive function of the autonomous and the passive progressive.

The results presented above regarding autonomous and passive progressive clauses point to the importance of the difference between them as regards perfective and imperfective aspect. The autonomous is used to denote punctual as well as durative events, while the passive progressive can only be used to express durative actions.[9] The differences observed above dealing with autonomous and passive progressive clauses, that is, text function in relation to the eventline, supporting functions, markers of personal perspective, and clause type, may be related to the contrast between perfective and imperfective aspect. As regards the variable text function in relation to the eventline, it was shown that the autonomous is used considerably more often than the passive progressive to denote actions as part of the eventline, 24% vs. 4%. As pointed out in 5.1, eventline actions are associated primarily with punctuality, and thus with perfective aspect. Further, the greatest difference found between the two constructions in the distribution across supporting functions concerns describing a setting, which is linked to imperfective aspect since the description of a setting is often built up by a durative event simultaneous to the one for which it provides a setting. The function to denote a setting is found considerably more often with the passive progressive (18%) than with the autonomous (< 1%). As for personal perspective, there is practically no difference between the autonomous and the passive progressive in the relative frequency of clauses containing such a perspective. However, great differences have been found concerning the linguistic markers of personal perspective, and these differences may relate to aspect. The most common marker of personal perspective found with the passive progressive is a verb of perception. Such verbs denote simultaneity of the perception with the action perceived and thus imperfective aspect. In the autonomous, on the other hand, the most common marker is direct speech, a marker which has no particular link to aspect. Finally, as shown above (5.1), the autonomous occurs more frequently than the passive progressive in main clauses, and main clauses are associated with eventline and perfective aspect (Hopper 1979). In all these cases, the main difference between the two constructions may be linked to the fact that the autonomous denotes mainly perfective aspect, while the passive progressive denotes imperfective aspect.

A factor connected with perspective and also worth taking into account in a comparative study of the autonomous and the passive progressive with regard to information packaging is the function of the progressive as opposed to the non-progressive. The view that the progressive (in English) has functions other than solely aspectual ones is generally accepted, although most scholars seem to consider the aspectual functions as the core functions from which non-aspectual functions are derived (see, for example Leech 1987, Palmer 1988, Quirk et al 1985, Rydén 1997, Scheffer 1975; for an overview and discussion of some accounts of the function of the English progressive, see Smitterberg 2002).

---

[9] In Chapter 2 it was shown that a small proportion (69/2,956 = 2%) of the instances of the autonomous in the database are combined with the active progressive, that is, they denote on-going actions.

Hübler (1998) is a study dealing with various grammatical constructions related to expressivity, that is, a dimension of human communication, which is based "in the personal setting of every communicative event in that it originates in a person (sender, addresser) and is directed at some other person (receiver, addressee)" (Hübler 1998: 1). Among other concepts connected to expressivity, Hübler investigates what he labels attachment, that is, the expression of the speaker's "emotional attitudes toward propositional states of affairs" (Hübler 1998: 15). One of the constructions studied by Hübler is the progressive, or expanded, form in Modern English. Hübler (1998) argues that a basic function of the expanded form is to express speaker attachment. Turning to the progressive in Irish, one of the few studies, to my knowledge, where the Irish progressive is analysed in detail with regard to function is Ó Corráin (1997), where the aspect system in Old and Modern Irish is investigated. Special attention is paid to the progressive, a construction that, according to Ó Corráin, has two important features that are related to aspect. First, the modern Irish progressive is imperfective, as opposed to simple tenses that express perfective aspect. Second, Ó Corráin (1997: 165) claims that the Irish passive progressive is introspective since it "looks at the internal contours of a situation"; thus the progressive contrasts with retrospective and prospective periphrastic constructions. These features of the Irish progressive, in turn, point to the "general tendency in Irish to grammaticalize the distinction between events, processes and states" (Ó Corráin 1997: 171). It is beyond the scope of the present study to analyse the functions of the progressive in Irish in terms of a progressive/non-progressive dichotomy. However, the fact that the progressive in English has been associated with non-aspectual functions, such as speaker attitude, should be kept in mind when considering what in the present study has been termed personal perspective.

I now turn to the third and final item to be discussed. The difference in topicality between patients and agents of the autonomous and the passive progressive, respectively, has important implications when it comes to the function of the autonomous and the passive progressive in relation to a passive/non-passive dichotomy. As mentioned previously (the Introduction, section 3), the definition of passive constructions usually involves the demotion of the agent in comparison to the corresponding active constructions. Thus, the agent of a passive clause typically displays lower topicality than the patient, since the demotion of a participant is normally associated with a decrease in topicality; in the corresponding active clause, the topicality of the agent is typically higher than that of the patient. Therefore, to return to the results concerning the level of participation of patients and agents in the subset analysis, the conclusion to be drawn is that to a considerable extent the Irish passive progressive is not used to demote the agent. Overt agents (63% of the instances of the passive progressive in the subset and 62% of the instances of the passive progressive in the main database are agented) are considerably more often given, continuous and co-referential with the subject of an active clause than patients. Consequently, the passive progressive does not quite match the definition of a passive construction with regard to function.[10] The autonomous, in contrast, in most instances displays a topicality pattern consistent with that of a 'typical' passive, that is, the demotion of the agent.[11] The results presented above show that in the autonomous clauses in the subset, patients are on average considerably more topical than agents. The low level of participation of agents is in itself hardly surprising since autonomous agents are always implicit. However, in the passive progressive, implicit agents seem to be slightly more topical than patients and also more topical than autonomous implicit agents. Consequently, the greatest contrast as regards topicality in the passive progressive is that between, on the one hand, patients and implicit agents, and, on the other hand, overt agents. These results concerning the passive progressive are somewhat contradictory since the contrast between implicit agents and patients of the agents-less passive progressive is very small, considerably smaller than that between patients and agents of the autonomous. Thus, the agent-less passive progressive seems to be used to demote the agent while not promoting the patient. These findings indicate that the autonomous, but not the passive progressive, is used to denote events where the patient is significantly more central in the text than the implied agent. In the passive progressive the agent, explicit or not, is more textually central than the patient. This, in turn, suggests that the autonomous, as opposed to the passive progressive, fulfils the function generally associated with the passive, that is, to promote the patient at the expense of the agent. With the passive progressive, on the other hand, the on-going character of the activity and perhaps a non-neutral perspective could possibly be seen as more prominent features of the construction than its function as a passive.

5.5 Summary

The aim of the present chapter was to further explore the functions of the autonomous and the passive progressive in context. For this purpose a subset of the instances of the autonomous and the passive progressive in the main database was selected. The analysis of the instances of the autonomous and the passive progressive in the subset concerns the text function of the autonomous and the passive progressive in relation to the eventline, the perspective of autonomous and passive progressive clauses in relation to a subject of consciousness, and the level of participation of patients and agents. The choice of variables was based on findings presented in Chapters 2 and 3, and on previous research (discussed in 5.1). The results discussed above have shown that there are great differences

---

[10] Similar results are found by Noonan (1994), as indicated in the Introduction, section 4. Compare Greene (1979: 133): "The earlier [Irish] language undoubtedly had a passive, but former passive constructions which survive are now either active or impersonal in meaning", and Hartmann (1954: 92), who defines the passive progressive as the progressive construction used when the process and the agent—instead of the patient—are foregrounded.

[11] Similar results are found by Noonan (1994), as mentioned in the Introduction, section 4.

between the autonomous and the passive progressive clauses in the subset as regards all three variables included in the study. These differences concern two aspects of discourse functions. The first aspect, comprising the variables text function in relation to the eventline and personal perspective, concerns the type of information contained in autonomous and passive progressive clauses, as well as the way in which these clauses contribute to the construction of the text. The second aspect concerns topicality, measured as the level of participation of patients and agents. The comparison of the topicality patterns of the autonomous and the passive progressive was based on the theory of how the degree of topicality of patients vs. agents of passive constructions contrasts with that of patients vs. agents of active constructions (see the Introduction, section 4).

As regards text function in relation to the eventline, it was shown above that the autonomous and the passive progressive differ from each other in two important ways. First, there is great variation between the two constructions with respect to the proportion of clauses where events are described as part of a sequentially ordered chain of actions. As displayed in Table 5.4, 24% of the autonomous clauses in the subset are used to express such events, whereas only 4% of the passive progressive clauses are used in that way. This difference is perhaps to be expected since the autonomous and the passive progressive contrast with each other as regards two features usually associated with the distinction between clauses that express events as part of an eventline and clauses that do not. The features in question are punctual vs. durative activity and main vs. subclause. The autonomous can be used to denote punctual as well as durative actions while the passive progressive cannot, since this construction, by definition, involves on-going actions. Further, as exhibited above, the autonomous occurs considerably more often in main clauses (47% in the main database and in the subset) than the passive progressive (13% in the main database, 14% in the subset). Considering this difference, it is evident that the autonomous is a far more likely candidate for expressing actions as part of a chain of events than the passive progressive. However, the two constructions differ when it comes to eventline clauses in yet another way. In the few cases (11/308 = 4%) where the passive progressive is used to express eventline actions, this occurs in a subclause in 9 instances (82%), while only 17% (12/70) of the autonomous clauses on the eventline are subclauses.

Thus, the first important difference between the autonomous and the passive progressive regarding text function is that the autonomous is used considerably more often to denote actions as part of an eventline than the passive progressive. The second important difference between the two constructions concerns the supporting functions, that is, the semantic functions of the clauses that are not used to express sequentially ordered events. For example, as displayed in Table 5.4, 30% of the autonomous supporting clauses are used to explain events described in the surrounding discourse, and 22% to modify an element. This is in contrast to the passive progressive, where a considerably smaller proportion of the supporting clauses fulfil these functions. The function to explain events is found in 20% of the supporting clauses, and the corresponding figure for the function to modify an element is 12%. A fairly common function among the passive progressive supporting clauses is indeed to describe a setting; such clauses occur in 18% of the instances of the passive progressive but only once (< 1%) with the autonomous.

With regard to personal perspective, that is, the presence of explicit connections between a proposition and a subject of consciousness (the author or a character in the text), the results presented in Table 5.5 indicate that such explicit links were found in 31% of the autonomous clauses, and in 33% of the clauses containing the passive progressive in the subset. There is thus very little variation between the two constructions in this respect. In contrast, considerable differences between the autonomous and the passive progressive were found regarding the linguistic device used to create a personal perspective. As shown in Table 5.7, direct speech is the favoured marker in the present material in connection with the autonomous (54%), while the most common way of linking passive progressive clauses to a subject of consciousness is the use of a verb of perception (50%). Further, it was found that there is variation between the autonomous and the passive progressive in yet another way concerning the variable personal perspective. While the subject of consciousness is a character in the text in 74% of the autonomous clauses displaying a personal perspective, the corresponding figure for the passive progressive is 53% (see Table 5.6). Thus the author's perspective is considerably more frequent in the passive progressive than in the autonomous. Finally, as suggested in 5.4, the contrast regarding perfective and imperfective aspect between the autonomous and the passive progressive is of particular interest to the features text function in relation to the eventline and personal perspective.

Turning to the second main aspect of the present comparison, the aspect of topicality or level of participation, the results presented above point again to considerable variation between the autonomous and the passive progressive. As discussed in 5.1.3, the level of participation is a measure of topicality. A comparison of the average levels of participation of patients and agents in the two constructions (displayed in Table 5.9) revealed that in autonomous clauses the most topical participant is the patient, while in the passive progressive, overt agents are more topical than patients. Passive progressive implicit patients and agents seem to be equally topical. Thus, the autonomous is used to demote the agent, while the passive progressive is used primarily in contexts where the overt agent is more central in the text. Consequently, as discussed in 5.4, the main conclusion is that the autonomous functions as a passive construction while the passive progressive primarily does not.

Summary and conclusions

The present study is a corpus-based survey of two Irish verb constructions: the autonomous and the passive progressive. The aim of the study is to investigate and compare the frequency, distribution and use of the autonomous and the passive progressive in a corpus of 20th-century Irish texts. A secondary aim of the investigation is to explore dialectal variation concerning the use of these two constructions. As accounted for in the Introduction, the corpus comprises narrative texts from the three main dialects of Irish: Connacht, Munster and Ulster (see the Introduction, Table 4). The corpus contains about 600,000 words, evenly distributed across the three dialects. From the corpus the instances of the autonomous and the passive progressive were extracted and gathered in a database, totalling 3,423 instances with 2,956 instances (86%) of the autonomous and 467 (14%) of the passive progressive. The study consists of three parts. The two main parts of the study were carried out on the whole database, while the third part of the study was conducted on a subset of the database, totalling 601 instances, 293 of the autonomous and 308 of the passive progressive. The first part deals with the classification of the autonomous and passive progressive clauses in the database with regard to verb and clause type (Chapter 2). The second part of the study concerns the classification of the patients and agents of the autonomous and passive progressive clauses, dealing mainly with the topicality of the different participant types (Chapter 3). The third part of the investigation is a more detailed study of the autonomous and passive progressive clauses from a contextual perspective (Chapter 5).

The main emphasis of the study is to investigate the two constructions from an information packaging perspective. As explained in the Introduction, section 3, previous research has pointed to differences between the autonomous and the passive progressive as regards information packaging, particularly in connection with topicality, that is, the degree of attention given to a participant in the text (Noonan 1994; see also Ó Siadhail 1989, Greene 1979). It has been suggested that the autonomous but not the passive progressive is used to promote a non-agent, and demote the agent. As for passive constructions in other languages, previous research has shown that in passive constructions, non-agents are more topical than agents (see Givón 1979b, 1983b, Pinkster 1991, and Risselada 1991). In the present study, the comparison of the use of the autonomous and the passive progressive with respect to information packaging focused on the topicality of patients and implicit as well as overt agents.

The autonomous and the passive progressive both conform to the general definitions of passive as a means to demote the agent and promote the non-agent (patient). Structurally, these functions may be realised in at least two ways: the agent may be unspecified, as in the autonomous, or the patient may appear in subject position, as in the passive progressive. The autonomous is formed with an inflectional suffix, while the passive progressive is formed with an auxiliary verb and a verbal noun phrase; optionally, an agent phrase is included. The patient of a passive progressive clause is in the subject position and the agent (when overt) appears in a prepositional phrase.

As mentioned above, the instances of the autonomous and the passive progressive in the database were classified according to three sets of variables. The first set of variables deals mainly with the verb types that are used in the autonomous and the passive progressive and the clause types where the autonomous and the passive progressive occur. The focus of the study of verbs and clauses was on the distribution across transitive and intransitive verbs, on the one hand, and the distribution across main and subclause, on the other. In addition, passive progressive clauses were classified with regard to finite vs. non-finite subclause structure and the presence or absence of an overt agent phrase.

The second set of variables deals with the classification of the patients and agents, overt as well as implicit, of the two constructions. autonomous and passive progressive. The aim was to compare the information packaging of autonomous and passive progressive clauses. The features studied were selected since they are factors that have been used in previous studies to measure the topicality of the participants in passive clauses in Irish and other languages (see the Introduction, section 3). The variables studied are: type of overt element, given vs. new, continuity, recoverability and co-reference with active subject. The main focus was on the measuring of the topicality of patients and agents.

The study of dialectal variation covers the frequency of the autonomous and the passive progressive, as well as the features concerning verbs and clauses, and patients and agents (Chapter 4). Previous research has suggested that the passive progressive is used differently in Munster compared to Connacht and Ulster (see, for example, Greene 1979 and Ó Siadhail 1989). Therefore, one of the main aims of the comparison was to investigate whether there are any dialectal differences with respect to the function of the autonomous and, in particular, the passive progressive.

The final part of the study is a closer look at the autonomous and the passive progressive from a contextual perspective. The variables investigated are: text function in relation to the eventline, function of the supporting clauses, personal perspective and level of participation.

The results of the classification dealing with verbs and clauses showed that there are great differences between the autonomous and the passive progressive in the corpus in this regard. The most salient difference between the two constructions concerns their distribution of transitive verbs taking direct objects across the categories mono- vs. ditransitive verbs. First, the proportion of monotransitive verbs is considerably larger in the passive progressive than in the autonomous (Table 2.2). It was also shown that the autonomous is predominantly used with verbs that take direct objects; only 11% of them occur with intransitive verbs, auxiliaries and monotransitive verbs that take indirect objects (Table 2.2). While the instances of the autonomous in the database are evenly distributed across main and subclause, the vast majority (87%) of the passive progressives occur in subclauses (Table 2.3). Finally, the results showed that the majority (64%) of the subclauses containing the passive progressive are non-finite (Table 2.5).

In the results regarding patients and agents, considerable variation was found between the two constructions. The most salient differences indicate that the degree of topicality varies considerably between the elements under investigation: patients, implicit agents and overt agents. All findings point to the same pattern: patients of the autonomous and overt agents of the passive progressive are the most topical elements, while patients of the passive progressive and implicit agents of both constructions are the least topical ones. The conclusion drawn from these results is that the autonomous is used to promote a non-agent and to demote the agent. The passive progressive, in contrast, is not used primarily to demote the agent and to promote a non-agent.[1] This difference between the autonomous and the passive progressive is indicated by the following findings. First, patients of the autonomous and overt agents are more often expressed as definite NPs than indefinite NPs, and more often refer to given participants than to new participants. Patients of passive progressive clauses, on the other hand, are more frequently expressed as indefinite NPs than definite NPs, and frequently refer to new participants than to given participants (Tables 3.1 and 3.2). Thus, autonomous patients are topical to a certain degree, a fact which, together with the implicitness of the agents, indicates that the autonomous is used to promote the patient (non-agent) of a clause. As regards the passive progressive, on the other hand, the results show that overt agents are considerably more topical than patients, which is inconsistent with the promotion of patients. Further, autonomous patients and passive progressive overt agents are more often continuous than passive progressive patients and implicit agents of both constructions (Table 3.8). In other words, the most topical participant categories are patients of autonomous clauses and, in particular, overt agents of passive progressive clauses since they refer to an element that occurs elsewhere in the same sentence or in the preceding or following sentence to a greater extent than passive progressive patients and implicit agents of both constructions. Finally, it was shown that the highest proportion of elements that are co-

---

[1] Similar conclusions are drawn by Noonan (1994). It should be noted, however, that there are several important differences between his study and the present one. The two studies are in many ways incompatible, which renders a comparison of the findings in Noonan (1994) and the present study difficult, as explained in the Introduction, section 3.

referential with active subjects is found among passive progressive overt agents (55%) and autonomous patients (18%), compared to implicit agents of both constructions and passive progressive patients (6–8%) (Table 3.9). This is further indication of the high topicality of autonomous patients and passive progressive overt agents compared to passive progressive patients and the implicit agents of autonomous as well as passive progressive clauses.

The final variable relating to patients and agents, recoverability, concerns implicit agents only. The results indicate that the two constructions are very similar with regard to the distribution of implicit agents across the different types of recoverability (Table 3.4). The vast majority of passive progressive as well as autonomous implicit agents are textually recoverable, that is, inferable from the surrounding (usually preceding) context. The second largest category comprises the non-recoverable implicit agents, that is, where no participant responsible for the action is implied. Considerably smaller proportions of the implicit agents of the autonomous and the passive progressive clauses belong to the remaining two categories of recoverability, that is, those that are generic or pragmatically inferable.

As mentioned, the results regarding verbs and clauses, as well as patients and agents were compared in the three dialects. This comparison revealed that there are both differences and similarities between the dialects concerning the use of the autonomous and the passive progressive. The most salient differences concern the frequency of the passive progressive and the distribution of agented vs. agent-less passive progressives. The distribution of the passive progressive is very uneven across the three dialects (Table 4.1). A great majority (73%) of the instances of the passive progressive in the database occur in the Munster texts. Considerably smaller proportions are found in the Connacht and, in particular, the Ulster material (22% and 5%, respectively). The autonomous is fairly evenly distributed across Connacht (38%) and Ulster (39%), but it occurs less frequently in Munster (23%) (Table 4.1). Apart from the great variation regarding the frequency of the passive progressive in the dialects, the most salient dialectal difference concerns the distribution of agented and agent-less passive progressives (Table 4.6). The largest proportion of agented passive progressives are found in the Munster texts, where the majority of the instances are agented (73%). In the Connacht and Ulster texts, on the other hand, a minority of the instances of the passive progressive are agented (36% in Connacht and 8% (two instances) in Ulster). As mentioned in 4.1, it has been noted by previous scholars that the passive progressive is used differently in Munster compared to the other two dialects. First, the passive progressive is reputed to be used considerably more frequently in Munster. Second, it is said that the passive progressive does not have passive function in Munster, as opposed to Connacht and Munster. The first of these statements is fully supported by the results of the present study. However, as regards the second statement, the study undertaken here of patients and agents (the variables investigated in Chapter 3) does not point to any significant differences between the dialects concerning the function of the passive progressive. Based on my findings, it cannot be argued that the passive progressive differs significantly with regard to passive function in Munster compared to Connacht and Ulster. There is little evidence that the primary function of the passive progressive in Connacht and Ulster is to promote a non-agent, except the fact that the passive progressive is most often agent-less in these dialects, which in itself is an indication of agent demotion. It should be kept in mind, however, that the number of instances of the passive progressive (agented ones especially) is considerably smaller in the Connacht and, in particular, Ulster texts, compared to the Munster material. Therefore, it is difficult to draw any valid conclusions regarding the use of the passive progressive in those dialects, as well as regarding variation between the three dialects. As for the classification of verb and clause type, the results do not suggest a clear pattern of difference among the dialects in the use of the autonomous and the passive progressive.

The results of the third part of the study, a closer look at the autonomous and the passive progressive from a contextual perspective, point to similarities as well as differences between the two constructions. One of the most salient differences concerns the variable text function in relation to the eventline. This variable distinguishes between clauses that contain material that is part of a sequentially ordered chain of events, an eventline, and clauses containing supporting material that is not part of an eventline. The autonomous is used to denote actions as part of an eventline considerably more frequently than the passive progressive, 24% compared to 4% (Table 5.3). The majority of clauses in both constructions are thus used to express supporting material, that is, material that is not part of a sequentially ordered chain of events. However, great differences are found between the autonomous and the passive progressive with respect to supporting functions, in particular the categories to explain, to modify, and to describe a setting (Table 5.4). While 30% of the autonomous clauses are explanatory, the corresponding figure for the passive progressive is 20%. Further, 22% of the autonomous supporting clauses modify an element, compared to 12% of the passive progressive ones. Finally, the passive progressive occurs considerably more frequently than the autonomous in clauses that describe a setting, 18% compared to less than 1% (one instance). The next variable investigated is personal perspective. A personal perspective indicates that the propositional content of the clause in question is attributed to a subject of consciousness, that is, a specific person. Two types of subject of consciousness are recognised: the author or a character in the text. The results show that the proportion of sentences containing the autonomous and the passive progressive where there is a personal perspective is about the same: 31% and 33% (Table 5.5). There is considerable variation, however, between the two constructions as regards the subject of consciousness to which the perspective is linked (Table 5.6). In the autonomous 74% of the personal perspective clauses are linked to a character in the text, compared to 53% of the passive progressive clauses. Thus, in the passive progressive clauses the author's perspective is present to a much larger extent than in the autonomous (47% vs. 26%). A personal perspective is established by the use of various linguistic markers. The comparison of the two constructions revealed that direct speech is the most common marker in the autonomous (54%), while it occurs in 25% of the passive progressive clauses. In the passive progressive clauses, on the other hand, the most favoured marker is a verb of perception (50%); this occurs in 1% (one instance) of the autonomous clauses (Table 5.7). As for the distribution of the remaining markers of personal perspective (verbs of cognition, verbs of utterance, and disjuncts), there is some variation between the two constructions, as shown in Table 5.7. Concerning the final variable, level of participation, the results for the distribution across the various levels of participation as well as the average level of participation showed that passive progressive overt agents appear on the highest level in the text, story-level, more frequently than the other elements and their average level of participation is the highest. Conversely, the highest proportion of instances on the lowest level of participation, single-occurrence sentence-level, as well as the lowest average level of participation, is found among implicit agents of both constructions as well as among patients of the passive progressive. As for the patients of the autonomous clauses, they have the highest relative frequency on the intermediate levels of participation, multiple-occurrence sentence-level and passage-level, as well as the second highest average level participation. These results indicate that the two most topical element categories are overt agents of the passive progressive and patients of the autonomous, while implicit agents of both constructions and patients of the passive progressive are the least topical element categories (Tables 5.8 and 5.9). Thus, the findings regarding level of participation tally with the other results relating to topicality (given vs. new, continuity, and co-reference with active subject).

The main conclusion to be drawn from the results of this study is that the autonomous and the passive progressive have different functions in the text in several respects. First, the results have shown that there is great contrast between the autonomous and the passive progressive with regard to passive function. The autonomous tends to be used when the patient is topical, or central, in the text. Thus, the autonomous fulfils a passive function. The passive progressive, on the other hand, is most often used with an overt agent. This passive progressive agent is considerably more topical than the patient. In agent-less passive progressives, patients and implicit agents are equally low in topicality. This seems to indicate that, in contrast to the autonomous, the passive progressive does not fulfil a passive function. Second, there are differences between the two constructions with respect to text function. As shown in Chapter 2, the autonomous occurs about equally often in main and subclauses, while the passive progressive is used primarily in subclauses, mainly non-finite ones. This finding tallies well with the results referred to above concerning the variable text function in relation to the eventline as well as the classification of supporting functions. In particular, the fact that the autonomous is used considerably more often than the passive progressive to denote events that are part of a sequentially ordered chain of actions seems to be connected to the contrast in the use of the two constructions in main and subclause.

This study contributes to the understanding of the concept of voice in Modern Irish and may serve as a point of departure for further research in this field, relating to the autonomous and the passive progressive, as well as to other constructions. By applying a corpus-linguistic methodology on a comparatively large material this study has provided empirical evidence of the many functional differences in use between the autonomous and the passive progressive.

Bibliography

Abraham, W., T. Givón, and S. A. Thompson. (eds.). 1995. *Discourse Grammar and Typology: Papers in Honour of John W. M. Verhaar*. Amsterdam and Philadelphia: John Benjamins.

Bäcklund, I. 1984. *Conjunction-Headed Abbreviated Clauses in English*. Studia Anglistica Upsaliensia 50. Uppsala: Acta Universitatis Upsaliensis.

Biber, D. 1999. *Longman Grammar of Spoken and Written English*. Harlow: Longman.

Bondaruk, A., and M. Charzynska-Wójcik. 2003. Expletive *pro* in Impersonal Passives in Irish, Polish and Old English. *Linguistische Berichte,* 195: 325–362.

Brown, J. D. 1988. *Understanding Research in Second Language Learning. A Teacher's Guide to Statistics and Research Design*. Cambridge: Cambridge University Press.

Chafe, W. L. 1976. Givenness, Contrastiveness, Definiteness, Subjects, Topics, and Point of View. *Subject and Topic*. Ed. by C. N. Li. New York: Academic Press. 25–56.

Cornelis, L. H. 1997. *Passive and Perspective*. Amsterdam and Atlanta: Rodopi.

Crystal, D. 1991. *A Dictionary of Linguistics and Phonetics*. Oxford: Blackwell.

de Bhaldraithe, T. (ed.). 1987. *English-Irish Dictionary. With Terminological Additions and Corrections*. Dublin: An Gúm.

Dillon, M. 1941. Modern Irish *atá sé déanta agam* 'I have done it'. *Language*, 17: 49–50.

English-Irish Dictionary, see de Bhaldraithe.

Foley, W. A., and R. D. Van Valin. 1985. Information Packaging in the Clause. *Language Typology and Syntactic Description. Vol. 1. Clause Structure*. Ed. by T. Shopen. Cambridge: Cambridge University Press. 282–380.

Givón, T. 1979a. *On Understanding Grammar*. New York: Academic Press.

— (ed.). 1979b. *Syntax and Semantics. Vol. 12. Discourse and Syntax*. New York: Academic Press.

— 1982. Transitivity, Topicality, and the Ute Impersonal Passive. *Syntax and Semantics. Vol. 15. Studies in Transitivity*. Ed. by P. J. Hopper and S. A. Thompson. 143–160. New York: Academic Press.

— (ed.). 1983a. *Topic Continuity in Discourse: A Quantitative Cross-Language Study*. Amsterdam and Philadelphia: John Benjamins.

— 1983b. Topic Continuity in Discourse: An Introduction. *Topic Continuity in Discourse: A Quantitative Cross-Language Study*. Ed. by T. Givón. Amsterdam and Philadelphia: John Benjamins. 5–41.

— 1987. Beyond Foreground and Background. *Coherence and Grounding in Discourse*. Ed. by R. L. Tomlin. Amsterdam and Philadelphia: John Benjamins. 175–188.

Graiméar Gaeilge na mBráithre Críostaí [The Christian Brothers' Irish Grammar]. 1960. Dublin: Mac an Ghoill.

Graiméar Gaeilge na mBráithre Críostaí [The Christian Brothers' Irish Grammar]. 1999. Dublin: An Gúm.

Greene, D. 1977. *The Irish Language*. Cork: Mercier.

— 1979. Perfects and Perfectives in Modern Irish. *Ériu*, 30: 122–141.

— 1979/80. Perfect and Passive in Eastern and Western Gaelic. *Studia Celtica*, 14/15: 87–94.

Guilfoyle, E. 1991. Light Verbs, Passives and A-Chains in Irish. *Proceedings of the Harvard Celtic Colloquium*. Ed. by W. Mahon and P. M. Freeman. Vol. 10–11: 46–68.

Haiman, J., and S. A. Thompson. 1988. *Clause Combining in Grammar and Discourse*. Amsterdam and Philadelphia: John Benjamins.

Hartmann, H. 1954. *Das Passiv. Eine Studie zur Geistesgeschichte der Kelten, Italiker und Arier*. Heidelberg: Carl Winter.

— 1977. Das Impersonale im Keltischen und Indogermanischen. Probleme der Dominanz. *Indogermanisch und Keltisch. Kolloquium der Indogermanischen Gesellschaft am 16. und 17. Februar 1976 in Bonn*. Ed. by K.-H. Schmidt. Wiesbaden: Dr. Ludwig Reichert Verlag. 159–203.

Hopper, P. J. 1979. Aspect and Foregrounding in Discourse. *Syntax and Semantics. Vol. 12. Discourse and Syntax*. Ed. by T. Givón. New York: Academic Press.

Hopper, P. J., and S. A. Thompson. 1980. Transitivity in Grammar and Discourse. *Language*, 56: 251–99.

Hübler, A. 1998. *The Expressivity of Grammar: Grammatical Devices Expressing Emotion Across Time*. Berlin: Mouton de Gruyter.

Irish-English Dictionary, see Ó Dónaill.

Keenan, E. 1985. Passive in the World's Languages. *Language Typology and Syntactic Description Vol. 1, Clause Structure*. Ed. by T. Shopen. Cambridge: Cambridge University Press. 243–281.

Langacker, R.W., and P. Munro. 1975. Passives and Their Meaning. *Language*, 51 (4): 789–830.

Leech, G. N. 1987. *Meaning and the English Verb*. London: Longman.

Mac Eoin, G. 1993. Irish. *The Celtic Languages*. Ed. by M. J. Ball and J. Fife. London: Routledge. 101–144.

Matthiessen, C., and S. A. Thompson. 1988. The Structure of Discourse and 'Subordination'. *Clause Combining in Grammar and Discourse*. Ed. by J. Haiman and S. A. Thompson. Amsterdam and Philadelphia: John Benjamins. 275–329.

McCloskey, J. 1996. Subjects and Subject Positions in Irish. *The Syntax of the Celtic Langugaes: A Comparative Perspective*. Ed. by R. D. Borsley and I. G. Roberts. New York: Cambridge University Press. 241–283.

McCone, K. 1987. *The Early Irish Verb*. Maynooth: An Sagart.

Müller, N. 1994. Passive and Discourse in Táin Bó Cúailnge. *Ulidia. Proceedings of the First International Conference on the Ulster Cycle of Tales, Belfast and Emain Macha 8–12 April 1994*. Ed. by J. P. Mallory and G. Stockman. Belfast: December Publications. 193–199.

— 1999. *Agents in Early Welsh and Early Irish*. Oxford and New York: Oxford University Press.

New Irish Grammar by The Christian Brothers. 1986. Dublin: C.J. Fallon.

Nolan, B. 2001. Passive Constructions in Modern Irish. *ITB Journal*, 3: 51–78.

Noonan, M. 1994. A Tale of Two Passives in Irish. *Voice: Form and Function*. Ed. by B. Fox and P. J. Hopper. Amsterdam: John Benjamins. 279–312.

Oakes, M. P. 1998. *Statistics for Corpus Linguistics*. Edinburgh: Edinburgh University Press.

Ó Cadhlaigh, C. 1940. *Gnás na Gaeilge* [Irish Usage]. Dublin: An Gúm.

Ó Corráin, A. 1997. Aspect in Irish with Particular Reference to the Progressive. *Miscellanea Celtica in Memoriam Heinrich Wagner*. Ed. by S. Mac Mathúna and A. Ó Corráin. Studia Celtica Upsaliensia 2. Uppsala and Stockholm: Almqvist & Wiksell International. 159–173.

— 2001. Aspects of Voice in the Grammatical Structure of Irish. *Béalra. Aistí ar Theangeolaíocht na Gaeilge* [Essays on Irish Linguistics]. Ed. by B. Ó Catháin and R. Ó hUiginn. Maynooth: An Sagart. 98–122.

Ó Dochartaigh, C. 1992. The Irish Language. *The Celtic Languages.* Ed. by D. Macaulay. Cambridge: Cambridge University Press. 11–99.

Ó Dónaill, N. (ed.). 1992. *Foclóir Gaeilge-Béarla* [Irish-English Dictionary]. Dublin: An Gúm.

Ó Murchú, M. 1985. *The Irish Language.* Dublin: The Department of Foreign Affairs and Bord na Gaeilge.

Ó Rahilly, T. F. 1976. *Irish Dialects Past and Present With Chapters on Scottish and Manx.* Dublin: Dublin Institute of Advanced Studies.

Ó Searcaigh, S. 1954. *Coimhréir Ghaedhilg an Tuaiscirt* [The Syntax of the Irish of the North]. Dublin: Oifig an tSoláthair

Ó Siadhail, M. 1989. *Modern Irish. Grammatical Structure and Dialectal Variation.* Cambridge: Cambridge University Press.

Palmer, F. R. 1988. *The English Verb.* Harlow: Longman.

Pinkster, H. 1985. The Discourse Function of the Passive. *Syntax and Pragmatics in Functional Grammar.* Ed. by A. M. Bolkestein, C. de Groot and J. L. Mackenzie. Dordrecht: Foris publications. 107–118.

Quirk, R., S. Greenbaum, G. Leech, and J. Svartvik. 1985. *A Comprehensive Grammar of the English Language.* London and New York: Longman.

Reynolds, H. T. 1984. *Analysis of Nominal Data.* Newsbury Park, California: Sage.

Risselada, R. 1991. Passive, Perspective and Textual Cohesion. *New studies in Latin linguistics.* Ed. by R. Coleman. Amsterdam and Philadelphia: John Benjamins. 401–414.

Rydén, M. 1997. On the Panchronic Core Meaning of the English Progressive. *To Explain the Present. Studies in the Changing English Language in Honour of Matti Rissanen.* Ed. by T. Nevalainen and L. Kahlas-Tarkka. Helsinki: Société Néophilologique. 419–429.

Sanders, J., and W. Spooren. 1997. Perspective, Subjectivity, and Modality from a Cognitive Linguistic Point of View. *Discourse and Perspective in Cognitive Linguistics.* Ed. by W.-A. Liebert, G. Redeker, and L. Waugh. Amsterdam: John Benjamins. 85–114.

Scheffer, J. 1975. *The Progressive in English.* Amsterdam, North-Holland and New York: Amercian Elsevier.

Shibatani, M. 1985. Passives and Related Constructions: A Prototype Analysis. *Language,* 61: 821–848.

Sjoestedt-Jonval, M. L. 1938. *Description d'un Parler Irlandais de Kerry.* Paris: Librairie Ancienne Honoré Champion.

Smith, C. S. 2002. Perspective and Point of View: Accounting for Subjectivity. *Information Structure in a Cross-Linguistic perspective.* Ed. by H. Hasselgård, S. Johansson, B. Behrens and C. Fabricius-Hansen. Amsterdam and New York: Rodopi. 63–79.

Smitterberg, E. 2002. *The Progressive in 19th-Century English: A Process of Integration.* Uppsala: Department of English.

Stenson, N. 1981. *Studies in Irish Syntax.* Tübingen: Narr.

— 1989. Irish Autonomous Impersonals. *Natural Language and Linguistic Theory,* 7: 379–406.

Thompson, S. A. 1987a. "Subordination" and Narrative Event Structure. *Coherence and Grounding in Discourse.* Ed. by R. L. Tomlin. Amsterdam and Philadelphia: John Benjamins. 435–454.

Thompson, S. A. 1987b. The Passive in English: A Discourse Perspective. *In Honour of Ilse Lehiste*. Ed. by R. Channon and L. Shockey. Dordrecht: Foris Publications. 497–511.

Thurneysen, R. 1980. *A Grammar of Old Irish*. Dublin: Dublin Institute for Advanced Studies.

Tomlin, R. L. (ed.). 1987. *Coherence and Grounding in Discourse*. Amsterdam and Philadelphia: John Benjamins.

Vendryes, J. 1956. Sur L'emploi Impersonnel du Verbe. *Celtica*, 3: 185–197.

Wagner, H. 1956. Review of Hans Hartmann, Das Passiv. Eine Studie zur Geistesgeschichte der Kelten, Italiker und Arier. 1954. *Zeitschrift für celtische Philologie*, 25: 141–5.

Weiner, E. J. and W. Labov. 1983. Constraints on the Agentless Passive. *Journal of Linguistics*, 19: 29–58.

Woods, A. 1986. *Statistics in Language Studies*. Cambridge: Cambridge University Press.

APPENDIX

Verbs used in the autonomous and the passive progressive

The verbs used in the autonomous and the passive progressive in the corpus are listed below in alphabetical order. Standard spelling (according to Ó Dónaill 1992) is used throughout. Their total frequency in each construction, as well as their frequency in the three dialects are given. An English translation is also included. When a verb has several meanings the translation reflects primarily its meaning or meanings found in the corpus.

Verb		Autonomous				Passive progressive			
Irish	English	Total	Co.	Mu.	Ul.	Total	Co.	Mu.	Ul.
abair	say	**134**	67	19	48	**14**	0	12	2
adhlaic	bury	**5**	0	0	5	**0**	0	0	0
agair	avenge	**0**	0	0	0	**1**	1	0	0
aimsigh	aim	**1**	0	1	0	**0**	0	0	0
ainmnigh	name	**1**	0	0	1	**0**	0	0	0
airigh	hear	**6**	0	6	0	**0**	0	0	0
áirigh	count	**2**	0	0	2	**0**	0	0	0
aistrigh	translate	**1**	0	1	0	**0**	0	0	0
aithin	know	**8**	3	1	4	**0**	0	0	0
aol	whitewash	**1**	1	0	0	**0**	0	0	0
ardaigh	raise	**5**	2	3	0	**1**	1	0	0
athainmnigh	rename	**1**	1	0	0	**0**	0	0	0
athraigh	change	**2**	0	0	2	**0**	0	0	0
bac	heed	**2**	2	0	0	**0**	0	0	0
báigh	drown, sink	**16**	6	3	7	**2**	2	0	0
bailigh	collect	**1**	1	0	0	**0**	0	0	0
bain	take (etc.)	**111**	34	39	38	**35**	1	33	1
baist	baptize	**8**	4	3	1	**0**	0	0	0
beannaigh	greet	**1**	0	0	1	**0**	0	0	0
bearr	cut	**2**	1	1	0	**0**	0	0	0
beartaigh	plan	**0**	0	0	0	**1**	0	1	0
beir	bear	**100**	36	26	38	**1**	0	1	0
beoigh	animate	**0**	0	0	0	**1**	1	0	0
bí	be	**77**	21	4	52	**0**	0	0	0
bligh	milk	**0**	0	0	0	**1**	1	0	0
bris	break	**24**	4	3	17	**4**	2	2	0
bronn	grant	**4**	2	1	1	**0**	0	0	0
brúigh	press	**0**	0	0	0	**1**	0	1	0
buail	strike	**55**	17	24	14	**3**	1	2	0
bunaigh	found, establish	**2**	1	0	1	**0**	0	0	0
caill	lose	**35**	22	6	7	**0**	0	0	0
cáin	tax	**2**	2	0	0	**0**	0	0	0
caith	wear, spend, throw	**103**	48	23	32	**24**	4	18	2
can	sing, speak	**11**	0	0	11	**1**	0	1	0
caoch	blind	**0**	0	0	0	**1**	1	0	0

Verb		Autonomous				Passive progressive			
Irish	English	Total	Co.	Mu.	Ul.	Total	Co.	Mu.	Ul.
caoin	*lament, weep*	1	0	0	1	2	0	2	0
cardáil	*card, discuss*	2	0	0	2	0	0	0	0
carn	*heap*	0	0	0	0	1	0	1	0
cas	*twist, turn, sing, meet with*	195	64	11	120	8	3	5	0
ceadaigh	*permit*	2	2	0	0	0	0	0	0
ceangail	*tie*	6	1	3	2	0	0	0	0
ceannaigh	*buy*	4	1	2	1	0	0	0	0
ceansaigh	*control*	1	1	0	0	0	0	0	0
ceap	*shape, think, compose, assign*	27	20	7	0	0	0	0	0
céas	*crucify, torment*	2	2	0	0	0	0	0	0
ceil	*conceal*	1	1	0	0	0	0	0	0
ceol	*make music*	1	0	0	1	0	0	0	0
ciap	*torment*	0	0	0	0	1	0	1	0
cinntigh	*confirm*	1	0	0	1	0	0	0	0
ciondáil	*ration*	0	0	0	0	1	1	0	0
ciontaigh	*convict*	1	1	0	0	0	0	0	0
ciorraigh	*cut*	1	0	1	0	2	0	2	0
cleacht	*practise*	0	0	0	0	1	1	0	0
cloígh	*wear down*	0	0	0	0	1	0	0	1
clois/cluin	*hear*	43	13	3	27	2	0	2	0
clúdaigh	*cover*	2	1	1	0	0	0	0	0
cnag	*knock*	1	0	0	1	0	0	0	0
cniog	*rap, strike*	4	4	0	0	0	0	0	0
codail	*sleep*	1	0	0	1	0	0	0	0
cogain	*chew*	0	0	0	0	1	0	1	0
coigil	*rake*	2	0	0	2	0	0	0	0
coill	*violate*	2	2	0	0	0	0	0	0
coiméad	*keep*	3	0	2	1	2	0	2	0
coinnigh	*keep, retain*	13	10	1	2	0	0	0	0
cóirigh	*arrange, dress, prepare*	3	1	0	2	1	1	0	0
coisc	*stop*	1	1	0	0	0	0	0	0
coisric	*consecrate*	2	0	0	2	0	0	0	0
comhair	*count, calculate*	4	2	2	0	0	0	0	0
comhairligh	*advise*	2	0	0	2	0	0	0	0
comóir	*celebrate*	1	1	0	0	3	3	0	0
connaigh	*accustom*	0	0	0	0	1	0	0	1
corónaigh	*crown*	6	5	0	1	0	0	0	0
corraigh	*move*	3	1	1	1	0	0	0	0
cothaigh	*feed*	1	0	0	1	0	0	0	0
cráigh	*agonize, distress*	1	1	0	0	1	0	1	0
creach	*ruin*	1	0	1	0	0	0	0	0
críochnaigh	*finish*	3	0	2	1	0	0	0	0
croch	*hang, lift, carry*	18	4	6	8	7	3	4	0
crom	*bend*	0	0	0	0	1	1	0	0
cruaigh	*harden*	1	0	0	1	0	0	0	0
cruinnigh	*gather*	1	0	0	1	1	1	0	0

Verb		Autonomous				Passive progressive			
Irish	English	Total	Co.	Mu.	Ul.	Total	Co.	Mu.	Ul.
cruthaigh	*create, form, prove*	4	0	0	4	0	0	0	0
cuach	*wrap*	1	0	0	1	0	0	0	0
cuardaigh	*search*	1	0	0	1	1	0	1	0
cuimhnigh	*remind*	1	0	0	1	0	0	0	0
cuimil	*wipe*	1	1	0	0	0	0	0	0
cúinneáil	*corner*	1	1	0	0	0	0	0	0
cuir	*set, put, sow, bury*	320	122	73	125	49	7	41	1
cúlaigh	*reverse*	1	0	1	0	0	0	0	0
cum	*form, compose*	7	4	0	3	0	0	0	0
dall	*blind*	0	0	0	0	4	0	4	0
damhnaigh	*materialize*	1	0	0	1	0	0	0	0
damhsaigh	*dance*	1	0	0	1	1	1	0	0
daor	*enslave*	1	0	1	0	0	0	0	0
dathaigh	*colour*	1	0	0	1	0	0	0	0
dealaigh	*separate (from)*	2	2	0	0	0	0	0	0
déan	*do, make*	174	85	42	47	71	11	58	2
dearmad	*forget*	1	1	0	0	0	0	0	0
díbir	*drive out, expel*	6	0	4	2	1	0	0	1
díol	*sell, pay*	5	1	3	1	0	0	0	0
dírigh	*straighten*	1	1	0	0	0	0	0	0
dluigh	*peel*	1	1	0	0	0	0	0	0
doirt	*pour, spill, shed*	11	7	0	4	1	1	0	0
druid	*close*	3	0	0	3	1	0	0	1
dúisigh	*wake*	1	1	0	0	0	0	0	0
dún	*close*	2	2	0	0	1	0	1	0
éadromaigh	*lighten*	1	0	1	0	0	0	0	0
éiligh	*claim, demand*	2	1	1	0	0	0	0	0
éirigh	*give up*	1	1	0	0	0	0	0	0
fág	*leave*	62	18	6	38	1	0	1	0
faigh	*get, find*	88	32	18	38	15	1	14	0
fáisc	*squeeze, press*	9	3	5	1	1	0	1	0
fan	*stay*	1	0	1	0	0	0	0	0
fás	*grow*	0	0	0	0	1	1	0	0
féach	*attempt*	1	1	0	0	0	0	0	0
féad	*be able to*	33	16	12	5	0	0	0	0
feann	*flay*	2	0	0	2	1	0	0	1
feic	*see*	125	50	9	66	0	0	0	0
feistigh	*fasten*	2	0	0	2	0	0	0	0
fiafraigh	*inquire*	5	4	1	0	0	0	0	0
figh	*interweave*	1	0	0	1	0	0	0	0
fill	*return (to)*	1	1	0	0	0	0	0	0
fógair	*call out*	3	0	0	3	1	1	0	0
foghlaim	*learn*	0	0	0	0	1	0	1	0
foilsigh	*publish*	1	0	0	1	0	0	0	0
folmhaigh	*empty*	0	0	0	0	1	1	0	0
foráil	*offer*	1	0	0	1	0	0	0	0
freagair	*answer*	2	2	0	0	0	0	0	0
friotháil	*attend*	1	0	1	0	0	0	0	0

Verb		Autonomous				Passive progressive			
Irish	English	Total	Co.	Mu.	Ul.	Total	Co.	Mu.	Ul.
fuadaigh	*abduct, blow away*	**3**	2	0	1	**1**	1	0	0
gabh	*take, go*	**5**	0	2	3	**2**	1	1	0
geal	*brighten*	**0**	0	0	0	**1**	1	0	0
geall	*promise*	**4**	3	1	0	**0**	0	0	0
géaraigh	*sharpen*	**0**	0	0	0	**1**	1	0	0
gearr	*cut*	**6**	3	2	1	**0**	0	0	0
géill	*yield*	**3**	0	0	3	**0**	0	0	0
gin	*originate*	**1**	0	0	1	**0**	0	0	0
glac	*take, accept*	**5**	4	0	1	**0**	0	0	0
glan	*clean, clear*	**2**	1	0	1	**0**	0	0	0
glaoigh	*call, cry out*	**9**	4	5	0	**3**	0	3	0
gleadhair	*beat noisily*	**0**	0	0	0	**1**	1	0	0
gléas	*prepare*	**1**	1	0	0	**0**	0	0	0
goid	*steal*	**6**	3	0	3	**0**	0	0	0
gortaigh	*injure*	**1**	0	1	0	**0**	0	0	0
gread	*strike, trounce*	**2**	0	1	1	**1**	1	0	0
grean	*engrave*	**1**	1	0	0	**0**	0	0	0
grian	*sun*	**0**	0	0	0	**1**	0	1	0
iarr	*ask, seek, attempt*	**15**	6	1	8	**0**	0	0	0
ídigh	*use, destroy*	**2**	1	1	0	**0**	0	0	0
imir	*inflict*	**1**	0	0	1	**1**	0	1	0
inis	*tell*	**28**	5	12	11	**2**	0	2	0
iompaigh	*turn*	**2**	1	1	0	**0**	0	0	0
ionsaigh	*attack*	**4**	4	0	0	**0**	0	0	0
ísligh	*lower*	**1**	0	1	0	**0**	0	0	0
ith	*eat*	**5**	2	1	2	**1**	0	0	1
labhair	*speak*	**6**	2	0	4	**13**	2	10	1
laghdaigh	*reduce*	**1**	1	0	0	**0**	0	0	0
las	*light*	**2**	1	1	0	**2**	0	2	0
lasc	*lash*	**0**	0	0	0	**1**	1	0	0
leag	*knock down, lay*	**19**	12	6	1	**1**	1	0	0
lean	*follow*	**7**	2	2	3	**0**	0	0	0
leasaigh	*improve*	**0**	0	0	0	**1**	1	0	0
leath	*spread*	**1**	0	1	0	**1**	0	1	0
léigh	*read*	**3**	0	0	3	**3**	2	1	0
leigheas	*cure*	**3**	1	0	2	**2**	0	1	1
léirigh	*explain, produce (a play)*	**3**	2	1	0	**1**	1	0	0
lig	*let, allow*	**45**	23	8	14	**5**	2	3	0
líon	*fill*	**7**	2	4	1	**2**	0	2	0
loit	*injure*	**3**	0	0	3	**0**	0	0	0
lorg	*seek*	**0**	0	0	0	**1**	1	0	0
luaigh	*mention*	**6**	5	1	0	**2**	2	0	0
luasc	*swing*	**0**	0	0	0	**1**	1	0	0
lúb	*bend*	**1**	1	0	0	**1**	1	0	0
luigh	*lay into*	**1**	0	0	1	**0**	0	0	0
maith	*forgive*	**10**	3	5	2	**0**	0	0	0
maraigh	*kill*	**23**	5	4	14	**3**	1	2	0
marcáil	*mark*	**1**	0	1	0	**0**	0	0	0

Verb		Autonomous				Passive progressive			
Irish	English	Total	Co.	Mu.	Ul.	Total	Co.	Mu.	Ul.
maslaigh	*insult*	0	0	0	0	1	1	0	0
meabhraigh	*recall*	1	1	0	0	0	0	0	0
méadaigh	*increase*	0	0	0	0	1	1	0	0
meall	*entice*	2	2	0	0	0	0	0	0
meas	*estimate, deem*	5	2	0	3	0	0	0	0
measc	*mix*	1	1	0	0	0	0	0	0
mill	*ruin*	2	1	1	0	0	0	0	0
mínigh	*explain*	1	1	0	0	0	0	0	0
mol	*praise, recommend*	7	2	0	5	1	0	1	0
mothaigh	*perceive, hear*	4	0	0	4	0	0	0	0
múch	*smother, extinguish*	2	2	0	0	2	0	2	0
múin	*teach*	6	0	6	0	1	1	0	0
múnlaigh	*shape*	1	0	1	0	0	0	0	0
múscail	*wake*	1	0	0	1	1	0	1	0
naomhaigh	*sanctify*	2	2	0	0	0	0	0	0
nigh	*wash*	2	1	0	1	0	0	0	0
nocht	*bare, become visible*	6	1	1	4	0	0	0	0
oibrigh	*work*	0	0	0	0	2	2	0	0
oil	*rear*	1	1	0	0	0	0	0	0
ól	*drink*	2	0	0	2	1	1	0	0
ordaigh	*order*	3	1	0	2	0	0	0	0
oscail	*open*	21	2	10	9	4	1	2	1
pacáil	*pack*	1	1	0	0	0	0	0	0
peacaigh	*sin*	1	0	0	1	0	0	0	0
pioc	*pick*	1	1	0	0	0	0	0	0
pléigh	*discuss*	1	1	0	0	1	1	0	0
plúch	*smother*	3	3	0	0	0	0	0	0
pós	*marry*	28	1	5	22	1	0	0	1
prioc	*prod*	1	0	1	0	1	0	1	0
rad	*throw*	0	0	0	0	1	0	1	0
ramhraigh	*fatten*	1	0	0	1	0	0	0	0
réab	*tear, shatter*	3	3	0	0	1	0	0	1
riastáil	*score, furrow*	0	0	0	0	1	0	1	0
rinc	*dance*	0	0	0	0	1	0	1	0
rith	*run*	1	0	1	0	0	0	0	0
robáil	*rob*	4	1	0	3	0	0	0	0
roinn	*divide, distribute*	4	3	0	1	2	2	0	0
róst	*roast*	1	0	0	1	4	0	4	0
ruaig	*chase*	2	2	0	0	1	0	1	0
sac	*thrust*	1	1	0	0	0	0	0	0
sáigh	*push, press*	0	0	0	0	3	0	3	0
sáinnigh	*corner*	1	1	0	0	0	0	0	0
samhlaigh	*imagine, appear*	10	0	0	10	0	0	0	0
saoirsigh	*work*	1	1	0	0	0	0	0	0
saolaigh	*be born, deliver*	5	1	4	0	1	0	1	0
saor	*free*	2	2	0	0	0	0	0	0
saothraigh	*earn, cultivate*	2	1	1	0	0	0	0	0
sáraigh	*transgress*	4	4	0	0	0	0	0	0

Verb		Autonomous				Passive progressive			
Irish	English	Total	Co.	Mu.	Ul.	Total	Co.	Mu.	Ul.
sásaigh	*satisfy*	1	0	1	0	0	0	0	0
satail	*trample*	2	2	0	0	0	0	0	0
scaip	*scatter*	1	0	1	0	1	1	0	0
scairt	*shout, call*	11	1	0	10	1	0	1	0
scaoil	*loosen, discharge*	9	2	5	2	1	1	0	0
scar	*separate*	2	0	1	1	0	0	0	0
sceith	*spread*	1	1	0	0	0	0	0	0
scoilt	*split*	1	1	0	0	1	0	1	0
scoir	*release*	1	1	0	0	0	0	0	0
scoith	*leave behind, break apart*	2	0	0	2	0	0	0	0
scól	*scald*	1	0	0	1	0	0	0	0
scríob	*scrape*	1	1	0	0	0	0	0	0
scríobh	*write*	19	10	2	7	2	2	0	0
scrios	*destroy*	2	1	1	0	0	0	0	0
scrúdaigh	*examine*	1	1	0	0	0	0	0	0
scuab	*sweep*	5	3	2	0	0	0	0	0
seachaid	*hand over*	1	1	0	0	0	0	0	0
séid	*blow*	2	0	2	0	4	0	4	0
seiftigh	*provide*	1	0	0	1	0	0	0	0
seilg	*hunt*	0	0	0	0	1	1	0	0
seinn	*play (music, musical instrument)*	2	0	0	2	4	0	4	0
seol	*send, direct*	2	1	0	1	1	0	1	0
síl	*think, consider*	5	3	0	2	0	0	0	0
sín	*stretch, lay flat*	5	0	4	1	1	0	1	0
síob	*blow, drive*	2	0	0	2	4	0	0	4
siortaigh	*rannsack*	1	0	0	1	0	0	0	0
siosc	*cut*	1	1	0	0	0	0	0	0
slog	*swallow*	1	1	0	0	0	0	0	0
sníomh	*wrench*	0	0	0	0	1	1	0	0
socraigh	*settle, agree upon, decide*	6	4	2	0	1	0	1	0
splanc	*spark*	1	1	0	0	0	0	0	0
spreag	*inspire*	1	1	0	0	1	0	1	0
srac	*tear*	0	0	0	0	1	0	1	0
sroich	*reach*	1	1	0	0	0	0	0	0
stad	*stop*	7	0	2	5	0	0	0	0
steall	*splash, pour*	0	0	0	0	3	0	3	0
stoll	*tear*	1	0	1	0	0	0	0	0
stop	*stop*	2	1	0	1	0	0	0	0
streachail	*drag*	2	2	0	0	1	1	0	0
stróic	*tear*	1	1	0	0	1	1	0	0
struipeáil	*strip*	1	0	1	0	0	0	0	0
stuáil	*stow*	2	1	1	0	0	0	0	0
suaith	*shuffle*	1	0	0	1	0	0	0	0
suigh	*sit*	2	2	0	0	0	0	0	0
súigh	*suck*	0	0	0	0	2	1	1	0
tabhair	*give, take, bring*	230	91	73	66	30	3	27	0

Verb		Autonomous				Passive progressive			
Irish	English	Total	Co.	Mu.	Ul.	Total	Co.	Mu.	Ul.
tacht	choke	4	0	0	4	1	0	1	0
taibhrigh	dream, show	1	0	1	0	5	0	5	0
taibhsigh	seem	2	0	1	1	0	0	0	0
tairg	offer	5	1	0	4	0	0	0	0
taispeáin	show	4	1	1	2	1	1	0	0
tar	come, come upon (etc.)	10	2	2	6	0	0	0	0
tarraing	pull, draw	10	2	2	6	6	0	6	0
tástáil	try	0	0	0	0	1	0	1	0
teagasc	teach	1	0	0	1	0	0	0	0
teann	press towards	3	0	3	0	1	0	1	0
téigh	go	9	1	3	5	0	0	0	0
téigh	heat	0	0	0	0	1	0	0	1
tiomáin	drive	0	0	0	0	1	0	1	0
tiontaigh	turn	3	1	0	2	0	0	0	0
tnáith	exhaust	0	0	0	0	1	0	1	0
tochail	dig	2	1	0	1	0	0	0	0
tóg	lift, take up, take	68	12	30	26	8	2	6	0
togh	choose, elect	5	1	0	4	0	0	0	0
tomhais	measure	1	0	0	1	0	0	0	0
tórraigh	hold obsequies of, wake	0	0	0	0	1	1	0	0
tosaigh	begin	15	8	2	5	0	0	0	0
traoch	wear out	0	0	0	0	2	0	2	0
treabh	plough	1	0	0	1	0	0	0	0
tréaslaigh	congratulate	1	1	0	0	0	0	0	0
tréig	abandon	0	0	0	0	1	0	1	0
triail	try	2	0	1	1	0	0	0	0
triomaigh	dry	1	1	0	0	0	0	0	0
tuairteáil	pound	1	1	0	0	0	0	0	0
tuar	bleach	0	0	0	0	1	1	0	0
tuar	forebode	1	0	0	1	0	0	0	0
tuig	understand, realise	86	18	61	7	1	0	1	0
tuirsigh	tire	1	0	0	1	0	0	0	0
tum	dip	1	0	0	1	0	0	0	0
ullmhaigh	prepare	0	0	0	0	1	0	1	0
úsáid	use	0	0	0	0	5	0	5	0

Index

ACTA UNIVERSITATIS UPSALIENSIS
Studia Celtica Upsaliensia
Editores: Mats Rydén, Ailbhe Ó Corráin & Karl Inge Sandred

1. *Ailbhe Ó Corráin* assisted by *Jan Erik Rekdal:* Proceedings of the Third Symposium of Societas Celtologica Nordica held in Oslo 1–2 November 1991. 1994.
2. *Séamus Mac Mathúna* and *Ailbhe Ó Corráin:* Miscellanea Celtica in Memoriam Heinrich Wagner. 1997.
3. *Ailbhe Ó Corráin* and *Séamus Mac Mathúna:* Minority Languages in Scandinavia, Britain and Ireland. 1997.
4. *Ailbhe Ó Corráin:* Proceedings of the Fifth Symposium of Societas Celtologica Nordica. 2001.
5. *Karin Hansson:* The Autonomous and the Passive Progressive in 20th-Century Irish. 2004.